CyclePro

HOW TO BUILD
HARLEY-DAVIDSON
HORSEPOWER

Tom Murphy

Motorbooks International
Publishers & Wholesalers ®

Contents

Acknowledgments and Dedication

This one is dedicated to Hans, the guy who got me into all this in the first place. Also, I'd like to thank Custom Chrome, Inc., San Jose Harley-Davidson, and Horsepower Express in Campbell, California, for all their help.

First published in 1997 by Motorbooks International Publishers & Wholesalers, 729 Prospect Avenue, PO Box 1, Osceola, WI 54020-0001

The information in this book is true and complete to the best of our knowledge. All recommendations are made without any guarantee on the part of the author or Publisher, who also disclaim any liability incurred in connection with the use of this data or specific details

We recognize that some words, model names and designations, for example, mentioned herein are the property of the trademark holder. We use them for identification purposes only. This is not an official publication

Motorbooks International books are also available at discounts in bulk quantity for industrial or sales-promotional use. For details write to Special Sales Manager at the Publisher's address

Library of Congress Cataloging-in-Publication Data Available

Murphy, Tom.
  How to build Harley-Davidson horsepower / Tom Murphy.
    p. cm. — (CyclePro)
  ISBN 0-7603-0150-6 (pbk. : alk. paper)
  1. Harley-Davidson motorcycle—Performance. I. Title.
  II. Series: Motorbooks International CyclePro series.
  TL448.H3M876 1997   97-12210
  629.28'775—dc21

On the front cover: This exotic Evolution engine sports fuel injections and four-valve heads. *Nick Cedar*
On the back cover: **Top:** The four camshafts on the Sporstster engine are installed in sequence. **Bottom:** The exhaust side of Rivera's four-valve setup feeds through a siamesed port into a single outlet. *Rivera*

Printed in the United States of America

Introduction

In *Harley-Davidson Big Twin Performance Handbook,* I covered various stages of engine performance, from Stage I street motors to Stage III big-inch race motors. In addition, I included a list of necessary aftermarket speed parts and their suppliers.

This book assumes you know what you want to accomplish and have a general idea how to get there. I'll cover three basic stages of performance and identify parts so we can begin from a common point. But I'll assume you know the difference between a camshaft and a crankpin, and that you understand how specific parts work—for instance, the effect of a cam with 0.490-inch lift versus one with 0.550-inch lift.

Just in case you don't have my first book (And why not?), this one will cover the different go-fast parts with short descriptions of how they affect performance. I'll start with the Stage I street motor—80ci and bolt-on parts. Then I'll progress to Stage II—a lot of aftermarket parts and some serious machine work, especially on the heads. I'll finish with the Stage III motor—lots of cubic inches, big cam, and high-flow heads, plus all the necessary machine work.

After covering what you'll need to dial in a high-performance engine, I'll detail exactly how to take a motor apart on the way to increased performance—be it simply a cleanup pass with a cylinder hone, or a complete teardown. Then step by step, I'll show how to put the mo-

Randy Snyder and Doug Morrow of Carl's Speed Shop pose with their Sportster-based land speed record machines. Note both engines sport intake scoops, not air filters. You can imagine what a few pounds of salt will do to the engine bores. This is OK for a racer that is rebuilt after a few runs, but definitely will drastically shorten the life of a street bike's engine. *Carl's Speed Shop*

tor back together, fire it up, and turn gasoline into noise.

Most of this information will cover the newer Evolution motor, like that in the 1995–1996 Dyna Glide. All the operations will pertain to the older engines in general, but I'll note differences along the way. Except with the Stage III engine, I'll assume you want to ride on the street at least occasionally, so I will build the engines with that in mind.

For someone who wants a smooth, everyday street machine, 75 horsepower is a good limit, and that's the Stage I engine. It idles OK, starts

easily, has a steady idle, and will supply you with a fair share of grins when you yank the throttle. Stage II takes matters a full step further, but it's one you should think about before you make it, because it might be a little too much in day-to-day driving for most people. Reliability isn't a problem—RevTech's 96-horsepower Old Blue has 25,000 miles and over 500 full-throttle dyno runs on her and still runs great. But rideability suffers when the horsepower climbs much above 85. An all-out 125-horsepower Stage III motor is strictly for racing.

First, I need to cover a few basics.

1 Equipment and Basic Rules

Safety and Proper Operating Procedures

Before beginning work on a Stage I engine, I need to say a few things about tool safety and general procedures. Always work on one part at a time. Clean and inspect all parts as you go. Be sure all holes are clear and passages are open. Compressed air is a terrific way to check openings, so this might be a good time to invest in an air compressor. I've had one for 25 years and would be lost without it.

If any parts are rusted or corroded, replace them if you can. If you must reuse them, remove the corrosion with a wire brush on an electric drill, or a bead blaster. You can also use vapor blasting, rust remover, abrasive cloth, or a hand wire brush. Clean any surface rust from machined surfaces. Once they're clean, spray machined iron parts with WD-40 to prevent surface rust. Strip rusted painted surfaces to bare metal, then prime and repaint, preferably with a two-part epoxy aircraft paint—DuPont's Imron, for ex-

ample. If the paint can withstand bug hits at 500 miles per hour, it can likely handle anything you can throw at it.

Once parts are clean, place them on a clean surface and cover with clean, lint-free cloth or paper. Butcher paper spread out on a bench works well. I used to cover engine parts with freshly laundered bath towels, but the other member of the household squelched that. Now I've found that surgical towels (usually blue or green and about 12 inches square) are lint-free and work perfectly. Either date a surgical nurse, or call a hospital or surgical center and find out if you can buy some. Hospitals typically use them only once, then wash and dispose of them.

When measuring machined parts, double-check your measurements and write them down. Measure what's there, not what you want to see. No matter how you hold a dial indicator, you can't add a thousandth of an inch to a bearing.

Don't be afraid to buy new nuts and bolts. Some race-engine builders use fasteners once and then discard them. Self-locking nuts, such as Nyloks, should fit tightly on their bolts—if they don't, toss them. Any screw or bolt with a semi-stripped head or slot is guaranteed to cost you a knuckle and maybe a broken part. If a bolt strips in aluminum, you can save the part with a thread insert, such as a Helicoil, but check the bolt threads for damage. If you find burred or nicked threads or damage of any sort on a fastener, discard it. Don't put it in the bottom of your toolbox or in a coffee can as a spare—throw it away.

A whole book could be written about fasteners. Suffice it to say that you should always use H-D bolts for special applications. When buying new fasteners, stick with Grade 5 or better. Graded hardware is marked on the bolt head with various lines denoting minimum tensile strength. Grade 5 has three lines across the head, Grade 8 has six.

Believe me, nothing is more frustrating than to have a bike down because a bolt snapped. Also, if you can think of anything that hurts more than skinning a knuckle across a cylinder fin on a cold night, let me know.

When installing any fitting with pipe threads, seal them with Teflon tape. Be sure no tape covers the opening of the fitting.

6

Going with a completely assembled "mountain motor"—96ci or so—from someone like Axtell might be the best route to performance if you've never built an engine before. All the hard work in the bottom end has been done for you; just heads, carb, pipes, and fire her up. *Axtell*

A bike support stand and a roll-around seat with tools underneath makes working on your bike much easier.

When you finally get the engine up on the table, you'll need something to hold it. This stand takes XL engines from 1957 to 1985. It'll work as your third hand. *CCI*

This is the stand you'll need for mounting a Big Twin. Either one can be bolted or clamped to the workbench to give you a solid foundation to work from. *CCI*

One special tool useful on any stage engine is a cam gear mike and gauge pins. These pins are made by Andrews and are used to properly determine cam and pinion gear size. Two sizes are available—0.105-inch diameter and 0.108-inch diameter. *CCI*

Don't over tighten any pipe fitting, as Teflon tape will let you run the threads all the way down until they disappear. Usually 1 to 1 1/2 threads should be showing.

Wiring, Hoses, and Lines

Rubber hoses more than one year old should be changed; replace them with metal-braided Teflon lines. It only takes one broken fuel line spewing gas on a hot engine to scare the living bejeesus out of you—especially if it hap-

pens at high speed. (No, I didn't catch fire, but I almost burned a 1971 XLH down to the hubs when a fuel line split at about 45 miles per hour: Lock up the brakes, throw the bike down in the dirt, throw the dirt on the bike, pray.)

Check all wiring. Replace any that have cracked insulation or loose connectors. With a combination wire crimping and cutting tool and a box of Stay-Con terminals, you can rewire a bike for about four dollars worth of wire.

Gaskets

This is an easy one. Never reuse gaskets or O-rings—ever.

Storing Information

You and I have been pullin' down Harleys for so many years that we absolutely know where all the parts go, even the little ones, but for those who don't have total recall, a little help is in order.

I highly recommend taking pictures of everything before it comes apart. Get a cheap Polaroid

Ashcroft pressure gauges can be used for a number of purposes; in this case, it's a valve-spring tester. *Jim's Tools*

Jim's also supplies a cam installation tool that keeps you from having to remove the pushrods, pushrod tubes, tappets, etc. The tool holds the tappets up in the lifter blocks while the cam is changed. *Jim's Tools*

Crane's "Tune-a-cam" kit comes with degree wheel dial indicator, TDC indicator, and lightweight checking springs. It can be used to check crank end play, cam end play, and shaft runout. *Jim's Tools*

camera with a built-in flash, and photograph how everything goes together. A Polaroid gives instant results, so you know right away if the pictures came out—not three days from now when everything's in boxes. As you take the bike down, shoot pictures of the procedure. Once the tank is off, take a few shots looking straight down. Shoot a picture of the motor mounts and attaching bolts. Shoot the throttle and choke linkage, or anything else you might not remember a month from now.

Bearing Care

Always clean bearings by soaking them in a safety solvent.

Don't use chlorine-based solvents such as Dichloromethane or Tetrachloroethylene (TCE), because they will remove all the protective oil film. Don't spin bearings with an air hose to dry them. I know it reminds you of your childhood to hear 'em whir, but try to resist the impulse— bearing races can chip or brinnel when spun without lubricant. Plus you don't want to look 12 years old, do you?

Tool Safety

Don't use regular, chrome-plated sockets on an air wrench— they can't stand the pounding; either the chrome will chip off or the socket will split. Wear safety glasses. You may think they look dorky, but blindness is a hell of a lot worse. If this were a bicycle book, I'd tell you to never point an air tool at someone, but since this is a Harley book, I don't have to, do I?

If you must use a hammer on a wrench, get a "striking face" wrench. Better yet, use a longer wrench for increased leverage.

OK, that's enough preaching from Father Murphy—let's see what it takes to build high-horsepower engines.

Tools and Fasteners

Basic tools for all engine stages consist of:
* A set of good screwdrivers, Phillips and straight blade. Throw worn ones away before you start rounding off screw heads or slipping and gouging the paint.
* A full set of Allen wrenches, 5/64- to 3/8-inch.
* Open- and box-end wrenches, 5/16- to 1 1/4-inch.
* Pliers and side-cutters with plastic-covered handles.
* A set of pry bars, 12-, 24-, and 36-inch.
* A 3/8-inch-drive socket set, 1/4- to 1-inch minimum, with extensions from 1 1/2 to 6 inches. A 3/8-inch-drive universal comes in handy too.
* Two 3/8-inch-drive ratchet handles, 8- and 4-inch, and a 12-inch breaker bar.
* A 1/2-inch-drive socket set, 5/8- to 1-1/4-inch, ratchet and breaker bar.
* Three adjustable wrenches, 6-, 8-, and 12-inch, preferably with plastic-covered handles.
* A ball-peen hammer, a brass hammer, and a 22-ounce claw hammer with a smooth face.
* Steel chisels and punches, various sizes.
* A brass drift, 3/8-inch by 12-inch.
* A rechargeable flashlight.
* Used-oil container.
* A couple of heavy, clean towels to use for tank and fender covers.
* Shop rags.
* Safety solvent and wash-down tank (An oil drain pan will do).
* Clothespins.
* Lock wire and pliers.
* Universal gear puller.
* Snap-ring pliers.
* Piston-ring compressor.
* Timing mark view plug, Harley part # HD-96295-65D.
* Oil-filter wrench.
* Valve-lapping tool.

Specialty tools you'll find useful, but not necessary, include: an inductive timing light, a cylinder compression gauge, a valve-spring compressor, a nylon valve-guide cleaning brush, an engine stand, a volt-ohm-amp meter (I use a Fluke 78), Corbin-clamp pliers, and a flywheel-truing stand. Experienced mechanics might also want an air wrench with impact sockets, both standard and Allen.

A good source for tools is Sears or your friendly Snap-On dealer. Jim's Tools (800-482-6913) handles Harley specialty items. Buy good tools and they will last you a lifetime. Buy cheap tools and you will be buying them your whole life.

2 Stage I through Stage III Big Twin Engines

The Stage I Engine

When building a hot-rod Evolution Harley, how much performance you end up with is largely a product of how much money you throw at the bike. It's a cliché, but the old adage is still true: "Speed costs money, how fast do you want to spend?" Stage I consists of bolt-on parts within a wide price range, but raising the stock Harley Evolution engine to 75 horsepower requires changes to the induction system, cam, ignition, and exhaust.

When planning changes, remember the engine is nothing more than an air pump. The more air it pumps, the more power it makes. Opening up only the output—exhaust—side of the pump without improving the intake won't provide much gain. All aspects of the pump must be improved for an overall gain, so it's better to wait until you've got enough money to work with the motor as a total package than to go about it piecemeal.

Improved breathing at the intake side must be balanced by a cam change to handle the additional airflow. Likewise, if you just slap on an aftermarket set of pipes, you'll likely be disappointed. Noise might increase, but that's about all—performance might even deteriorate if you make no other changes.

To obtain the most for your

dollar, you should treat the engine as a complete assembly, from air cleaner to exhaust tips. The best approach is to figure out on paper what you want to change, how much it will cost, and when your checkbook can handle it.

The 75-horsepower engine will give you a suitable increase in performance—around a mid-13-second elapsed time and 95 miles per hour in the quarter-mile. If you're not interested in tearing down the engine every 20,000 miles or so and want to be able to go touring a bit without any problems, this is fast enough for a street motor. Granted you won't be blowing off Kawasaki ZX-11s, and it will take at least two leaps to clear tall buildings, but it will take the worry out of being close—like when you try to pass one Peterbilt and another appears in the opposite direction.

For the Stage I engine, limit revs to 6,200rpm, which produces a piston speed of 4,500 feet per minute. Much higher than this and reliability suffers and original pieces—like engine cases—get replaced by very expensive aftermarket parts. That's OK on a 125-horsepower engine that covers asphalt a quarter-mile at a time, but not for a street motor built on a budget.

Done correctly, changing the carb, cam, ignition, and exhaust can net you 25 horsepower over the current 51-horse, 50-state engines. Start with the correct tools for the job. You'll need to open up the timing case to change the cam, so your tool kit should contain more than the usual collection of screwdrivers, adjustable wrenches, and hammers.

The Stage I engine requires pretty much the same types of parts as the Stage II, just not so many of them, so I'll wait until Stage II before getting deep into detail. At Stage I, most of the

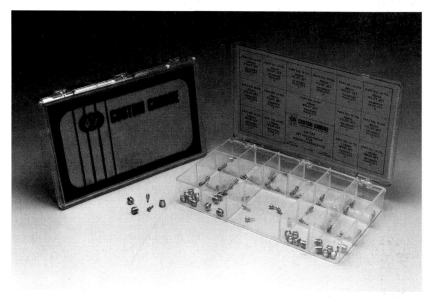

An assortment of main and pilot jets is handy for a stock bike and essential for major engine work. *CCI*

work is bolt-on; only the cam requires involved work, and that will be covered under Stage II. Later in the book, we will get down to how to open an engine, install a stroker kit, true flywheels (which involves magic), and install an aftermarket cam and oil pump. Disassembly and assembly will be pictured in detail.

For now, I'll start with a list of the aftermarket parts needed to raise power to the 75 horsepower level. I'll pick parts by brand name to make a combination, but remember, there are many ways of getting to the same point. If I include Rich Products exhaust system, that doesn't mean Super-Trapp's isn't equally as good. It's just a choice of products that I'm more familiar with—you can pick as you wish.

If I could only afford minimal changes, I'd go for an aftermarket cam with a lift around 0.500 and 234 degrees of duration or better. The stock pipes would get a 1-inch drill punched through the baffles, balanced by a set of carb jets for the factory fuel-mixer, and a low-restriction air-filter element from K&N. The bike would still

retain a factory stock appearance, with power greatly enhanced.

Package Specifications for Stage I Engines
75-80 horsepower
Approximate cost in 1996—
$1,400

Kit #1
1. S&S Super B Carb & Teardrop Air Cleaner
2. Crane Hydraulic Cam Part # 1-1101
3. Jacobs Energy Team Ignition, Part # 379126
4. SuperTrapp two-into-one exhaust

Kit #2
1. Mikuni HS40 Carb
2. K&N Air Filter Part # ML-092B
3. Competition Cams V-Thunder, Part # Evo-3020
4. MSD MC1 Ignition
5. Drag Specialties Python II Pipes

These are but a few ways to gain up to 75 horsepower on a stock displacement bike. Other companies market equivalent

1995-96 Dyna Glide Engine Specifications

General
Number of Cylinders 2
Type................................4-cycle, 45-degree V-twin
Horsepower....................69 @ 5,000rpm
Torque............................82 foot-pounds @
....3600rpm
Bore ....3.498 inches
Stroke ....4.250 inches
Piston Displacement ....81.7ci (80ci nominal)
Compression Ratio 8.5:1

Valves
Guide fit
Exhaust ....0.0015–0.0033 inch
Intake..............................0.0008–0.0026 inch
Seat width.......................0.040–0.062 inch
Stem height from head ...1.990–20.024 inch
Outer spring free length..2.105–2.177 inch
Inner spring free length...1.926–1.996 inch

Rocker Arm
End clearance ....0.003–0.013 inch
Bushing-rocker arm fit.....0.004–0.002 inch
Shaft-bushing ....0.0005–0.002 inch

Rocker Arm Shaft
Shaft-rocker cover..........0.0007–0.002 inch

Oil Pump Pressure
12–35psi @ 2,000rpm

Piston
Cylinder clearance ....0.00075–0.00175 inch
Ring gap—compression ...0.007–0.020 inch
Ring gap—oil...................0.009–0.052 inch
Piston pin fit....................0.0001–0.0004 inch

Cylinder Head
Valve guide to head ....0.0020–0.0033 inch
Valve seat to head ....0.0020–0.0045 inch
Head surface distortion...0.006 inch

Connecting Rod
Pin fit.............................0.0003–0.0007 inch
Flywheel side play...........0.005–0.025 inch
Rod to crankpin..............0.0004–0.0017 inch

Hydraulic Lifters
Guide fit in case ....0.000–0.004 inch
Guide fit ....0.0008–0.002 inch

Gearcase
Breather gear end play ...0.001–0.011 inch
Cam gear shaft ....0.00075–0.00175 inch
Cam gear shaft
in bearing.......................0.0005–0.0025 inch
Cam gear end play ....0.001–0.050 inch
Oil pump drive shaft
to bushing......................0.0004–0.0025 inch

Flywheel
Rim runout......................0.000–0.010 inch
Runout at shaft...............0.000–0.002 inch
End play ....0.001–0.005 inch

Ignition Timing
Retarded.........................TDC
1,100–1,500rpm..............20 degrees BTDC
Spark-plug gap................0.038–0.043 inch

parts that will do the same job. Some are shown below. Addresses and phone numbers are in the Appendix at the back of the book.

Cams

Andrews EV3, EV13, EV46
Bartels BP20, BP40
Crane 1-1000 (requires you check piston clearance)
Sifton 140-EV, 145-EV

Ignition

Andrews
Dyna

Exhaust

Bub Enterprises Bad Dogs
Kerker
Rich Products 2 into 1

Basically, you can mix or match any of the above, but keep in mind you need to change all four—intake, cam, ignition, and exhaust—to get the full benefit. The one you pick depends on your own preferences; any of these combinations will pull horsepower out of a Big Twin in sufficient quantities to make riding a great deal more fun. You might even be able to win a dollar or more in some sort of speed contest.

The Stage II Engine

If you happen to be the type of person who thinks a .44 Magnum is cute, or that the 405-horsepower ZR-1 was the only Corvette with any power, you just might not be satisfied with 75 horses at the rear wheel. You don't want to blow most people's doors off, you want to take the windshield and fenders too. No matter how much horsepower you extract from an engine, there's always someone with five more than you. With that in mind, it's now time to build a radical street machine—the Stage II engine, which boots up 96 real horsepower at the rear wheel.

This motor will take you into the realm of serious racing bikes that only occasionally see the street. Reliability won't be as good as with the Stage I engine—if only because you can't resist turning the throttle. After all, the boot-in-the-back feeling you get every time the engine climbs up the torque curve is why you go through all the time and expense to build a fast bike.

There are two ways to make power. One is through the use of multiple cylinders turning over at a good percentage of the speed of light. The Japanese are the absolute masters at this, getting 100 horsepower out of a 600-cc four-cylinder spinning 14,000rpm. Power builds like a Singer sewing machine on steroids—the engine turns faster, you go faster.

The other way is through large amounts of low-end torque. A great number of us are certifiable power junkies. We live for that punch when the carb goes wide open and the revs jump. Most of the riders I know enjoy the rush of power but would really rather not have to put up with a machine that turns 7,000rpm at 65 miles per hour and makes little power until the tach passes 8,000. We prefer to run down the freeway at a leisurely pace, engine turning around 2,700rpm, and be able to twist the grip and have things happen without a downshift or three.

Torque at low rpm is what makes Harleys jump. Old Blue, RevTech's test mule, on the RevTech dyno, had 75.6 foot-pounds of torque at 3,000rpm, with a peak of 91.9 foot-pounds at 4,700rpm. For comparison, a Suzuki GSX-R1100 makes 47 foot-pounds at 3,000rpm and peaks at 74.8 at 7,000rpm. The Suzuki makes 125.6 horsepower at 9,500rpm, while the RevTech bike hit 96 at 6,300rpm.

In order to get the rated 96 horsepower out of an Evo engine, you need to change quite a few parts, as well as make some fairly expensive decisions. If you plan to use all the power on a regular basis, you should think about replacing the stock engine cases with a stronger aftermarket set. A lot more power can, and will, make the stock Harley cases flex and eventually crack. A set of cases from S.T.D. or Sputhe Engineering will eliminate that problem.

This is where the expenses begin to climb, though. Above and beyond the go-fast parts, expect to spend at least $900 to $1,000 for a set of cases, but that's a lot cheaper than having to redo the engine when a stock case cracks and lets go. On the stock crankcases, a crack usually shows up as an oil leak behind the primary case. This can happen from applying too much horsepower too many times, but sometimes a case will crack because of a seemingly unrelated problem.

For the street, there really isn't any good reason to build an engine that has to go to 7,000rpm to make power. Old Blue would run up to that range quite easily, but it wasn't really a bike to cover a 300-mile day. It really wasn't happy trying to run around 2,500 to 3,000rpm, where the typical Harley spends 90 percent of its life on the road.

Parts and Machine Work

Building an 80-inch Evo to 96 horsepower will take some serious work on the heads. Getting an Evo to flow enough air to maximize the rest of the parts is a major consideration. Again, if you think of the engine as an air pump, that pump has to flow a lot of air to make 90+ horsepower.

The intake and exhaust valves regulate the amount of air flowing into the engine. The size and

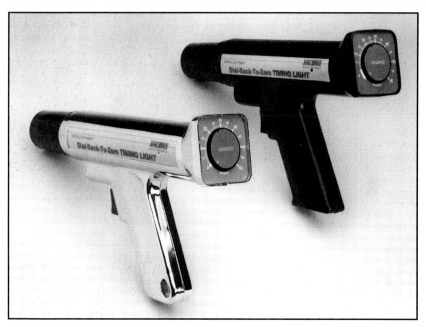

Jacobs Electronics has a couple of different versions of their "dial back to zero" timing lights. They all operate on the same principle of setting the total timing advance in the window, then checking the timing at 2,000rpm. The timing mark should show in the center of the timing opening. *Jacobs Electronics.*

A spark plug gapper is a nifty tool, but not an essential one. Jacobs spark-plug gapper sets the proper clearance and keeps the outside electrode parallel to the center one. *Jacobs Electronics*

amount of time the valves are open play major roles in making horsepower. Ideally, the intake and exhaust valves would be located so all the air-fuel mixture possible could flow through the engine with the least interference.

On an H-D Evo V-twin, with its narrow cylinder angle and single carburetor, this just isn't possible. Once past the air cleaner, incoming air must turn constantly on its way through the engine.

When flowing through the engine, the air-fuel mixture will be slowed by any obstructions on the way to the combustion chamber. The pressed-in valve seats usually have a ridge around their outside edges, which causes power-robbing turbulence. Even if the seat is cut to remove this ridge, after a few thousand miles it will begin to reform through wear. Valve-to-seat contact areas must be renewed to smooth this area,

and the valve seats must be ground so that the valve touches evenly all around its face. This is what is done during a "valve job."

Maximum airflow and heat transfer are obtained with 0.060-inch contact between the intake valve and seat. The exhaust valve needs 0.010-inch more area, since valve-to-seat contact provides cooling. Intake valves are cooled by the incoming mixture, but exhaust valves are constantly exposed to hot exhaust gases, and need more surface area to transfer heat to the head. Some exhaust valves have a hollow stem filled with a low boiling point metal—such as sodium—to help transfer heat away from the valve face. Exhaust valves can actually turn cherry red and burn away if not sufficiently cooled.

Aftermarket valve manufacturers often use stainless steel to insure longer life, while more expensive ones use titanium for its

strength, light weight, and heat resistance. The stems are hard-chrome-plated for better wear, and the tips hardened for the same reason. For maximum airflow, the joint between the stem and head is radiused and smoothed.

Purchase the best valves money can buy. Saving $10 just to have a stem pull off at 6,000rpm is a poor way to economize. One broken valve will cause an engine to deposit a lot of very expensive parts in the bottom of the cases.

Manley lists a set of two 1.850-inch intake valves at $70. For titanium (1.90-inch or larger) expect to lay down $270, plus expenses for larger seats in the head. Racing-only engines benefit from titanium valves because their increased strength and light weight mean they have less inertia to overcome, so they can accelerate faster and place less stress on the valve spring when they close.

The dyno results are compiled by the computer and can be read on the screen or saved for a printout.

A dyno is the ideal place to tune your engine, and also a good place to see how much more horsepower you got for your money. To run a bike on CCI's dyno, a rider has to be on it to shift gears and run the throttle. Due to the very high noise level, all personnel inside the dyno room must wear hearing protectors at all times. I pulled one muff away from my left ear as the engine crossed 6,000rpm, and poof—no hearing for the rest of that day.

One of the screens available shows a simulated tach and speedometer. The speedo is only accurate if the rolling diameter of the rear wheel is plugged into the computer. This is done by inputting the tire's outside diameter. All readings are taken in top gear, so it's quite common to see 6,750rpm and 160 miles per hour.

Good valves require good valve guides. Manley offers two types: silicon-aluminum-bronze for the race track and cast-iron for the street. For valve-to-guide clearance, Manley recommends 0.0015-0.0020-inch for intakes, and 0.0020-0.0025-inch for exhausts. Manley's Teflon/metal, or all-Teflon valve-guide seals should be installed on all street engines. These seals keep oil from being drawn down the valve stems into the combustion chamber, and reduce carbon build-up on the back side of the intake valve.

The Stage II engine requires either professionally modified stock heads or a set of ported aftermarket heads. For an owner unfamiliar with porting and modifying heads, you're better off with an aftermarket set. Not that you couldn't get it right and extract maximum airflow from your own heads by judicious use of a grinder, but the chances of doing it wrong far outweigh the possibilities of getting it right. Rather than ruining a set or two of heads with your Dremel tool, contacting someone like Airflow Research and perhaps letting them build a set would be a better way to go.

Labor for a basic port, polish, and valve job costs $700, parts extra. For an all-out racing head with larger valves, titanium retainers, and locks, expect to pay $1,700, machining and welding included. S.T.D. Development provides a complete set of fully ported and flowed heads, along with a matching intake manifold, for $2,500.

Individual head work typically runs as follows:
1. Flow test and
   head calibration................$150
2. Mill head deck...................$80
3. Valve job
   (no new parts)...........$85-$100

Intake and exhaust ports are typically rated in cubic feet per minute (cfm) of airflow at a constant pressure drop and specific valve opening. Typical flow rates for a stock Harley head with 1.850-inch intake and 1.600-inch exhaust valves are 228-cfm intake and 159-cfm exhaust at 0.500-inch valve lift, testing with 25 pounds of pressure. Porting and polishing should lift the figures to 275-cfm intake and 192-cfm exhaust at the same 0.500-inch lift. Trick heads, with 1.940-inch intakes and 1.625-inch exhausts, will flow 297/198cfm—enough to make them worthwhile for serious racing.

Aftermarket Heads

Another way to increase airflow to the engine is through a set of aftermarket heads—let someone else have the dubious pleasure of doing all the flow and porting work, you just sign the check. The principal benefit is knowing the heads will be done right. You need to talk to the company building the heads, and know what other mods you're doing—cam, carb, compression ratio, exhaust—so the company can tailor the heads to your engine.

It's possible to simply write a check to a company like Rivera Engineering and order a set off the shelf, but you'd be far ahead by actually calling the company and talking to the engineers before spending your money. Let them advise you about what head is best for your particular engine setup.

Sputhe Engineering builds high-performance two-valve heads and advertises that they will outperform Rivera's four-valve setup. Like Rivera, Sputhe heads are special castings, not modified stock heads. Sputhe uses the same aircraft-grade aluminum that Harley-Davidson used in its XR-750 heads.

Sputhe raises the inlet ports higher than stock for better flow, then fares the intake valve guides for smoother airflow and increased valve-guide support. On the exhaust side, the guide fairings improve exhaust scavenging and help remove heat from the valves and guides. Valve seats are Inconel, and guides are either aluminum-bronze or manganese-meehanite. Stainless intake valves are titanium-nitride coated, as are the one-piece austenitic-forged exhaust valves. The company will supply valve springs to match your cam—another reason you should contact the manufacturer and provide an exact list of parts in your engine.

Intake valves in the Sputhe heads range from 1.973 to 2.100

This particular day, CCI was testing this motor combination with a SuperTrapp exhaust. The difference between 6 and 14 plates was quite noticeable, both in sound and dyno performance.

All measurements and modifications must be taken for even the most basic parts of the engine. Here, pistons and wrist pins are being weighed, and the weight recorded.

inches, depending on specific use. Engines in the 95-to-104-ci range best benefit from 2.000-inch intake valves, matched to a 1.750-inch exhaust valve. For drag-racing purposes only, Sputhe builds finless heads with 2.100-inch intake and 1.875-inch exhaust valves. Most street motors running the stock 80-ci bore size (3.780-inch) work best with 1.937-inch intake and 1.710-inch exhaust valves. Whichever way you go, expect to write a check in excess of $1,500 for a set of heads from Sputhe.

A quick aside. Sputhe manufactures 60-degree V-twin engines (stock is 45, but you knew that), running in displacement from 101ci for the street to 125ci for fuel dragsters. These engines are few and far between, but offer the rider looking for absolute performance a bolt-in way to go. This engine is designed to be the ultimate air-cooled, pushrod V-twin. It bolts to stock Big Twin motor mounts and takes a cone-motor inner primary. It runs two Lectron 44-millimeter carbs, a Dyna ignition, a street roller cam of various grinds, and comes as a completely assembled unit. Just bolt it in and hang on. It's fair to say that 101 inches will take the worry out of being close.

Custom Chrome's (RevTech) answer to the head question starts with its "Street-Legal" stock-compression heads. These are manufactured from 356 T-6 aluminum and are ready to bolt to your cylinders. The intake ports have been reshaped from stock and are raised 0.100 inch using a D-shaped port to increase flow. They will still work with the stock intake manifold, although I'd advise using an aftermarket manifold rather than the stocker.

Combustion chambers are the "bathtub" shape that many other head builders use today—including H-D. Intake valves are 1.940-inch, and exhaust valves are 1.610. These sizes work well with 10.0:1 compression in stock displacement motors, though the pistons must be cut for valve clearance. Valve springs will handle up to a 0.600-inch lift cam up to 6,500rpm without float. RevTech's heads showed a flow of 230cfm at 0.600-inch valve lift when the heads were set up on a Super Flow SF3500 flow bench with 25-inch pressure and a #5 orifice.

RevTech advocates using these heads with a complete performance package of cam, carb,

The rod gets supported at the balance point, then the small end is weighed.

CCI has numerous bikes undergoing modifications at any one time. Each new part has to be logged out to the particular bike, then road-tested. The amount of road-test time goes into the same log. The mechanics are forced to ride a different Harley at least once a week, for a couple hundred miles. No—it won't work: I've already volunteered to test for free.

exhaust, and ignition for maximum performance. RevTech heads are milled for dual plugs and come with a pair of socket-head plugs if only one plug per head is used. Go with the dual plugs.

Edelbrock offers a set of high-performance racing heads

street-legal in all 50 states. They use a unique combustion chamber shape with a 72-cc volume, which increases compression from 8.5:1 to 9.5:1. A D-shaped exhaust port is used for better flow. Installation is bolt-on, but requires Edelbrock's intake manifold.

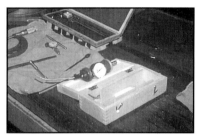

Matt Negherbon, the RevTech R&D mechanic, had this set of micrometers in the top of his toolbox. Well-worn, they see a lot of use each day.

The brains behind Accel's ignition system. Light, compact, low-amp draw, custom engine cutoff, and no more double-fire ignition. *Accel*

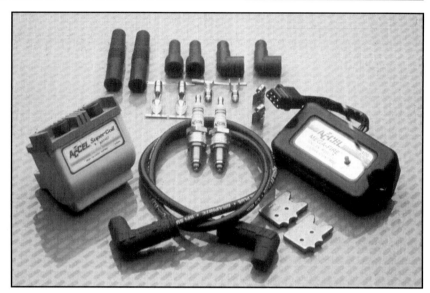

Accel's ignition system kit includes everything from spark plugs to an ignition module with a built-in adjustable rev limit. *Accel*

Accel also produces a complete fuel injection system for Harleys. It's still a bit pricey—$3,000 or so—but big brother and the smog police will soon see to it that all bikes come with a system as efficient as this one controlling the sparks and fuel. *Accel*

Stroked H-D twins often require a reworked intake manifold. Since stroker cylinders are often taller than stock, the intake ports are farther apart from one another, so stroked motors often require a wider intake manifold to bridge the gap. The intake manifolds can be spec'd to fit up to 0.125-inch stroker cylinders with heads that have been milled 0.050 inch. Or, they can be fit to stock-length cylinders with the same 0.050-inch cut.

Volumetric Efficiency and Compression Ratio (CR)

The Stage II engine, with a tuned intake tract and an exhaust system operating at maximum efficiency, will produce a Volumetric efficiency (VE) close to 100 percent. VE is the percentage of cylinder fill during engine operation. A street Harley turning at its torque peak will typically have a VE of 80

to 85 percent. Improving the engine's breathing will improve the VE, which can actually exceed 100 percent in well-designed high-performance engines.

Once you've improved engine breathing, bumping the compression is a simple way to increase power. Everything else being equal,

there's a direct proportion between compression ratio and horsepower—raise compression 10 percent and you'll get a 10 percent bump in horsepower as well. Unfortunately, it's not that simple, since raising the compression ratio typically hinders an engine's breathing, because the smaller combustion chamber often

Planning Performance

Once you've gotten over the newness of your Harley and decide a little more "go" might be in order, you can save yourself a lot of extra work, anguish, broken parts, and money by stepping back and taking a long look at what you really want to accomplish with any modifications. When someone asks me about making his bike run harder, I usually take the time to explain "Total Concept Performance."

It doesn't matter if the plan is to build an out-and-out racer for the quarter-mile or add power to an overloaded touring machine, my concept is always the same. Look at the entire bike as an integral machine—one unit—not just a collection of motor, transmission, front end, and all that stuff in the back.

The salient point is that any change you make to one part will affect the rest of the bike. Growing another 25 horsepower will put more strain on the clutch, create more energy for the brakes to dissipate in heat, and cause the stock suspension to work harder. The whole machine feels the change.

This means that when you make a large boost in power, you need to look at the rest of the bike to see what the additional power will do to the other components, then modify them to handle the increased load.

For instance, when you build an engine for more horsepower, you probably will want to use it whenever possible. More power transmitted to the rear wheel will increase the load on everything from the primary chain to the swingarm and wheel bearings. The rear shocks will have to work harder to control the rear wheel, especially if you plan to run any land-speed attempts or any competition that revolves around the top end of the performance spectrum. At best, the stock Harley suspension is adequate for what the engine is built to do, but the operative word is "adequate." Take a bone-stock Dyna Glide, capable of 100 miles per hour at most, and try to run it 125+ at El Mirage dry lake, for instance, and you'll definitely put a greater load on the stock components than they were designed to handle.

Hard street running, or hammering the throttle up to 110 miles per hour in the quarter-mile, requires that the bike be able to stop at that speed with some degree of reliability. I know none of you would exceed the speed limit on our nation's highways, but hypothetically speaking, think about the additional load placed on the brakes and suspension when you come cooking over the top of a hill at 29 percent of the speed of light, only to have someone in a Buick pull out of a driveway at 0.0005 miles per hour, 100 yards in front of you. I won't ever admit to having done anything that dumb, but I have learned that stock H-D brakes really don't want to stop that fast, and the front fork, after it hits bottom no longer controls where the bike goes. (I missed the Buick, but only by using the oncoming lane as an escape road.)

So now I advocate modifying the bike as a whole. When you budget money for the engine, be sure to think about better suspension to put all that increased power to the ground. When you plan to run 125 miles per hour and better, make sure the front end won't visit you with a good case of front-wheel wobble. It takes only one high-speed tank-slapper to give you religion. Bad triple-clamp bearings can induce shimmy, but worn-out bearings in the swingarm can also make the front end take strange and interesting paths.

Look at the odometer. If it reads 25,000 miles, or more, and you're planning some major horsepower surgery, be sure to consider the suspension and brakes in your budget. After 25,000 miles, stock shocks just aren't going to handle a major horsepower transplant. Go for an aftermarket set built to take the load. The front end will definitely be happier with a set of high-performance damper tubes, stiffer springs, heavier oil, and a fork brace.

And I know this will sound simple to some, but buy a set of new tires rated to take the increased speed. If you plan to go 125+, install a pair of tires rated for sustained speeds above that. For instance, Avon Super Venoms and Dunlop K591 Elite SPs both offer a V rating, good for a sustained 149 miles per hour. Don't try to get by on a set of standard—or worse, worn—H-rated tires.

In all Stage I through Stage III engines, the cam is changed. Unless you are an expert, one cam pretty much looks like another, but their performances can be 180 degrees apart. The only way to be sure as to what you have is to read the instruction sheet that came with the cam and mike the lobes to check lift. *CCI*

A kit like this matches the rest of the valvetrain to your new camshaft. Consisting of lifter galleys, lifters, pushrods, and all the needed fasteners, the kit makes for a balanced setup. *Competition Cams*

shrouds the valves so they don't flow as well. Also, higher compression tends to cause detonation, or pinging, which also lowers horsepower as well as causing other more serious problems.

The stock compression ratio—also called the mechanical compression ratio—is simply the volume of the combustion chamber when the piston is at bottom dead center (BDC) compared to the volume when it's at top dead center (TDC). Actual compression ratio when the engine is operating is called the Operational Ratio (OR). OR changes depending on the volumetric efficiency; as VE increases, so does the operational compression ratio.

Harley's Big Twins run a mechanical CR between 8.3:1 and 8.5:1 depending on assembly tolerances. A bump to 9.5:1 is usually necessary to make any noticeable increase in power. Racing engines can run compression up to 12.5:1; running strictly on racing gas, an Evo makes excellent drag-racing power with a 12.5:1 compression

ratio, but you have to realize parts go away at a much faster rate. Racing engines get opened up frequently, so this isn't a problem. Bearings can be changed before they fail, and other parts can be inspected and replaced as necessary. But when you start trying to make a 12.5:1 Harley run on the street for any length of time, you'll run into problems.

Just finding fuel that the engine can digest without pinging is a major hassle, since most engines with over 10.5:1 compression ratio can't handle even 92-octane gasoline. Now that alcohol is being added to the fuel, the problem is even worse. Some new multivalve combustion chamber designs will let a motor run on ultrahigh compression, but you'll still run into excessive engine wear when the ratio gets over 12.5:1.

You have to consider how much extra money, time, and effort you're willing to spend to keep a racing engine running. What type of detonation control will be used? And, perhaps most importantly, how much more go will you really

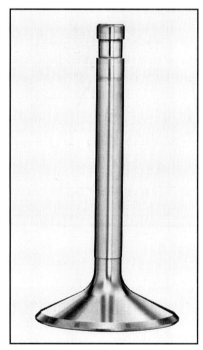

Again, a valve pretty much looks like every other valve. It's the materials in its construction that make the difference. An exhaust valve can be stellite tipped or sodium filled for better cooling. Titanium valves tend to get a bit pricey, but their combination of light weight and strength make them a must for high-rpm race engines. *Manley.*

RevTech's adjustable breathing valves allow the engine builder to precisely match the engine's breathing to its displacement. A larger engine will increase the total volume of the crankcase, and the pistons will have to fight against the increased pressure if the breather isn't set spot on. *CCI*

The length of the rocker arms will affect the total lift of the valve. More lift will of course flow more fuel-air mixture, but too much lift can result in the edge of the valve striking the head. *Florida Caliper*

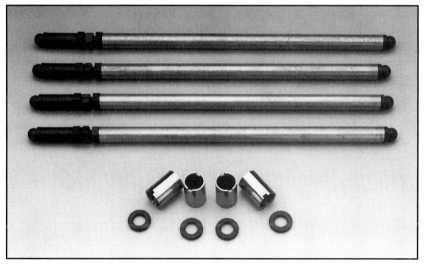

A lot of aftermarket cams require running solid lifters and adjustable pushrods. These rods from CCI come with hydraulic deactivators to change your stock hydraulic lifters to solids. *CCI*

These Sifton adjustable tappets for Sportsters are to be used with solid pushrods only. Some strokers have such an angle between the rocker and cam lobe that the thicker adjustable pushrod will rub against the pushrod tube. Non-adjustable 7/16-inch rods must be used in these cases. *CCI*

Jim's Machining has a set of precision roller tappets ground with a 0.0002-inch fit, which eliminates most causes of pumpdown for all Evo motors, including Sportsters up to 1990. *CCI*

get by stepping on the compression so hard? Engine life may not be a problem if all you do is run it a quarter-mile at a time, but if it has to live on the street, the problems inherent with ultra-high compression just aren't worth the small performance gains.

Something to consider when bumping the compression and changing heads is that combustion benefits greatly from a second spark plug. You can either buy heads set up for two—such as RevTech's—or have your stock heads modified. Running two plugs improves combustion efficiency, makes for easier starting, and allows you to run more compression before the onset of detonation. Any ratio increase above 12:1 really needs the additional plug.

The only engine that won't benefit from twin plugs is the low-compression (7.5:1) Shovelhead engines of the last decade. That engine will still rattle a bit on hot days or under a heavy load below 2,500rpm, but it hasn't been manufactured since 1984 and, frankly, isn't the way to go for a performance engine. Matter of fact, the Shovel is starting to head toward collector status, which means most owners will be looking for stock parts, not go-fast equipment.

Keep in mind that you don't want to let the compression get in front of the engine's ability to breath. Having a lot of squeeze without the ability to get the fuel-air mixture through the combustion chamber is self-defeating. The cam, carb, and exhaust all have to be balanced with the compression. Too much piston sticking up into the combustion chamber can create breathing problems, which cuts power at elevated rpm. Better to run a lower ratio than try to compensate for poor breathing with increased compression.

Also, running a high-compression engine for long periods at high revs increases the possibility of detonation and subsequent engine damage. Going for land-speed records requires a lower compression ratio than running at the drag strip. And any oil allowed into the combustion chamber can, and will, bring on detonation in short order. Straight pipes and ear plugs inside a helmet can make it almost impossible to hear detonation. Usually you'll notice it only when the power goes away. By that time, it's too late to prevent piston damage.

High-compression engines get a better seal between the head and cylinder by using an O-ring in place of a head gasket. Axtell "BT-EV" drag-racing cylinders come with O-ring grooves already cut. Here again, when ordering a kit like this,

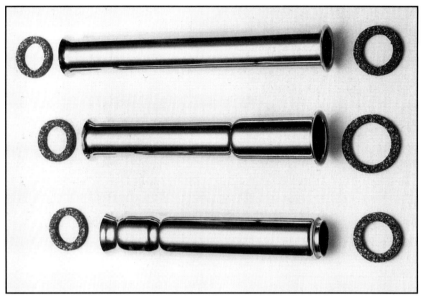

Sometimes you will have to resort to slightly thinner pushrod tube covers to keep rubbing to a minimum. *CCI*

Buy spark plugs by the case and change them frequently. Don't save the old ones in the bottom of the toolbox as spares. Plugs are too cheap and too important to take a chance with an old one. *CCI*

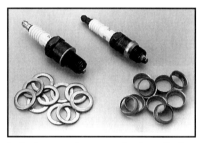

Indexing washers can be installed to help line-up the side electrode away from the incoming fuel-air mixture, promoting better performance. *Jacobs Electronics*

specify bore, stroke, compression, and application of your particular engine. Expect to pay $1,100 for the special-order-only kit.

Compression is one of those things where a little more is good, but a lot more can put the pistons in the bottom of the cases. You can expect a really nice power boost on the street with a 9.5:1 motor. A heavy touring bike with two people aboard can suffer detonation on a long uphill climb if the ratio is much higher, but a

lighter Big Twin can get away with a little more without hurting reliability. Expect to shorten component life by a factor as much as 50 percent if you squeeze the compression over 10.5:1 and make frequent use of all the new-found power.

Pump gas can be mixed with 100LL aviation gas or racing gas to support a higher compression, but if you feel the engine missing or hear any detonation, back off the throttle and run a plug check.

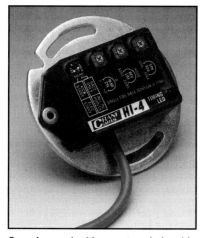

Crane's new ignition system is legal in all 50 states. They mount to the ignition timing plate, and the "race" version has adjustable rear cylinder timing. All models have adjustable rev limits, and the advance curves can be tailored for kick or electric start.

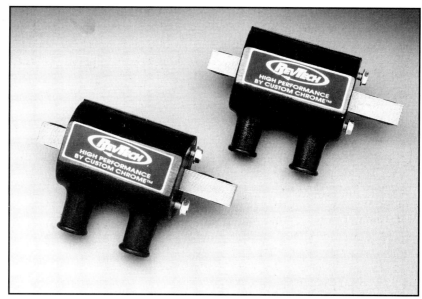

RevTech's hi-po coils put out up to 30,000 volts in both single-plug and dual-plug iterations. *CCI*

The insulator should be a light brown with almost white at the tip. Look for a brown fuel ring at the bottom of the insulator. Detonation damage is typically indicated by flecks of aluminum on the insulator, or a cracked insulator.

Pistons

Changing the compression of a Big Twin entails opening the engine for a piston swap. Companies such as Axtell Sales, Inc., Wiseco, and CCI build pistons in various bore sizes and compression ratios for all Evo engines.

Axtell also specializes in building large-displacement "mountain motors" using flat-top forged pistons. These pistons also are available as an angle-top design, which feature a 30-degree angle on top, as opposed to a flat surface. The head has corresponding area cut into the combustion chamber for clearance. Axtell claims the design maintains turbulence and improves flow over a flat-top piston, and that the angled dome forces the mixture toward the spark plug for better flame propagation. Motors can run a 10:1 compression ratio with these pistons without problems, Axtell claims, but timing and jetting must be altered for optimum results. This is where access to a rear-wheel dyno would come in handy.

Axtell can set you up with anything from a cast-iron stock displacement Pro Street kit with 10:1 pistons, to an elephant-stomping 114.1-ci engine—11.1:1 compression ratio optional. The latter engine is definitely not for the meek of checkbook, because installing the big 3 13/16 bore cylinders requires the stock head-bolt holes to be downsized and heads counterbored and a 30-degree angle cut in the combustion chamber.

Cylinders this big and larger, up to 40.0 inches in diameter, really should be mounted on a set of aftermarket cases. The stock ones will hold up for a while, but you will eventually get to replace them: either all at once when the engine goes blooey, or when enough cracks appear to make oil loss a problem.

To keep tabs on what your electrical system is doing, Dyna offers electrical system monitors that are built to primarily watch battery voltage in total-loss ignition systems. They are a great add-on for a race-only bike; takes the wonder out of battery condition. *CCI*

Let's say you want to run something a little bigger than stock, and you want it to have a life expectancy longer than a mayfly's—what size cylinders and flywheels should you choose? Here's where I'd start talking to the guys who make the stroker motors. For anything close to 100ci or bigger, plan to change the cases to handle the larger bar-

Cylinders and Strokers

Table 2
Engine Displacement (cubic inches)

Bore (Inches) Stroke (inches)	3-7/16	3-1/2*	3-5/8	3-11/16	3-3/4	3-13/16	4	4-1/4
3-31/32	73.6	76.3	81.8	84.7	87.6	90.6	99.7	112.6
4-1/4*	78.8	81.7*	87.6	910.0	93.8	97.1	106.9	120.6
4-1/2	83.5	86.5	920.0	96.2	99.3	102.8	113.1	127.7
4-5/8	85.8	88.9	95.5	101.4	102.2	105.5	116.3	131.2
4-3/4	88.1	91.3	980.05	105.1	104.8	108.5	119.4	134.8
5	92.7	96.1	103.2	106.8	110.3	114.1	125.77	141.9
5-1/4	97.5	1010.0	108.4	112.2	1160.0	119.8	132.1	149.1
5-1/2	102.1	105.8	113.5	117.5	121.4	125.6	138.24	1560.08

* = stock 81.7ci

rels and the added power. Actually you'd be better off opening your checkbook rather than building a stock H-D motor into a 100-inch fire-breather. You won't have many Harley parts left when you're through.

You'll need to change crankcases, cylinders, pistons, flywheels and rods, bearings, heads, cam, pushrods, lifters, oil pump, breather, ignition, fasteners, valve covers, and exhaust headers, and that's just for starters. About the only Harley parts you'll have left will be inner and outer primary covers, and those might go too. You might be better off to just buy a preassembled engine and throw it in the frame. That way you'd know it's right and the actual cost probably wouldn't be all that much more than building one out of pieces.

Axtell makes complete short blocks from 97ci and up. They can be had with either S.T.D. or Delkron cases and stock or S&S flywheels. Depending on size, prices start at $2,900 and go up from there.

To put this in perspective, figure a set of S&S cases alone costs $1,000. An Axtell 97-ci cylinder kit is $825. S&S rods—$300. So far you've spent $2,100 and still need bearings, flywheels, crankpin, pistons, rings, and gaskets. Don't forget the labor to put it all together, open the breather, lap the bearings, and finally balance and true the bottom end. I can't do it for $3,000, and unless you have been building engines for a lot of years, and your uncle owns a Harley shop, neither can you.

You will still need a carb and manifold, a set of heads and pipes, cam and kit, and all the other small parts, so figure at least another $3,000 before the motor makes noise. Some of the expense can be recouped by selling your stock motor to another biker. Its worth depends on condition, miles on the engine, time of year, and year of the motor, but it should bring at least half the cost of the new one.

Building a bigger engine by increasing the stroke is an efficient way to go with a V-twin. Stock bore and stroke is 3.5 by 4.25 inches. This is what's known as an "undersquare" motor—the bore is smaller than the stroke. A

"square" motor is one whose bore and stroke are equal—40.0 by 40.0 inches for example. "Oversquare" motors have a bigger bore than stroke. Japanese motorcycle engines are usually oversquare; the Suzuki GSX-R1100, for example, is 75.5millimeter x 60.0 millimeter.

As a general rule, undersquare motors make maximum torque at lower rpm than oversquare motors of the same displacement. The road to horsepower and quicker quarter-miles on a Harley is through bigger engines with longer strokes. Stroking an engine boosts displacement by increasing the distance the piston travels in the cylinder. Boring increases the diameter of the cylinder so it uses larger pistons.

Big Twins gain horsepower most effectively through lengthening the stroke—increasing the distance between the crankpin centerline and flywheel centerline. Twice this distance is the stroke of the engine, because the crankpin moves the rod from TDC to BDC for the total piston travel.

Move the crankpin centerline away from the flywheel centerline

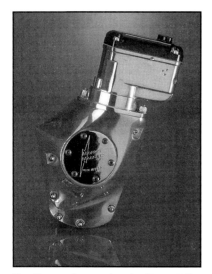

For those of you who don't want the hassle of a battery, Morris Magnetos are the way to go. This M-5 model features automatic advance and kicks out a hot enough spark to fire an engine no matter how slow it revolves. *CCI*

CCI's products cover the range from rectifiers to rebuild kits. They put out a catalog with over 800 pages based entirely on Harley-Davidson. *CCI*

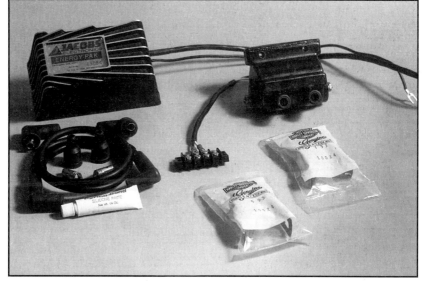

For those of you who think 30,000 volts of power isn't enough, RevTech has a 40,000-volt coil available for all Evos with the V-Fire III electronic ignitions. *CCI*

Jacobs Electronics has primarily concentrated on four-wheeled devices for their "Energy Pak" ignition systems, but lately they've branched out into motorcycle ignition. *Jacobs*

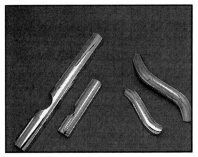

Not many people like the looks of shields on their header pipes. I was one of them until, through no fault of my own, the bike I was riding slowly settled to the right. Luckily the bike never hit the pavement as my inner calf cushioned the fall by supporting the exhaust system—I now have shields, and the burns are almost healed, thank you. *CCI*

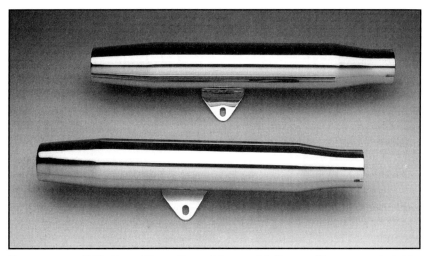

If you own an FXR, these "Dyno Power" low-restriction mufflers are a straight replacement for the stock mufflers. *CCI*

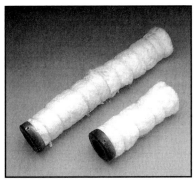

Something else that probably will become necessary with a set of low blow pipes is the fiberglass packing used to cut down the noise level. Ordinary fiberglass will only work for a few short hours before it goes out the back as sparklies, whereas this stuff is made specifically for mufflers and will last. *CCI*

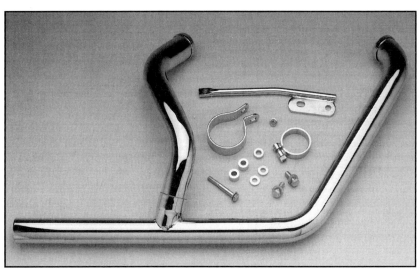

Many people don't like the look or sound of the factory headers with the crossover tube right in the middle. All aftermarket header manufacturers make at least one set of pipes that are two-into-one and missing the crossover. These happen to be from RevTech. *CCI*

and the stroke increases. This results in an increase in leverage on the crankpin for increased torque, increased displacement, and increased horsepower.

Nothing is free, however. As the stroke increases, piston speed also rises for a given engine speed, with resultant accelerated cylinder wear as a possibility. This isn't a problem on frequently rebuilt racing engines, but it can pose difficulties on a street engine, especially if you don't observe a reasonable redline.

The best way to utilize the increased torque of a stroker engine is to shift below 5,500rpm and let the torque do the work. Running much past that figure provides little gain but a lot more wear. Racing is a different story. If the mo-tor makes large horsepower at 7,500rpm, it's going to get spun up there. In racing, the idea is to be first, not worry about wear.

Sputhe, Axtell, and CCI will help you build a big motor. Axtell's finless racing cylinders range in size from 3.5 to 4 inches and can handle up to a 5-inch stroke. S.T.D. big-valve heads, with raised ports and a 30-degree cut for compression relief and an eight-bolt pattern, start around $2,200. Rods designed by Jim McClure, S&S, or Carillo are just about bulletproof and designed to hang together through sub-8-second runs. The McClure rods are sold only as special-order items with races, wrist pin bushings, bearing cages, crankpins, and nuts included as a kit.

Camshaft, Lifters, and Pushrods

The cam in the Harley engine has more influence over the engine's total performance than any other single component. Factory cams are designed to make the engine turn over, produce some power, and most importantly for H-D, pass new bike noise and exhaust emission standards. It's not designed to make maximum torque or horsepower, just to be adequate—if you can call 52 horsepower out of 81.7ci adequate—and pass 1996 emission regulations. This makes for fairly mild performance in the Big Twins.

A profusion of aftermarket cam builders can fill your need for a good cam—Red Shift, Andrews, Competition Cams, RevTech, Crane, Sifton—the list goes on. All of them have one thing in common: Each builds a product guaranteed to wake up your motor big-time. Cam replacement is very important, but it must be matched with all the other components. It does little good to install a high-lift, long-duration cam in a stock displacement engine without major work on the induction and exhaust.

Lift can be discussed in two different ways; net cam lift and total valve lift. Net cam lift is the size of the bump on the camshaft, measured from the heel to the toe of the cam. Total valve lift is how far the valve actually moves out of the valve seat.

To calcuate total valve lift, the rocker arm ration must be fac-

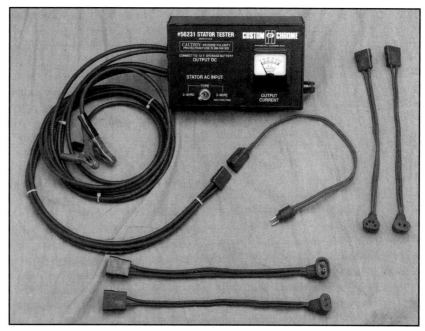

Sometimes figuring out where the electricity went is the hardest problem an average builder faces. You start out with a fully charged battery, everything runs well for a while, then no more sparks. Charge the battery again, and everything is good for another hour. Well, maybe your stator has given up and no more 12-volt current is being generated. What you need is this stator tester to check the charging system, then maybe a new stator. *CCI*

tored, as shown in the following formula:

Cam lobe lift x rocker arm ratio = total valve lift

For example, a cam with a lobe lift of 0.560—like in RevTech's Old Blue—provides the following net lift:

0.560 lift x 1.625 ratio = 0.910 total valve lift

So the valve will actually lift off its seat a total of 0.910 inches. Maximum lift doesn't happen at TDC, though, or the valve would hit the piston. Intake valves start to open while the piston is traveling up the cylinder near the end of the exhaust stroke. They stay open all through the intake stroke and into the beginning of the compression stroke, to insure a complete charge in the cylinder. When

the piston reaches TDC, the cam has opened the valve only a fraction of total valve lift.

In our example above, intake valve lift is only 0.128 inch at TDC. Among other things, this insures the piston stays away from the valve. At 6,000rpm the crank is rotating 100 times a second. This doesn't leave very much room for error if the clearances grow when the engine gets hot.

In this book, valve lift and cam lift are appropriately labeled. Bear in mind, however, that catalog companies often list valve specifications without noting whether the lift is cam lift or valve lift. Before you purchase a cam, you should contact the company that builds the cam and get a good specification sheet which lists total valve lift, cam lift, duration, overlap, spring travel to coil bind, spring free travel, and degrees at which the intake and exhaust valve open and close.

Since each stroke in a four-stroke engine runs a full 180 degrees—half a crankshaft rotation—a four-stroke engine fires each cylinder every 720 degrees (4 x 180 = 720), or two complete crank rotations. During a crankshaft rotation, the number of degrees of crankshaft rotation that the camshaft is open is referred to as its duration or timing.

Although you might think the camshaft should open the intake valve only during the 180-degree intake stroke, it takes a few moments for the mixture to begin flowing from the intake port into the cylinder. As a result, it helps to give the intake charge a "head start" into the cylinder, by opening the valve a bit before top dead center. Similarly, at the end of the intake stroke, the mixture continues to move through the intake port, so it helps to keep the valve open a bit after the piston reaches bottom dead center, to allow some of this late-arriving mixture into the cylinder.

The same thing happens on the exhaust side, though the high pressure in the cylinder means the exhaust valves can open sooner than the intakes because the hot gases will force their way out of the cylinder. Exhaust valves don't, however, stay open as far past top dead center, so that the incoming mixture—the intake valve is starting to open, remember—won't simply scoot out the open exhaust valve.

As a result, camshafts keep the valves open more than 180 degrees. How much more depends on the type of camshaft; the higher the performance, the longer the valves stay open past 180 degrees. The way cam grinders denote duration is by showing the number of degrees before and after top dead center that each valve—intake and exhaust—remains open. Those two figures, plus 180, give you the camshaft's duration. Our

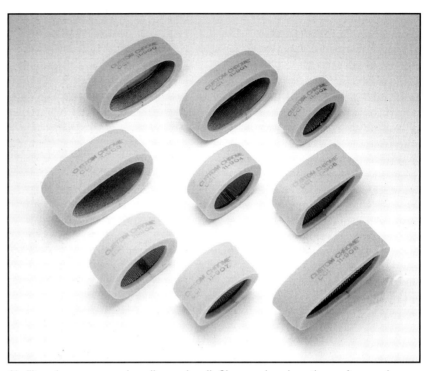

Air filters keep your engine alive and well. Clean and replace them often, and your bike will live long and prosper. Here's nine different washable types from CCI. They can be ordered to fit just about any combination of carb and air cleaner. *CCI*

reference cam has 260 degrees of duration on the intake side and 270 exhaust. The valve timing is represented like this:

Duration @ 0.053 inch—Intake 260; exhaust 270.
Valve Timing Open/Close— Intake 24/56; Exhaust 61/29

Note that if you add 180 to the opening and closing for the intake and exhaust timing, the result is the cam's duration (24 + 56 + 180 = 260 intake; 61 + 29 + 180 = 270 exhaust). The measurements are all taken after the cam has begun to lift the valve off its seat. The 0.053 inch is the valve lift off the seat. This measurement is used because all cams ramp open differently: some slowly, some rapidly, but very little actual flow occurs until the valve is open at least 0.053 inch.

The amount of degrees rotation that the intake and exhaust

valves are open at the same time is called overlap. Having both valves open at the same time lets the outgoing burnt gases draw the intake charge into the cylinder. Some camshafts allow a small bit of mixture to follow the exhaust out the port to cool the exhaust valve, but these also cause exhaust emissions to go sky-high, so they're not used by the factories on stock engines. Cams on fuel-injected engines can use this cooling feature, however, since fuel is injected only after the exhaust valve has closed.

Overlap allows the outgoing gases to help draw in the fresh intake charge, by creating a low-pressure wave in the exhaust port as the burned gases exit the combustion chamber. At certain engine speeds, some of the unburnt charge is lost through the exhaust, true, but it's made up by the supercharging effect of the incoming mixture. In effect, the increased velocity of the air/fuel helps pack the cylinder with more charge than if there were no overlap. This is how engines can achieve more than 100 volumetric efficiency at certain rpm.

Here's a perfect example where some is good, but more isn't better. At low rpm, overlap can cause more of the intake mixture to flow out the exhaust valve than is wanted; power drops in the process, and the engine often refuses to idle at a reasonable speed. The charge loss happens less at high rpm, which partially accounts for a high-perf engine "coming on the cam." But bottom line, select a cam with small overlap for the street.

To select a cam for your particular engine combination follow these steps:

1. Write down the displacement, head type, carb, ignition, and header system.
2. Decide what kind of engine you want: street torquer, Pro Street, Pro Stock, or whatever.
3. Call at least four cam grinders and get their spec sheets. Check the spec sheets to determine if they all use the same starting points and reference points for figuring cam specs. If they have a service department, talk to a rep and tell him what you're building and ask his advice.
4. **Take The Advice!** It will save you from building an engine totally unsuitable for your needs.

Camshaft Kits

The valvetrain for any engine can be ordered as a complete kit composed of valves, springs—including a third harmonic-damper spring, steel or titanium collars, machined keepers, pushrods, lifters, and camshaft. S&S's 0.630-inch lift valve spring and

Mikuni's HSR 42 is a good choice for large-displacement engines. Roller bearings on the slides keep it from sticking open. This particular carb fits all Big Twins from 1990 to present. *CCI*

collar kit will control valves up to 7,500rpm without float. The kit runs 460-pound open-spring pressure, needed if you are going to turn the motor at high revs. For cams with up to 0.780-inch lift, S&S makes a 780 racing-only kit—definitely a setup for the track, not the street.

Lift above 0.550 inch is almost useless on the street. RevTech's Old Blue had a cam with 0.560-inch lift and that was really much too radical. Unless you're willing to live with an engine that idles at 1,200rpm and doesn't want to run much below 3,500, stick with a milder lift cam, something like an Andrews EV-5. It has 0.530-inch lift, 252-degrees duration, and works between 4,500rpm and 6,500rpm. Set your rev limiter to 6,250rpm, and if all else is right in the engine, it should last for many a mile. This cam will require heavier springs, plus solid lifters with a set of adjustable pushrods. Big-lift cams have such radical specifications

that increased valvetrain wear can become a problem. Increased spring pressure accelerates valvetrain and valve-seat wear much more than with a stock setup.

Installing high-lift cams and the valve springs needed to control them requires that you check for clearance between open valves and the piston-to-valve clearance. You must check that there's no interference between the pushrods, pushrod tubes, and the cylinder head.

You'll also need to avoid coil bind, which occurs when a cam compresses the valve springs to a point where the coils actually touch. What really happens is that parts wear out at a frightening rate. It's entirely possible to have such a bad case of spring bind that the top of the valve pulls through the keepers and continues into the top of the piston—not good.

The heads should be off the engine to check installed spring height. This is the distance from the top of the bottom collar to the

Rev Limiters

A corollary to the increased revs these cams allow is the possibility of a missed shift at high revs, which can definitely do some serious damage. Miss the first-second shift at 5,500rpm and not much happens. Miss the same shift at 7,500rpm with the engine pulling like a Nile River water pump, and you'll spend your afternoon picking up hot, broken engine parts. A rev limiter will save you from those embarrassing moments when your transmission develops nothing but neutrals and 3,000 people are watching. Bouncing off the rev limiter after a missed shift isn't even remotely as embarrassing as blowing your motor up.

bottom of the top collar—or the height of the installed valve spring. The distance should be no less than 1.800 inch on Evo motors.

To check for coil bind, figure out the actual valve lift provided by the camshaft, then raise the valve to its fully open position. Ensure there's at least another 0.060-inch travel before any spring coils contact another. If there's less, you'll have to use a thinner spring collar, or grind the spring perch deeper into the head, but don't let the total spring height get more than 0.040 inch above the 1.800-inch installed height.

Once the heads are torqued onto the engine and the rocker arms installed, check clearance between the rocker arm and valve-spring retainer. Rotate the engine while watching the rocker arm's relationship to the collar. A too-long valve stem, poor rocker-arm geometry, or incorrect rockers can result in the arm hitting the collar during its stroke. If there's a problem, check your assembly, or call the cam grinder for recommendations for different rocker arms.

During break-in, remember that newly installed valve springs don't have their final operating pressure. When a freshly rebuilt engine starts for the first time, the valve springs need to come to operating temperature to take a set at their operating pressure. Allowing the engine to warm up slowly (with the valves set at manufacturer's specs), then cool to ambient, will break in the springs, helping to eliminate early breakage.

Lifters

Although there was a time when any performance engine used solid lifters, the choice is not so automatic these days. The biggest problem with solid lifters is cylinder growth as the engine heats and expands, which causes valve lash to change. With hydraulics, clearance valve lash is handled by oil flow in the lifter. Stock H-D lifters, however, often pump up when the revs climb near 6,000rpm. When this happens, valves don't close fully and the engine quits making power.

For lower redlines you can still use the stock lifters, but most cam grinders recommend adjustable pushrods. When using adjustable pushrods with stock hydraulic lifters, you will have to collapse the lifter for correct operation. Start with a cold engine. Rotate the crank to the lowest lifter position. Set the adjusting screw so that all the free play is taken up. Then turn the ad-

juster out 4 to 4 1/2 turns or until the lifter bottoms. Remember that oil takes time to bleed out, so don't hurry this procedure. All remaining pushrods are adjusted this way.

S&S offers an HL2T limited-travel lifter kit that works a little differently. Crank down the pushrod until the lifter bottoms, then back off the adjustment until the pushrod turns freely between your finger and thumb. Tighten the locknut, and recheck the clearance. Do the same for the remaining three. Remember to rotate the crank slowly to make sure valve clearance is adequate. Never use the starter motor to turn the engine, this can bend expensive pieces.

Competition Cams makes its Velva Touch hydraulic roller lifter kits for use with CC or other cams. They control valve action up to 6,700rpm, so they will work well with a 6,250-rpm redline. Velva Touch lifters won't bleed down like stock lifters, so the engine won't go flat at higher rpm.

Out-and-out racing engines that spin 7,500rpm or better use solid lifters for accurate valve control at high rpm. They can be used on the street without problem, but you must watch the clearances with high-lift cams to ensure the valves don't touch the piston or each other.

Pushrods

For any type of performance engine, plan to buy aftermarket pushrods. Stock pushrods work fine in a stock engine, but they have no place in a modified engine. Furthermore, on an Evo bike the cams can't be changed with the engine in the frame because the pushrods can't be removed without pulling the heads. Changing to adjustable pushrods solves the problem. Use a pair of good side-cutters to cut the factory pushrods and pushrod tubes in half, then after the cam change,

Pingel builds a petcock for every reason. These are but a few of what he has. He can build one with a separate nitrous oxide system outlet, or individual feed to a Thunderjet. *Pingel*

screw the adjustable pushrods all the way down, slide the adjustable tubes over them, and install the pushrod and tube at the same time.

Some books advocate using one-piece chrome-moly pushrods and solid lifters with adjusting screws. This works fine provided you have some way to change the pushrods should you miss a shift and bend one. My personal preference is solid lifters and adjustable pushrods. Non-adjustable pushrods have to be cut to exact size for each valve, then fitted with ball ends. You lose any advantage if one bends at the track and it can't be changed without pulling the engine. Even if you brought spares, trying to cut one to fit using a hacksaw will only wear out blades.

Once again, stroker motors provide an additional complication with pushrods, due to their longer cylinder barrels. Andrews recommends chrome-moly pushrods with any of its cams, and manufactures extra-long pushrods with only one end finished for stroker

engines with longer cylinders.

Years ago, some adjustable pushrods had a reputation for loosening up and going out of adjustment with the usual power loss problems. These days the aftermarket parts don't have that problem. Once set, they stay there. If you try really hard, you can bend one, but not unless something is seriously wrong in the engine or you really don't know when to shift. Bending pushrods below 7,500rpm is a good indication of serious mechanical problems, like a valve hitting a piston or a coil-bound valve spring.

Carburetion

As with everything else, proper carburetion is a trade-off. Depending on actual use—not what you think you want to do but what the bike is really going to do— you're going to have to give up a little on the top for all-around good performance. This also applies to camshafts, heads, exhaust, and all the rest. Not everybody

If you stick with the stock Keihin on your earlier bike, this adjustable main jet can help tune out any flat spots up high. *CCI*

who buys this book wants to go racing, but all of you are interested in making your Harley run harder or you wouldn't be reading this.

Pulling 96 horsepower out of an 80-ci engine will require much better airflow than the stock mixer can supply. Airflow increase can be handled by many different carbs; S&S Super G or Super D, Mikuni HSR-42, or CCI's Accelerator II are among the popular replacements.

The Super G comes with a 2 1/16-inch throat at the butterfly, narrowing to 1 3/4 inch at the venturi. This is too much carb for a low-compression, stock displacement engine; the 1 7/16-inch Super E will work much better. If you aren't really sure which size to use, go with the Super E, as it will provide better low-end response in any case.

As with other S&S carbs, both Super G and Super E use a two-cable throttle. All aftermarket carb manufacturers recommend the second cable to ensure the throttle is positively closed. Also note: While these eliminate the possibility of a stuck carb butterfly at wide-open throttle, they don't eliminate the need for an electrical kill switch to shut down the engine if things really go wrong.

The S&S carb comes as a kit with all the necessary bits and pieces—everything from the air filter to the California Off-road disclaimer. Tuning it for racing or street use is fairly simple. It provides adjustments to cover all operating ranges.

Initial settings work best by gently turning the idle-mixture screw all the way in, then backing it out 1 1/4 to 1 3/4 turn. Intermediate jetting usually runs between 0.032 inch and 0.036 inch. The main jet—the one you use during wide-open throttle—is where all the high-speed tuning takes place. The main jet that provides the strongest run through the gears is the right one for your particular engine.

The high speed jet begins to come on between 3,000-to 3,500rpm. By 4,500rpm the engine is running fully on the high-speed jet. The best way to determine proper size is by actually running the engine and seeing how your time is affected at the drag strip or by using a dynamometer to measure horsepower directly.

Metering numbers for the main jets are stamped on the end of the jet, and measure the meter-

The Thunderjet mounted on an S&S carb provides for another high-flow charge of fuel when the engine's running WFO. It needs a good supply of fuel, preferably straight from the petcock. That's why a petcock like Pingel's is so important. It will allow enough fuel to flow to produce maximum horsepower.

ing orifice in thousandths of an inch. A tag attached to the carb or a number written on the shipping box gives you the initial jet size. Record this, along with any other changes you make to the carb, and keep it in your toolbox with the spare jets.

Make the first run, watching speed and engine rpm at the finish. Bump up the high-speed jet one size and make another run, recording the information. Keep upping the jet size until the speed begins to fall off, then back down one size for best top-end performance. Under racing conditions, this will be where the power peaks, then drops off. Shift at this rpm. This jetting will also serve well for the street if you make the other settings mentioned.

CCI's Accelerator II carb has enough interchangeable parts so that it can grow with your engine. Venturi size is easily changed with replaceable 38-millimeter, 42-millimeter (standard), and 45-millimeter venturis. The carb has an accelerator pump that injects 0.5cc of fuel into the center of the venturi when the throttle's cracked, providing quick engine response.

CCI provides no choke plate; instead, a three-position enrichener helps start the engine. Flick it all the way over, hit the starter, and quickly bring it back off. I found that the engine would start without using the enrichener if it was fairly warm, but if it sat for any length of time and cooled, the enrichener had to be used. The trade-off is that no choke plate interferes with airflow, which is well worth any extra effort.

Like most other aftermarket carbs, the Accelerator II is set up with replaceable high- and low-speed air bleeds and fuel jets. Sizes cover any practical application I can imagine. For instance, the high-speed fuel jet comes in sizes from 1.40 millimeter to 2.80 millimeter. Low-speed fuel jets run from 0.56 millimeter to 0.84 millimeter. Standard sizes in the kit are 1.60-millimeter or 1.80-millimeter high-speed fuel jets and 0.64-millimeter and 0.68-millimeter low-speed fuel jets. Anything bigger can be bought in a kit including six different sizes. Bear in mind that a 2.80-millimeter high-speed fuel jet is like having a 7/64-inch hole delivering fuel, almost like running without a jet installed. Jets this large are needed only on very large engines or when running alcohol.

Mikuni's HSR 42 smoothbore carb is available across the counter for $395. It's a straight bolt-on to your existing manifold and requires little, if any, modification to the bike. For a 95/5 street/racing operation, a better choice is Mikuni's 40-millimeter HS40. This gives better atomization of air-fuel mixtures during street riding while still offering good high-end performance.

Mikuni airflow rates run slightly better than some of the other aftermarket carbs, because the lack of a throttle butterfly makes up for the flow reduction by eliminating obstructions in the venturi. Testing shows a greater airflow through the 42-millimeter Mikuni than with another brand's 52-millimeter (2 1/4-inch) butterfly carb when both are running at full throttle using an air filter and stock manifold. Further, the smaller bore provides higher velocity through the carburetor, improving fuel/air mixing and response.

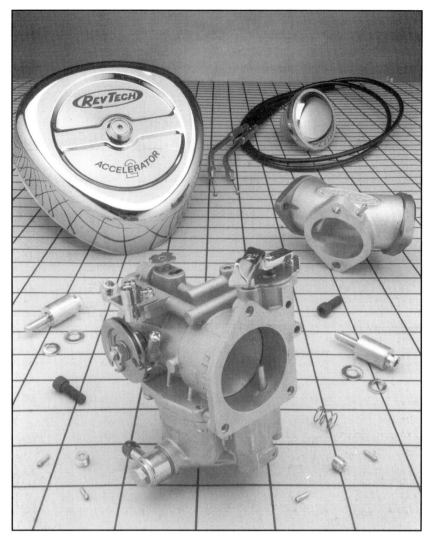

RevTech's Accelerator II carb comes with enough jets to fit any size engine from 883cc to whatever you build. One of its better features is an accelerator pump (hence the name) that gives a 1/2-cc blast of fuel into the venturi as soon as the throttle is cracked. *CCI*

Setting up the Mikuni HSR 42 is similar to working with any of the S&S products. You'll need a number of runs over a measured distance to establish the correct jet size for maximum performance and lowest E.T.

To ensure adequate fuel delivery at elevated revs, be sure the petcock can flow enough fuel to keep the carb from starving. Engines over 100ci will burn up to 300 percent more fuel than a stocker in a quarter-mile run. Even a highly modified stock displacement engine can get fuel-starved. A Pingel Enterprise petcock and fuel filter will ensure decent fuel flow and eliminate those embarrassing moments when a piece of crud blocks a jet and all the horses go to sleep.

Carburetor Tuning

When installing any carb, be sure the throttle closes all the way with the handgrip before you start the engine. Having a brand new, fresh, cold, expensive engine jump to 6,000rpm in the first few seconds of operation just because the butterfly is stuck 1/32-inch open will upset your composure at the least, and break an engine at worst. I've watched more than one engine wind itself past valve float because the throttle spring didn't close the butterfly completely. It takes only a very small throttle opening to run an unloaded engine past redline.

Contrary to popular belief, there is no magic to tuning a carb. Drag-strip tuning begins by warming the engine fully before staging. Operating temperature makes a considerable difference in your launches, and a warm engine is less likely to sneeze just as you nail the throttle. Also very important, make jetting changes one at a time, and don't change anything else—such as timing—without checking its effect as well.

Certain cam and exhaust system combinations can create flat spots at a particular rpm, making an engine difficult to tune. Eliminating this flat spot can cause a power loss at higher rpm, causing the engine to stumble or back down on power from an overrich mixture. The idea in racing is to tune the engine to eliminate any flat spots in the rpm range used on the track. The street is different. You can live with a flat spot up high—where the engine spends little time—but you want a smooth power flow down in the useful range.

Carburetion, cam overlap, exhaust back pressure, or a combination might produce a big flat spot at 3,000rpm, but because a correctly geared racing engine will only see this once during a run, it won't figure as much in tuning as if it were to happen at 4,500rpm.

Checking state of tune through spark-plug readings is a good idea on engines run on the

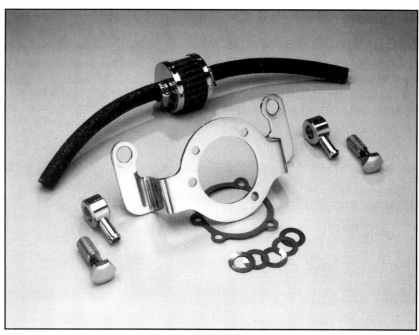

The newer CV-type carbs found on Evo Big Twins from 1993–up require a different support bracket and breather system to enable aftermarket air cleaners to be mounted to the stock intake manifold and still utilize the cylinder head crankcase breather system. *CCI*

street, but is mostly wasted on anything that runs at full throttle at a drag strip. Frankly, 1,320 feet just isn't enough distance to develop accurate plug readings, except in extremely lean conditions where the insulator will be very white and possibly blistered. If this occurs, the engine is way too lean, or the timing is far too advanced. At this point, quit all tuning runs, recheck the ignition timing, and install the richest jets you can lay your hands on. Don't start running again until you solve the problem, or you may get to rebuild the engine after a very short time.

The large number of cams, headers, displacements, and other factors means that pulling one carb out of the box and having it right will be virtually impossible. You'll only reach maximum performance by continued trial and error. That's why it's so important to keep records of each tuning change and what happened with each step. What works today

when it's 67 degrees and 45 percent relative humidity won't work for 100 degrees and 80 percent humidity.

Street running is another matter altogether. The carb must work, and work well, over a wide range of riding conditions, one of which might be racing.

Exhaust

More misinformation, ignorance, sales hype, and myths exist about exhaust systems than any other engine modification. After all, hanging a single-fire, dual-plug ignition on the engine really doesn't do much to impress passersby. Making a lot more noise and looking cool drives sales of a lot of aftermarket exhaust systems, even if the performance gain is strictly imaginary. In some cases, changing only the pipes and making no other modifications can cost you as much as 4 horsepower.

Joshua Cho, editor of *Thunder Alley*, took his bag-stock FXR and hung a set of straight pipes on it with no other modifications. He put his bike on the dyno and ran it twice, just to make sure he got a correct reading. He did—power dropped to 56 horsepower, a 2 horsepower loss. Swapping the straights for a SuperTrapp 2 into 1 gave 60 horsepower with a smoother power curve.

Cho made no other changes to the engine, just a pipe swap. The open pipes had a flat spot between 2,500- and 3,200rpm, right where most of us ride. The tuned system started the power curve right when the throttle was opened at 2,600rpm and continued upward to a higher peak than the open pipes.

Engines above 100ci will need pipes of at least 2-inch diameter. For very large engines, 2 1/4-inch pipes, or larger, are almost a necessity. When we get into racing Sportster-derived bikes on road racing tracks, we'll cover exhaust systems that deliver best power over a wide rev range while still meeting race-track noise levels. Today's exhaust systems are approaching levels of performance only available with open headers only a few years ago.

On an 88-ci Sportster built by Ron Dickey from Axtell, optimum pipe length was determined to be 46 inches long and 2 1/4 inches in diameter. He based his calculations on what was in the motor, valve size (Manley titanium 2.150-inch intake and 1.750-inch exhaust), 723 Red Shift cam, acoustic resonance, and back pressure. Lots of experience helped when it came to designing the bike: He's the current owner of Axtell and has invested 23 of his 46 years into the company. Spring-mounting the pipes helps keep them from cracking from vibration when the horsepower gets wicked on. Performance to date has been a 10.11 at 134 miles per

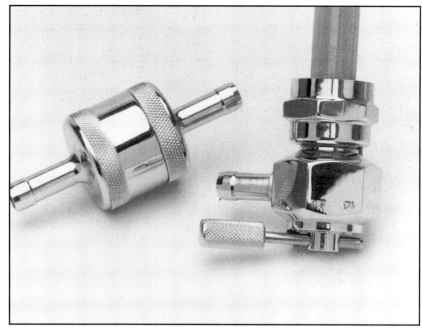

Pingel also makes chrome petcocks and fuel filters for show bike installations. *Pingel*

hour run at Memphis, with no air shifter or wheelie bars.

Big Twin engines, 100ci and larger, need pipes 42 to 50 inches long, measured from valve face to end of pipe. Most important is to ensure both pipes are within 0.50-inch total length of each other for equal performance. Each cylinder functions independently of the other, and it's entirely possible to have one making more horsepower than the other—not a good situation.

Presuming you aren't planning to run open pipes on the street, a set of headers with tuned mufflers, or a single muffler, works the best. Rich Products, SuperTrapp Industries, and Bub Enterprises manufacture dyno-tested exhaust systems for Big Twins and Sporties. Any one of these systems will allow your modified engine to make more power.

Ignition

The best thing I can say about the stock twin-fire ignition is that it's provided a great market for the aftermarket. The stock unit fires both plugs at the same time, regard-

less of which one's on compression stroke. This steals a little power and makes for a rougher idle.

A system like a Dyna Single-Fire is set up to use two ignition modules, each firing one plug at a time. Dyna uses the Harley-type mechanical advance, but relies on an electronic trigger to fire the plugs. The kit includes a programmable two-stage rev limiter, along with coils, wiring, high-tension plug wires, and instructions.

I advise using a Dyna on a scooter with an alternator. This unit pulls a lot of amps, so racers running a total-loss ignition system should use a battery less than one year old and hook it to a trickle charger between runs. Normally a total-loss system won't have the voltage and amp-hours available to support ignition throughout an extended run, unless the battery is 100 percent. It's really embarrassing to be halfway through a run and have the ignition run out of zaps.

Running at the dry lakes or Bonneville requires either an ignition with a low-amp draw or a

Bracket or Class Racing

Through the past I've learned that trying to run a combination race bike/street bike really doesn't work. If you go racing because it's fun and you like the adrenaline rush, then a modified street bike might be OK. Going for real racing, however, requires a dedicated racing bike in today's world. Too many people are running purpose-built race bikes for you to be able to approach their times with a street motor.

For a fast street bike that occasionally winds up pointed down the quarter, the best way to bring home a trophy or two is to find a class where you think you have a good chance of running in the top ten, and build your bike to run there. Once you have the bike sorted out, you will find that learning to race and improving your abilities will do more for lower ETs than another 5–10 horsepower. One excellent way to hone your talents is through bracket racing.

Bracket racing depends more on reflexes and consistency than out-and-out performance. The way it works is to first run the bike in practice enough that you're turning consistent times, run after run. Then you pick a bracket to run in—say 13.01 seconds to 13.41 seconds or whatever setup the track or sanctioning body uses—and go racing against another competitor, either in your own ET bracket, or one completely different from yours. Brackets can be as far apart as 2 seconds or more; the timing lights make up the difference by giving the slower bike a head start.

The starting lights on the Christmas Tree are staged in such a way as to theoretically have both bikes cross the finish line at the same time. Should you run faster than your bracket, you lose. For instance, run in the 13.01-to-13.41 bracket and turn a 12.99, and you're out.

Reaction time off the line makes all the difference. You have to anticipate the green light and be moving as soon as it flashes. Wait until you see the green and you'll end up sitting by yourself at the starting line, wondering where the other guy went. Bracket racing definitely favors the racer with the fastest reflexes as opposed to the fastest bike.

This type of racing started off as an effort to keep costs down for the average racer, relying more on the rider's ability than on his checkbook. As in a lot of racing, motorcycle drag races can often be won by an average rider on a "money-no-object" bike, unless there's some form of control over the bikes. Believe me, it's easy to get to the point where you debate about whether you pay the water bill or buy a set of tires.

A lot of people are interested in owning the fastest street Harley, period. This is where the expense comes in. Anyone can have a 120-inch, 135-horsepower bike built with lights and turn signals, if he's willing to open his checkbook, but this type of racing ultimately only proves who has the fattest checkbook. "Run what you brung" racing predates pneumatic tires. It's interesting to see where technology takes bikes, but it leads to such things as $45,000 Top Fuel bikes costing $1,500 per pass—if nothing breaks.

Kosman Specialties builds racing bike frames for Top Fuel Harley, Pro Stock Harley, and EVO Sportster. Kosman's philosophy on racing is realistic:

1. Realize all parts have a lifetime, and racing parts have a short one.
2. Constantly inspect all parts to determine their condition. Discard or repair any part if its condition is even questionable.
3. Understand that greater care and maintenance are required on racing parts. Racing parts are made with light weight and strength in mind; they require more care and frequent replacement, and will not last as long as those designed for 100,000 miles of street use.

Kosman's Pro Stock Harley chassis, from fuel tank to racing slick, runs $12,500 and is one of the best ways to get started in professional racing. Top Fuel racing is another matter entirely. Kosman offers a chassis set up for Jim McClure's engine cases and a three-speed racing transmission. Frames can be built around any combination of engine and gearbox, depending on your needs. The rear section takes up to a 12-inch-wide beadlock wheel and can be set to an 84- to 86-inch wheelbase. Price? Call for information, according to Kosman.

You need to plan what to do with a competition bike before opening the checkbook. Designing, building, and tuning the bike—not just the engine—requires a lot more knowledge than bolting on a carb and a set of pipes and going racing.

Some of the most enjoyable riding for me has been when running a "sleeper," or "Q-ship." Q-ships were anti-sub warships designed to look like slow-moving freighters. Phony cargo on the decks hid a lethal assortment of weaponry inside crates and boxes. The idea was to entice the U-boat to surface to use its deck gun to sink the ship instead of launching an expensive torpedo. When the U-boat was fully committed to surface work, with its hatches open and gun manned, the Q-ship would run up its flag, drop the phony decking, and fire away.

S.T.D. cases and heads, S&S stroker kit, Axtell Big Twin 98-ci cylinders, 10.5:1 pistons, Dyna Ignition, and a Mikuni HSR 42 combine to produce 118 horsepower at the rear wheel. Stuffed into a fairly new Dyna Convertible—replete with windshield and bag mounts—that kind of power makes the perfect Q-ship. Not that I advocate betting money on impromptu racing, but I'd make sure someone neutral held the money.

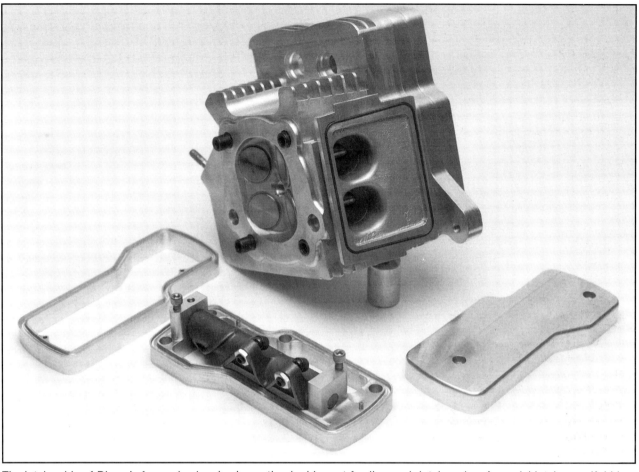

The intake side of Rivera's four-valve heads shows the double port feeding each intake valve. A special intake manifold is used, along with a dual carb setup. One carb feeds from each side of the engine. *Rivera*

charging system to sustain the sparks over a long duration. Warming up, waiting in line, then running three miles one way—with less than one hour to make the return run for a record—puts a lot of strain on a total-loss system. If you really don't want to run a charging system, bring a spare battery.

Accel builds a single-fire, programmable ignition system for Harleys. MSD has its multiple-spark MC1 ignition that will provide easier starting, less plug fouling, and quicker engine response. It will operate reliably up to 12,000rpm, a range few Harley engines will see no matter how long the throttle is held open. MSD's rev limiter incorporates a "soft-touch" feature to keep the

engine from cutting instantly, and an air-shifter cutoff comes standard for racing.

Jacobs Electronics is a company usually associated with cars and boats, but has branched out into the motorcycle ignition business. Jacobs guarantees its Energy Team ignition will outperform any other system. The brains behind the brawn is the Energy Pack microprocessor, which Jacobs claims tailors each spark to its individual cylinder based on feedback from the plugs. The voltage ranges from 12,000 volts to a peak of 60,000 volts, based on computer feedback to determine the spark intensity needed to fire the mixture. It can't burn through steel plate, but it can detect a

fouled plug and up the voltage enough to zap through the gunk.

Jacobs states the system will produce up to 2,550 watts peak spark wattage at the plug, but hold the current draw through the transistors to 0.056 amps. This is below the 3.50 amps of the stock system, and the 0.50 amps of the typical single-fire system.

Most companies recommend that all components in an ignition system be installed as a kit. In Jacob's case, this consists of the processor, two 40,000-volt coils, metal core ignition wires, and a complete set of instructions.

Spark Plugs

Fresh plugs, fresh plugs, fresh plugs. There, that should cover just about everything you need to know about spark plugs. It makes no sense to drop a lot of money on cams, carbs, and pipes, but neglect to keep a good set of plugs screwed into the heads. A plug with a rounded electrode can take up to 40 percent more voltage to fire. Most of the new hi-voltage ignition systems are capable of firing a plug through a popsicle stick, but that's still no reason not to ensure new plugs are in the engine before each event.

Automotive engineers have been able to extend plug life to 30,000+ miles through electronics and unleaded fuel, and most people change them at least once during vehicle ownership, but this doesn't mean they should sit in the head until they rust. A lot of racers change them before every race, making sure the old ones end up in the circular file, not in the bottom of the toolbox as "spares." Plugs are cheap—buy 10 at a time and you'll never be out.

Jacobs also has a number of tools and other products for tuning your bike, including a set of plug-gapping pliers capable of setting spark-plug gap from 0.025 to 0.085 inch while keeping the side electrode centered over the plug. Dial up the required gap, drop the plug into the recess, and squeeze the handle.

Before installing a spark plug, take the time to index the electrode. With a felt-tip pen, draw a line on the plug body in line with the electrode. Install the plug, then note where the line falls. Use different-thickness brass washers to align the plug so the side electrode points away from the intake valve, so the side electrode doesn't shroud the incoming fuel mixture from the center electrode. Jacobs manufactures washers in various sizes, 30 washers per pack, so proper alignment is easy.

Reading spark plugs doesn't

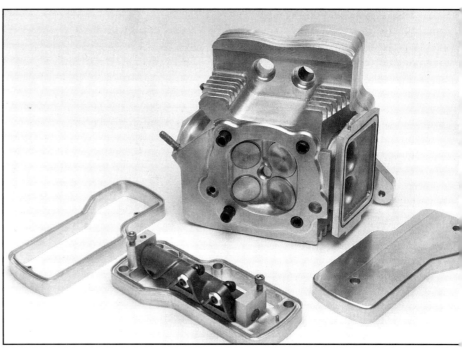

For the ultimate in Big Twin breathing ability, a set of Rivera four-valve heads will really make a Stage III engine come alive. *Rivera*

take a long white beard, black robe, and pointed hat. A good magnifying glass is helpful, though. On a street engine, take plug readings—on new spark plugs—after every major modification. Run the bike hard for a mile, then stop the engine with the kill switch and pull in the clutch or shift to neutral. Don't let the bike slow down on compression with the engine running, as this will give a false plug reading.

Spatters of aluminum indicate things are hotter than hell inside the engine, and the piston top is starting to melt. Either the timing is too advanced or the mixture needs to be fatter. The mixture also needs to be richer if the ceramic below the center electrode becomes glazed. Neither electrode should turn color or have any rounded corners. Down at the bottom of the ceramic insulator there should be a brown ring of fuel.

Too far to the cold end of the heat range can lead to fouling, while a hot plug can cause pre-ignition and engine damage. Much better to start on the cold and rich side than to try to go lean and hot—spark plugs are a lot cheaper than pistons or valves. Aside from Top Fuel engines, which live under strange and interesting conditions, no one ever cooked an engine because of a fouled plug.

Timing

All Evo engines left the factory with the timing preset, and a stock motor usually won't need the timing changed before it rolls over 100,000 miles. The stock system is relatively easy to check if you have reason to believe the timing has gone adrift.

The hardest part with a kick-start, or run-and-bump-start bike is to figure out a way to roll the engine over while watching for the timing mark without ending up with 700 pounds of steel and aluminum laying on your nice new shoes. Electric-start bikes have it a bit better, but race bikes require some way to lift the back wheel off the ground. A motorcycle stand capable of picking the back of the bike up by the swingarm will make timing and other jobs much easier. Around the shop, a motorcycle lift like Zipper's Quicklift will save you a lot of grief. It's good for 17 inches of lift, and one person can operate it.

Get the bike on the stand and remove the timing plug between the cylinders on the left side of the engine. Remove the plugs, but leave the front plug hooked to the wire. Ground the plug to the engine, and with the ignition on, slowly turn the engine over until the plug fires. Look into the timing hole and see if the line on the flywheel lines up in the center of the hole. Assuming the timing mark lines up as it should, the timing is OK.

If it doesn't align, drill out the pop rivets holding the timing cover on the cam case and remove the cover. The inner cover and gasket have to come off to get to the cam position sensor plate. Loosen, don't remove, the screws holding this plate. Move it in small amounts and recheck the plug firing until it coincides with the timing mark; this sets the static timing.

If you are assembling the engine for the first time and the timing mark doesn't even come close to when the spark fires, stop right there. Something is badly wrong inside the cases, and you can't proceed until it's corrected.

Most Evo motors, Sporty or Big Twin, shouldn't get out of time during their lifetime, but when you go changing parts, it's a good idea to check. After making sure the static timing is

close, procure a timing light, hook it to the battery or a 12-volt source, and clamp the induction lead over the front plug. The best way to time an engine after installing an aftermarket ignition is with a "dial-back-to-zero" timing light. This light allows you to set the total timing advance on a dial on the back of the light so that the mark on the flywheel shows even when the ignition is fully advanced.

Install a clear-plastic timing hole plug (any shop or dealer has it) so oil doesn't spray out when the engine is running. Set total advance for your particular engine/ignition combo on the back of the light and run the engine up to 2,000rpm. The timing mark should be in the middle of the hole. If it's at the rear, the timing is advanced approximately 5 degrees—at the front of the hole, retarded by the same amount. Again, move the sensor plate to bring the mark into the center, then tighten the set screws. Remove the timing light, replace the plug, and go run the bike to see if all the parts work as advertised. Then go find someone to race!

Summary

A Big Twin weighing 775 pounds with rider, a half-tank of fuel, and a 92-horsepower motor will turn between 12.05 and 13.5 seconds in the quarter-mile, depending on whether the pilot rides like he makes the payments or like speed is more important than money. Touring bikes don't spend much time running the quarter, but in the real world of steep hills, heavy loads, and approaching Kenworths, these modifications will make riding a greater pleasure. Somewhere between a Stage I engine and a Stage II, 90+ horsepower setup, will provide all the go you could want from a 850-pound road-burner.

Package Specifications for Stage II Engines

96+ horsepower

Approximate cost in 1996— $2,700 to $3,000 in parts, plus machine work and labor, which can double the cost.

Kit #1

1. S&S Super E or G carb with air cleaner
2. Crane hydraulic cam part # 1-1003
3. Jacobs Energy Team ignition
4. Bub Bad Dogs pipes
5. Axtell cylinder kits, 87- to 96ci
6. Carillo rods
7. Ported stock, or aftermarket heads with dual plugs
8. Adjustable pushrods

Kit #2

1. Mikuni HSR 42 Carb
2. K&N air filter
3. Competition Cams #EVO-3050
4. MSD MC1 ignition
5. Rich Thunderheaders 2 into 1
6. S&S Sidewinder 3 5/8 cylinders & pistons
7. Edelbrock Performer heads
8. Chrome-moly pushrods

Kit #3

1. CCI RevTech High-Performance kit (@ 90 horsepower)
2. (Optional) Sputhe or S.T.D. engine cases—this goes for all engines, Stage II and higher, if semi-serious racing is contemplated.

Kit #4

1. S&S Super G
2. Andrews cam
3. Dyna ignition
4. Sputhe 95-ci Street engine
5. S&S oil pump
6. Crane roller rockers
7. Rich Thunderheaders

Kit #5

1. Axtell 97-ci Mountain Motor
2. S&S Super G
3. MSD ignition
4. SuperTrapp 2 into 1

Add to all these kits the small parts, gaskets, nuts and bolts, case studs, machine work, and 10-percent fudge factor (remember Murphy's Law), and the entire motor, in the bike and running, will cost between $6,000 and $11,000. For semi-serious bracket racing, add at least half that amount for maintenance through a season and you will have an idea of the cost to go fast.

The Stage III and Stage IV Engines

Both Stage III and IV levels of performance require essentially the same parts. Stage IV just gets more and bigger, so we will look at them as a single entity—Stage III only—rather than as separate levels. These are serious war weapons, intended to take the battle to the track. A 100+ horsepower engine can be run on the street—sorta'—if the cam is mild enough and the compression is down around 12:1, but why? You can get the same level of street performance and a lot more reliability out of an 80- or 86-inch engine and not spend half the money.

On the other hand, if racing is what you want, then let's build a MOTOR. An old bearded adage says: "There's no substitute for cubic inches." Today it reads "... cubic money," but the original idea still applies for most of us: Bigger is better.

Taking it From the Top

Here's where we get into the realm of scratch-built motorcycles. Take a look at a serious dragsters these days and here's what you'll find. Start with a custom rigid frame held off the ground by a set of Drag Forx split over a Goodyear KR 133 250/275-18 racing tire from Kosman in the front. Another Goodyear sits at the back, a D1633 slick pinned to a 10-inch rim. Not too much in the way of Harley parts so far.

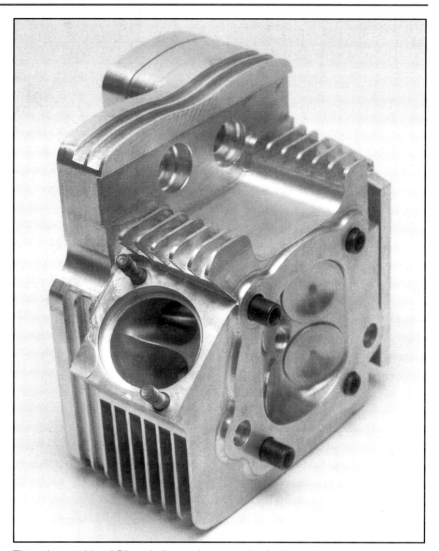

The exhaust side of Rivera's four-valve setup feeds through a siamesed port into a single outlet. This eliminates the need for a four-pipe exhaust header. Almost any good aftermarket set of pipes can be run. *Rivera*

Next up is an engine, pumping 121ci with every revolution of the crank, that's 60.5ci per hole—1,000cc, the displacement of a 1981 Sportster engine in each cylinder. A closer look shows names like S.T.D., S&S, Edelbrock, Rivera, Crane, and more. Still no Harley parts in evidence. Wait, the transmission looks like a Harley part. Uh-uh, it's a Zipper RaceCase fully auto five-speed set up for a Sportster or Bandit SuperClutch.

Actually, there are no Harley parts anywhere on the bike. It's a V-twin racing machine with only a passing resemblance to what sits at the local hog shop, but that's all. These days, that's what you'll find in the upper classes running the quarter-mile. The engine might be Big Twin- or Sportster-based, but all the hard parts come from aftermarket suppliers.

My philosophy about racing V-twins is this: If you want something from Harley-Davidson, go buy a T-shirt. If you want to win races, start from scratch.

RevTech's entry into the custom, free-breathing head department is this 50-state legal 230-cfm, two-valve head. Intake valves run 1.940 inch and exhausts are 1.610 inch. Either single or dual plugs can be run. If single plugs are selected, a pair of socket head plugs are included to block off the second spark-plug hole. *CCI*

Pro Stock Kit

First and foremost, I don't recommend you build a 120-ci Pro Stock bike as your initial project. Not that it can't be done—it's only parts. But you should work up through a few classes before investing big bucks.

That said, if you decide to go ahead and build a 150-horsepower shaker, you'd better have a good idea what you want before you start writing checks. The bills are going to cross the $40,000 mark real fast.

At the same time, this isn't going to be a detailed blueprint on how to build a Pro Stock bike. Rather, it's a general outline of what you need to go professional

racing, with a rough idea of cost set as of summer 1996. I'll take the bike part by part and develop a comprehensive list of what you'll need before turning a wheel in anger.

Specific non-Harley parts needed for a pro bike:
Front fork
Front wheel
Triple clamps
Front brake assembly including disc and stainless lines
Frame
Steering damper
Fuel and oil tanks
Motor plate and primary guard
Countershaft support kit
Rear wheel adjusters with wheelie bar mounts

Wheelie bars
Rear wheel
Rear slick
Rear brake assembly with peg and pedal kit
All bodywork
Battery box, coil mounts, chainguard
Countershaft sprocket
Rear sprockets (3)
Engine
Transmission
Fuel lines, battery, and miscellaneous parts, nuts, bolts, and washers
Ignition
Spark plugs (10)
Custom paint

Carburetion

When engines grow to the 100 + cubic inch size, airflow through the carburetor becomes paramount. Carb choices include Mikuni HSR 42, RevTech's Accelerator II, or two from S&S—the Super G or Super D. The Super G starts with a 2 1/16-inch throat at the butterfly, narrowing to 1 3/4 inch at the venturi. This is way too much carb for stock displacement engines, but works well on big ones. When used on very large engines—120ci or better—the Super G can be bored out another 0.100 inch for increased airflow.

Another alternative for big engines is Sputhe's Dual Lectron setup. Lectron carbs were used on Harley's XR-750 racing engine, and at one time Harley offered them as high-performance options on Sportsters and Big Twins. Their main drawback was their long-travel throttle spools. These took up too much space, so the carbs never caught on for street use.

Lectron and Sputhe got together and developed a second-generation specifically for high-performance Harley motors. It incorporates two carb bodies on a common manifold. Different carb sizes are available, including 40 millimeter, 41.3 millimeter, and 44 millimeter—all taper bores. As you can imagine, manifolds and air cleaner are quite different from a single-carb setup, and Sputhe includes the manifold, couplers, and K&N air filter in the kit. The carbs use the stock throttle and choke assemblies.

Pro Stock Costs

I could save you a lot of time and figuring by telling you that building a Pro Stock dragster will set you back $50,000, but some of you won't believe me. So here's a partial breakdown on the big stuff—all off-the-shelf items that take just a checkbook to bring home:

Pro Stock frame w/engine plates, wheels and tires, fuel tank, bodywork (no paint), brakes, oil and battery containers, wheelie bar, and assorted sprockets—$13,450
Engine—Sputhe 120-ci V-twin (40.00 x 4.75 inch bore and stroke), with heads and ignition—$8,475
Transmission—RaceCase five-speed auto—$7,200
Primary drive and clutch—Bandit SuperClutch on 3-inch belt drive—$1,375
Carburetion—S&S Super D kit w/manifold—$385
Shifter—air-shifter w/button, gauge, lines, and compressor—$575
Headers—Hand-fabricated straight pipes—$400
Paint—your choice—$2,500
Tachometer w/shift light—$175
Machine work, custom fabrication, mounts, and miscellaneous fasteners—$3,500 (and that's low)

Grand total—over $38,000, and you haven't even started the engine. You still need fuel, oil, filters, rollers, battery, battery charger, etc. Plus, no race bike runs without a few spare gear sets, pushrods, gaskets, spark plugs, chain and drive belt, plus 108+ octane racing gas at $5.35 per gallon.

Figure on opening the engine at least twice a season if you don't abuse it and it opens all by itself. You'll also go through the transmission at least once.

Cost to freshen engine—$2,500 x 2 = $5,000.
One transmission rebuild—$1,300.

My personal figures showed a cost per run—be it practice or racing—to be right at $500. This covered everything from leathers to motels and meals, all the money I spent to race, entry fees included. And I have enough tools to outfit a small shop already, so I don't count those.

Using the $500/run figure and figuring 21 runs in a year, direct operating costs are $10,500. Together with the bike cost, count on your first year's operation to run near $60,000.

This is why I say start with a sheet of paper before you decide to go run Pro Stock, Top Fuel (much more expensive!), or any professional class. Start hanging blowers or turbos on the engine and double the cost for the motor. Also, the blower will create 50 percent more maintenance and parts replacement, either directly or indirectly related.

Most people wouldn't give a starter drive gear much thought. I mean, it just has to turn the engine over, right? Well, that's what I thought until the one on my 11.75:1 motor turned into a pulley. The stock gear wouldn't take the extra abuse for very long. *CCI*

Another alternative is Rivera's Eliminator II, which is based on the English S.U. carburetor. S.U. (Skinner's Union—I don't know why) carburetors were universal on British cars during the 1950s and 1960s. Once upon a time, I thought I was going to set the world on fire from the seat of a race car. I don't know what prompted me to select English sports cars ("The parts that fall off this car are of the finest British manufacture"), but I managed to get a fair education in S.U. carbs.

Rivera has done a lot of work on the carb, and provides two different main jets and fairly comprehensive instructions—which is good. Set up right, the S.U. will feed a V-twin engine better than most other types, and the constant-velocity design provides good throttle response, but the Eliminator II needs to be tuned carefully for each engine combination.

In my last book, I put down S.U. carbs, but that's because up until now, no one made the bloody things perform right on a bike. With all Rivera's modifications, the S.U./Eliminator does do a good job of feeding four-valve heads. Like all good British hardware, it has a multitude of adjustments—vacuum-controlled venturi, replaceable main jet, replaceable tapered needle, bi-metallic temperature compensator, and all. It doesn't use an accelerator pump, which can make cold starts a bit interesting, but the engine response makes the trade-off worthwhile.

A great deal of performance problems that people attribute to a "cammy" motor can actually be traced to poor carburetion, caused when a cam change is made without retuning the carb. With the increased sophistication of today's carbs, a cam once thought of as racing-only can be used under much wider applications. In addi-

Not for street use, these finless Evolution drag cylinders are made from ductile iron for bore sizes 3 1/2 inch to 3 3/16 inch. Any stroke can be used. Axtell builds these cylinders to take an eight-bolt head pattern. *Axtell*

Street use requires fins for cooling. The left cylinder fits Big Twins; the right Sportsters. Again, bore sizes up to 3 3/16 inches are available. *Axtell*

tion, increasing the motor size without rejetting the carb will produce lean spots, usually in the low end and mid-range but occasionally throughout the powerband.

Heads

Big engines move a lot of air through the combustion chamber—the more air pumped, the more power made. To get the job done, numerous manufacturers have come out with their own ver-

sions of high-performance heads. Sputhe, S.T.D., and Rivera make heads that will fit up to 40.0-inch bores. S.T.D. big-valve heads, with raised ports and a 30-degree compression relief cut, are available for $2,200, set up for eight-bolt cylinders.

Choice of heads depends on your preferences and recommendations from professional engine builders. Talk to a lot of racers, send for brochures from head

Flowbench Test Pressure Conversion
by Steve Feree

Airfflow benches are designed to measure airflow at different pressures. A higher test pressure will show a higher cfm for the same port design. There is no standard test pressure, so the formula below must be used to compare flowbench results at different test pressures.

First, divide the desired test pressure by the existing test pressure. The square root of that figure is you conversion factor, as shown below:

$$\sqrt{\frac{\text{desired test pressure}}{\text{existing test pressure}}} = \text{conversion factor}$$

Next, multiply the test results by the conversion factor to calculate cfm at the new pressure.

Test results (cfm) x conversion factor = Test results (cfm) at desired test pressure

For example, let's say that you have one result of 325 cfm taken 28 pounds of pressure that you want to compare to another result of 206cfm taken at 10 pounds of pressure. First, you would calculate your conversion factor:

$$\sqrt{\frac{28 \text{ pounds}}{10 \text{ pounds}}} = \sqrt{2.8} = 1.673$$

Now, you can convert the result taken at 10 pounds (206cfm) of pressure so that can be compared to the result taken at 28 pounds of pressure (325cfm).

206cfm x 1.673 = 344.638cfm

Keep this in mind when you are comparing different head, porting, valve, or other work that uses flowbench results to indicate performance. In order to compare these results, you'll need to gather three bits of data:
1. cfm
2. Test pressure used
3. Correction to standard temperature and atmospheric pressure.

builders, and then make a few phone calls. Any of these manufacturer's products will outperform a modified stock head, so there's no reason to use the stock product, especially when building large motors.

In addition, all the racers I talked to while researching this book said it was much cheaper to buy a set of aftermarket heads set up for racing than to try and make the stock heads work. One particular builder, who shall remain nameless, modified a stock set of heads and spent almost twice as much as an aftermarket set would have cost, and the performance difference between the two wasn't measurable.

Fueling four-valve heads use stainless-steel valves, silicon-manganese-bronze guides, chromemoly seats, 8620 steel rockers, chrome-moly pushrods, and dualcarb intake. The theory behind four-valve heads (two intake—two exhaust) is that two smaller valves will flow more air than a single valve with the same surface area, and keep the velocity higher while doing it. Each intake valve has its own port and manifold runner, while the exhaust exits through one common port per head.

Two carbs with their related cables and gas lines are used, increasing the cost over a two-valve design, but the top-end performance is worth the additional expense. The heads retail for $2,399, and a second carb and air cleaner will set you back $400 to $450.

Piston Speed for Stroked Engines

When you're thinking about building a stroked V-twin, one thing to consider is piston speed—how fast the pistons must move through the cylinder bore. High piston speed—above about 4,800 feet per minute—will cause excessive piston, rod, and ring wear. Normal piston speed for a stock 4.25-inch-stroke Evo is 3,750 feet per minute at 5,300rpm. Piston speed is found by multiplying the stroke by the rpm, then dividing by six.

Increase the stock stroke by 3/4 inch to 5 inches and the piston speed climbs to 4,400 feet per minute at 5,300rpm. Not a problem if the red-line stays there, but bump the rev limit to 7,000rpm and the piston speed jumps over 5,800 feet per minute. This speed will wear out rings, bearings, and cylinder bores in very short order—unacceptable in a street engine you want to last a few years.

Racing engines are another story. If the 5-inch-stroke engine peaks at 7,000rpm on the dyno—well, that's where it's going to run—plus another 10 percent for a shift at 7,700rpm. The idea in racing is to be first, not to make the engine last. With luck, you'll open the engine often enough to catch any wear problems before they become critical.

Rivera also offers four-valve billet heads for Big Twins. The company's flow-bench testing shows 325cfm at 0.600 inch lift on the intake side, 210cfm on the exhaust at the same lift. See the flow chart for all the specs.

These four-valve heads are a 1994 design and are available in two versions, one street and one race-only. The street version fits cylinders up to 3 13/16-inch bore; the race heads are good for 4 1/4 inches. All the ports are polished and flow-tested before being shipped. A single spark plug sits between the two intake and two exhaust valves. The plug's central location means dual plugs aren't needed with a four-valve combustion chamber.

Rivera heads also have a siamesed exhaust port, so the stock header pipes will fit; however, the intake manifold is different—feeding a dual port plenum on each head. A single carb will work, providing it can flow enough air to take advantage of the dual intake valves. A Mikuni HSR 42 or Rivera's own S.U.-based Eliminator II carb will work.

The four-valve heads really don't do much for performance until the revs climb above 4,500. However, from there on up, they will outperform any two-valve setup when it comes to airflow. For anyone seriously contemplating racing, they are almost a necessity if you want to see the other end of the strip first.

Jim McClure (Master Performance Racing, 804-566-0544) runs a set of four-valve heads he's modified to take a 4 1/2-inch bore. He's gone 6.93 seconds and 200.27 miles per hour with his Sportster-based 150-inch engine. That's more than double the stock engine size, and there are few stock Sportster parts between the front motor mount and the Rivera belt drive. It takes a one-piece crank to stay together with that many cubic inches making horsepower, and so far he's had good luck with the setup. He'd be a good guy to talk to if you're going racing, especially with a Sportster.

Cylinders, Rods, and Crankcases

Make the holes bigger and the pistons go up and down farther, and presto—a larger engine. Build a 4-inch-bore by 5-inch-stroke motor for 126ci, and the problem becomes getting it to breathe enough to make use of a 50-percent displacement increase. The heads and carbs mentioned in the prior pages will handle anything up to 138ci easily, but engine size has a direct relationship on rate of wear of moving components.

A set of 4-inch cylinders and a 5-inch stroke increase the displacement 54 percent. All these parts simply won't fit in a stock set of cases, though. You'll need aftermarket cases with a wider-spaced cylinder-bolt pattern, and the bolt pattern on the heads must match the cylinder. Sputhe, Axtell, and RevTech can provide all the parts to build 125-ci stroker motors. Axtell offers eight-bolt finless cylinders in sizes from 3.5 inches to 4 inches, with up to a 5-inch stroke.

A good set of bulletproof rods from Jim McClure (Axtell) will set you back $795. They are sold as a special-order-only kit complete with races, wrist pin bushings, bearing cages, crankpin, and nuts.

Aluminum cylinders with steel sleeves, sizes 95.4ci to 104ci, are also available from Sputhe. These are high-pressure cast in 383 aluminum alloy by being injected into a steel die at 5,000psi.

Bonded to a cast, chrome-moly sleeve made out of "Lascomite," these provide a structure much more rigid, yet less brittle, than H-D factory parts.

Cylinders on the 95.4-ci engine can be removed with the engine in place; longer-stroke motors require pulling the engine from the frame. Solid copper O-rings replace the head gaskets, and seat in a groove in the cylinder deck for a positive seal. Cylinder spigots in the cases have to be 4.010 inches to accept the bigger 95-ci cylinders. You can bore out the stock cases, but you really should go with a set designed for the bigger spigots.

Aftermarket cases will take the additional stress from larger motors that would break a set of stock cases in short order. Sputhe's Big Twin cases are built to take the raised loads imposed by big-inch engines spinning 7,000+rpm. Aluminum castings (356A-T6) are CNC-machined with shrunk-in steel bearing inserts, extra case bolts, and increased wall thickness in critical areas. Sputhe's chrome-moly heat-treated cylinder studs have rolled, as opposed to cut, threads to help relieve stress on the threads, while a high thread finish allows more-accurate torquing. Studs and cases can be ordered for $864.

Using dished pistons with Fueling or Romanelli heads on top of Sputhe's 104-ci engine will give a 12.2:1 compression ratio with a 52-cc chamber volume. S.T.D. heads and flat-top pistons combine to produce ratios from 9.5 to 10.3:1. Other ratios and sizes are available on special order. Sputhe states the engine must be rebalanced because of the lighter pistons, but any modified motor should take a trip to the machine shop for a rebalance, no matter its size.

As a final alternative to rolling your own, call up the

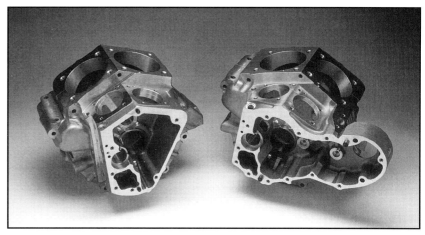

When engine sizes grow above 100ci, a set of aftermarket cases, like these from Delkron, are necessary. The cases have additional webbing where stress is concentrated. Oil passages, O-ring grooves, and stator plug location have been moved to eliminate weak areas or thin castings. They are available to fit a wide range of conditions, from a 1970 alternator case to big-bore cases for Evolutions. *CCI*

people at Sputhe and talk real nice ($$$$$), and they will build you a 60-degree 120-ci long block, set up for fuel or gas racing. It's designed to be the ultimate air-cooled pushrod V-twin, and any frame that takes an Evo motor will accept it. Sputhe's motor looks like a V-twin, but not a Harley V-twin. Expect to spend $8,000 without externals.

Cams

With a serious, big-inch race motor, here's where you can use a lot of cam, with lift like a hotel staircase and duration measured in months. Big-inch motors with straight pipes and high airflow can take a cam with over 0.630-inch valve lift and 268 degrees of intake duration. Sifton offers its 147-EV grind for just such an engine. It comes on at 3,000rpm and makes serious power up to 6,500rpm. Total valve lift is 0.640 for both intake and exhaust.

Here again you have to check all clearances very carefully before starting the engine. Valve-spring spacing, free travel, and ignition drive gear clearances need

to be carefully measured. Turn the engine through by hand and watch the valve springs. When the valve is fully open, the springs must not bind, or the valve touch the top of the piston. Be sure to use the right lifters, solid or hydraulic, with the cam.

Valve-spring free travel can easily be checked by assembling each valve in the cylinder head with the valve-spring collar and keeper in place, but without the springs. Run the valve up and down in the guide to check for any binding; then measure the distance the valve can move before the underside of the collar touches the top of the valve guide. This is the free travel and can be checked against the dimensions in the cam instruction sheet. To increase the free travel, the top of the guide can be ground away. Try to turn off just enough to give correct clearances, as the valve guide should be as long as possible to help hold the valve straight as it moves, and for longevity.

Reassemble the valves with the springs. Measure the distance the valve travels until the spring coils just touch. Normally this happens only on one side of the spring, so don't try to force the valve down past this point. Since springs vary in length at coil bind, it's necessary to check each spring set. If the spring travel to coil bind specification in the cam chart is 0.570 inch and the actual spring travel is greater than this, shims can be added to the top of the valve-guide flange. Not enough travel will require the head to be milled so the valve guide can be set deeper in the head.

Installing high-lift cams, with their bigger springs, might require the spring pockets on the heads to be cut to accept the larger-diameter springs. Lower collars have to sit perfectly flat on the head without the spring touching any part of the casting.

The distance from the top of the bottom collar to the bottom of the top collar, with the springs installed, is the installed spring height. This should be 1.80 inch for Evo motors.

To check valve-to-valve and valve-to-piston clearance, the engine must be fully assembled with all gaskets and correct torque on all the studs and bolts. Turn the engine to TDC with both valves in the overlap position. Insert a 0.040 wire through one of the ports, intake or exhaust, and check to see that the wire passes between the valves while the crank turns from TDC to 5 degrees after TDC. If they won't clear the wire, the valve heads must be beveled at a 45-degree angle.

At the same time the valves are checked for clearance, you can check the valve-to-piston clearance by placing a layer of clay on top of the piston before the engine is assembled. After checking valve-to-valve clearance, turn the engine through two more times and disassem-

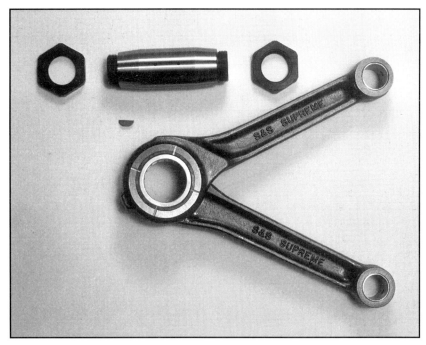

The best way to keep all those horses in a stroker motor working in the same direction is to install a set of S&S rods. Balance will have to be checked when new pistons are mounted on the rods. *S&S*

ble the heads. There must be 0.080 inch of clay remaining under the valves, or the piston top must be cut down to obtain that thickness.

One clearance a lot of people forget to check is the rocker-to-rocker box. Prior to bolting the engine into the frame, install the rocker boxes with their gaskets and tighten them down. Rotate the engine by hand, and if it stops turning, or strange noises come from the top of the head, loosen the rocker boxes and turn the engine again, watching them rise off the lower boxes. This will give you an idea as to how much material must be ground off the inside of the rocker covers for clearance.

High-lift cams change the angle of the pushrod from lifter to rocker because of their increased lobe rise, sometimes causing interference between pushrod, pushrod tube, and/or cylinder head. All 7/16-inch-

diameter pushrods should work without problems in clearance. Remember, all four pushrods are different lengths; longest goes to the front exhaust—farthest from the cam. Next longest goes to the rear exhaust. The remaining two short rods fit both intakes. Different angles leading to the rockers from the cam make for different pushrod length.

When setting up a drag-racing motor, you want a cam that lets the power peak 10 percent below the shift point. This keeps the engine from falling off the power when the next higher gear is selected. For instance, say your 121-ci motor shows peak horsepower at 7,000rpm on the dyno. Ten percent of 7,000 is 700, so shift at 7,700rpm. Be sure to set the rev limiter above this point to ensure you aren't using the power cutoff as a shift point, which could cause engine damage.

Compression Ratios and Pistons

An Evo engine makes excellent power with a 12.5:1 compression ratio running on racing gas of 108 octane, or better. Higher ratios can be used—14.5 to 15.5; however, wear and parts replacement become major factors. You need to know if the volumetric efficiency (VE) of the engine will support so much compression before using such high ratios.

VE is at 100 percent when the cylinder is filled to its maximum capacity. A street engine, turning at its torque peak will have a VE of 80–85 percent. Running the same engine at its horsepower peak will show a lower VE because, at higher rpm, the cylinder won't fill as completely as it will at the lower torque peak. As the engine's intake system is improved, the VE will increase. A racing engine with a tuned intake tract and an exhaust system operating at maximum efficiency will compress the fuel/air mixture and run a VE exceeding 100 percent.

Once the VE begins to drop off, the cylinder fill declines from 100 percent, causing torque to fall. When the torque drops faster than the rpm climbs, the horsepower peak has been reached.

Operational compression ratio is the actual CR reached when the engine is running. A change in VE will cause the operational compression ratio to change.

In a theoretical engine, the intake valve would close just as the piston begins rising in its compression stroke from BDC. This ensures maximum compression when the piston hits TDC. However, the incoming mixture has momentum and mass, so it takes time for the cylinder to fill. As the rpm climbs, there is less time for this to happen, so the intake valve has to open sooner and close later, after the piston has started up on

Wiseco builds pistons for any size, any compression H-D. These are Sportster pistons. Note the flat cuts for valve clearance on the domes. You will still have to check valve-piston clearance by assembling the engine with clay on the top of the pistons, over the area where the valves operate. At least 0.040-inch clearance is necessary. If the valves touch the pistons, the piston faces will have to be cut. *Wiseco*

the compression stroke. When the revs are down, the rising piston pushes part of the mixture back past the valve, resulting in reduced fill and less power. Higher revs take advantage of momentum and cam duration to push the air-fuel mixture past the valve during part of the compression stroke.

Using a cam with long duration will allow the cylinder to fill better at high rpm because of the length of time the valve is open in comparison to crank rotation. This will also cause a loss in VE when the revs are down, with a resulting drop in power.

More bang through increased cylinder pressure (compression) is the key to power. Everything you do to modify the engine is aimed at increasing power through more efficient breathing and improved combustion by more efficient cylinder filling and raising cylinder pressure on the power stroke.

The mechanical CR of Harley's Big Twin runs between

8.35 and 8.5 to 1, depending on tolerances. Ideally a raise to 9.5:1 is needed to make any type of decent power. Of course, racing engines respond better to higher ratios, providing detonation doesn't become a problem.

Axtell builds Evolution Big Twin cylinder kits with CR from 8:1 up to 10:1 for Pro Street. Bore and stroke range from stock 81.7ci to 114.1ci. Sportster kits' CR depends on application and covers engine sizes from 73.3ci to 114.1ci. Bigger cylinder sizes will require stock bolt holes to be downsized and heads counterbored to match the cylinder. A 30-degree compression relief cut into the head is recommended for both types of engines.

A 4-inch bore piston is available from Axtell for street or strip use in engines of 100ci and up. It can be set up with any compression ratio depending on application. Pistons can be ordered with a ceramic coating on the domes and composite film lubricant on the skirts. This is one area where you definitely need to call Axtell while you're still in the design stages of engine building.

Sputhe has a Big Twin cylinder kit that will open the engine up to 104ci. It uses the cylinders from their 95-ci kit with a set of 4 5/8 inch stroke flywheels, preferably from S&S. The stock cases can't be used, but they aren't strong enough to handle the horsepower anyway. It just so happens that Sputhe makes a set of cases that will take their big 4-inch cylinders. They come with extra socket-head case bolts for increased rigidity, pinion bearing race, shrunk-in steel bearing inserts, and increased wall thickness to handle the boost in torque from 100+ci engines. The 4-inch-bore cylinders require a 4.250-inch spigot diameter, and the cases that take these cylinders have a 0.125-inch cam chest offset for clearance. Put aside $950 for a set of cases and just under $1,000 for the 104-ci cylinder and piston kit.

With any big bore/stroker cylinder kit, engine mount dimensions must be checked. Some of the taller cylinders in the various kits require different engine mounting bolt holes in the frame. Up to 100ci isn't usually a problem, especially with the kits from Sputhe, but past that be sure to check cylinder length before you find yourself down on your hands and knees trying to fit a tall engine into a too short space.

Gasoline and Fuel

Now comes the fun of trying to get your brand new, high horsepower motor to run. If most of your riding is street-oriented, finding gasoline that will allow a compression ratio above 10.5:1 is going to be a problem. Detonation will raise its ugly head. On a hot day and with low rpms the engine

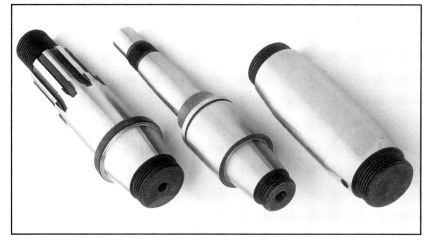

Accel is now in the crankpin, pinion shaft, and sprocket shaft business. They are set up for the severe duty of running in a big-inch engine. Shaft threads are annealed to allow torquing up to 100 foot-pounds over factory specs. The bearing surfaces are deep heat-treated to Rockwell 60–63 hardness. In plain terms, this means that any surface that has to take a bearing's motion has been toughened for a longer life. This also means no machining or polishing can be done to the shafts without removing the heat-treating. *CCI*

When bolting a used, stock inner primary case to a set of Delcron or STD cases, have the case X-rayed for cracks. Visual inspection will find larger cracks but won't pick up the small ones that form around places like bolt holes.

will rattle badly, with possible piston damage as a result.

Racing gas can be added to 92-octane pump gas to give a mixture that will run without pinging, but it's very expensive—$4.15 to $7.15 per gallon depending on rating—and carrying a 5-gallon can full of the stuff on a long ride is rather difficult.

Aviation gas, known as 100LL, will help in a marginal situation but requires an airport and gas cans, again a lot of work for a street bike. Octane boosters are advertised as "power in a can," capable of raising octane levels five points or more; however, most of the products do a good job of lightening your wallet and little else.

Face it, if you are going to run on the street 95 percent of the time, some compromise on compression must be made. Stick to no more than 10.5:1 and you'll have no problems.

You can run higher than 10:1 CR on the street with a lot of involved head work. Hot street engines running upwards of 12:1 CR require a redesigned combustion chamber to eliminate dead spots where detonation takes place. Some head builders are reshaping the combustion chambers for better quench—area in the head that "squishes" the air-fuel mixture toward the spark plug—and improved gasflow. All this increases turbulence, making the mixture burn faster, and supports combustion better than a stock head, plus allows much higher CR without resorting to domed pistons.

Flat-top pistons have less interference with the combustion wave front during its travels across the combustion chamber than do domed pistons. Although pistons with an angle top, like Axtell's, do help increase compression through better squish.

Fuel for racing at the drags or Bonneville is a different game entirely. High CR, all the way up to 15:1, requires very high octane fuel. Compared to the cost of your bike and related racing expense, paying $7.15 per gallon for 118-octane fuel really isn't much of a consideration. You won't be using enough of the stuff to really make much difference in the cost of racing. About $100 worth of fuel will see you through a long weekend with some left over for the lawnmower.

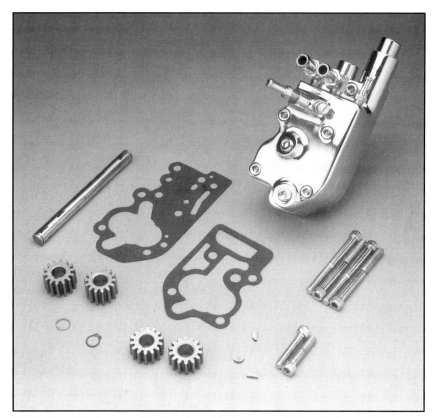

Oilflow is critical on modified engines. Harley never designed the stock oil pump to develop much pressure, as roller and ball bearings don't require as much as do plain bearings. The gerotors inside the pump must be checked for chips if a used pump is going back on the engine. I highly recommend installation of a high-flow pump on any new engine. *CCI*

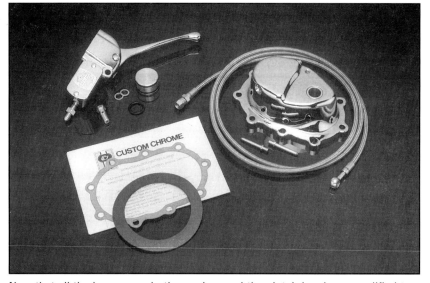

Now that all the horses are in the engine, and the clutch has been modified to take the power; you say you can't hardly pull in the clutch lever, eh bunkie? Well, don't feel alone. It's happened to so many of us that a hydraulic clutch is now available for most Harleys. It comes with a braided metallic line that controls expansion and gives a better, more positive feel during operation. *CCI*

A wide variety of parts exist for Stage III engines. Trying to list them all would produce a book more along the lines of a parts list for a 747 and still leave someone out through my own fault. So what I've listed here is a few of the basic combinations available. Any part not listed means the same part, like ignition, is common to Stage II engines.

Package Specifications For Stage III Engines Approximate cost in 1996— $4,500 and up

Kit #1
1. Axtell BT-EV drag-race kit, finless barrels, forged pistons, rings, and related components.
2. S.T.D. cases
3. Competition Cams EVO-3060 (.585 lift) w/Velva-Touch lifters
4. S&S Super G carb
5. Rivera 4-valve heads

Kit #2
1. Sputhe 104-ci Big Twin cylinder kit
2. S.T.D. cases
3. S.T.D. heads
4. S&S 4 5/8-inch flywheels
5. S&S Super D carb
6. S&S 33-5080 cam (.630 lift)

Kit #3
1. Axtell 4-inch Big Bore cylinders
2. S&S 4 5/8-inch flywheels (116.2ci)
3. Mikuni HSR 42 carb
4. Crane 1-1003 cam (.550 lift)

Kit #4
1. S&S cylinders w/Axtell pistons
2. S&S stroker crank w/rods
3. Red Shift cam and springs
4. Zipper's Hi-port heads w/ big valves and 30-degree squish
5. S&S Super G carb

In order to handle the increased torque put out by highly modified engines, the transmission gears and shafts need to be improved. Rather than modify stock pieces, install parts from RevTech or Andrews. All shafts are hard chromed; gears are back-cut for smoother shifting; and most of the gears are made from 8620H chrome moly. A 2.94:1 close-ratio first gear is available through RevTech. Andrews also has a complete line of close-ratio gears for four-speeds and five-speeds. *CCI*

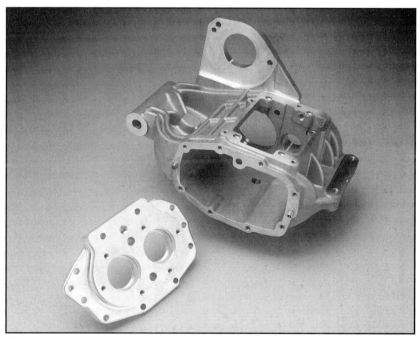

Five-speed, rubber-mounted transmission cases and bearing supports as they come from the factory will run forever behind a stock engine. It's when you start adding copious quantities of power that the stock parts begin to fail. Delcron builds their cases out of 356-T-6, permanent mold cast-aluminum. They have beefed up wall thickness in all stress areas, put in heavier webbing on the primary mounting ears, and will take stock components or Andrews gears. A chain final drive must be used with this case. *CCI*

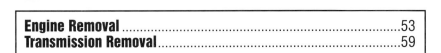

Now we get into the actual nuts and bolts of working on the engine. Actually, I should say you get to work on the engine; I'm just going to sit here and watch you sweat. And sweat you will, if this is the first engine you've torn down. Looking back from here, a teardown is easy when you follow directions, which I didn't the first few times, and for my troubles, got to do it over again, but the first time is a learning procedure.

Before you open up the toolbox, hang on a minute, and let's take a look around. Where, exactly, are you going to do all this work? Do you have a place to store all the parts while the bike's down? How 'bout coffee cans for nuts, bolts, and studs? Good idea to have some masking tape and a marking pen so you can wrap all of one group of bolts together and name them. For instance, the seven bolts and one stud holding the cases together need to be kept separate from everything else. Once they are out of the engine, write on the roll of masking tape: "Case Bolts & Front Upper Stud," then wrap it around all eight and put them in a can marked "Engine Right Side."

Little things like writing on the masking tape before it's unrolled seem petty, but five weeks later when you try to read your writing, you'll be glad you didn't try to wrap the bolts first, then write on the tape.

Have you a clean, well-lighted place to work? How about a soft surface on the floor? A piece of carpet helps your knees and keeps dropped parts from leaving for places unknown. Nuts and washers don't roll as far on carpet as on concrete. My whole garage is carpeted thanks to a neighbor who installed new wall-to-wall in his house. Makes for a warmer place to work, and is easier on the knees than concrete. When the oil stains get overwhelming, off to the dump it goes. The best place I've found to pick up large pieces of carpet is from a business building undergoing remodel. Call a carpet company and ask them if you can come get their next tear-out; saves them money to have you haul it, and you gain a free carpeted garage in the process.

I've got six four-bulb fluorescent lights spaced evenly down the garage, hanging 10 feet above the floor. They do wonders for erasing shadows. On sale, they can be had for under $10 per fixture. There's no such thing as too much light.

A workbench is a necessity to get the engine up high enough to handle comfortably. Even a card table will work, but something with a little more heft is better. Used furniture stores carry worktables with a Formica (no scratching the parts) top, usually in the 2-foot 8-inch by 7-foot size, or something similar. Two of them grace the north side of my garage; think I paid $15 apiece for them five years ago. I don't recommend bolting anything like a vice to them, as they are made out of pressed wood chips and won't take much load. I had an ammo reloading press, secured with two 3/8-inch bolts, on one of them, and it tore off within a very short time. (Hit me in the bloody knee, it did.)

I went to a sheet metal shop that fabricates air conditioning ducts and had them bend up a piece of 16 gauge sheet metal to fit on the table. Now the loading press bolts through this, and the sheet metal spreads the load. Works so well, I hung a 15-pound vice to one end of the table a year ago; still there after truing numerous flywheels.

The necessary tools, rags, solvent, etc., should already be close at hand. Buy a cheap Polaroid camera and three rolls of film. A standard camera can be used, but waiting for pictures to be developed is a hassle. And, what do you do if they don't come out and the engine is already occupying coffee cans? Considering the outgo for a performance motor, $50–$70 for a Polaroid is cheap.

Take pictures of all stages of disassembly. I know you've got a mind that retains information better than an IBM PC, but the other guys reading this book might not. When you figure there's 37 pieces, bolts, gears, and assorted widgets related to the gearcase cover and timing gears alone, the need for a camera becomes apparent. The pictures will pay for themselves in one rebuild.

Start with a picture of the whole bike. Make sure it's against a neutral background so individual parts stand out. Take a series of shots of the engine from both sides, then shoot pictures every time a major part comes off. I used a Nikon 35mm for shooting the pictures in this book, so it takes a couple of days to get my prints back. Looking at them, it's obvious how much I've forgotten in just a few days, so expecting to remember all the parts and where they go after a five-week, or more, span of time is almost impossible.

Notes:

1. The actual teardown covered here refers to 1995 and 1996 Dyna Glide models. Other bikes, different models, or prior years may have some variations; however, the sequence and operations will basically be the same. Sportsters will be covered in their own section. Only Evo engines are covered here.

2. Special tools will be listed before the particular section dealing with their use.

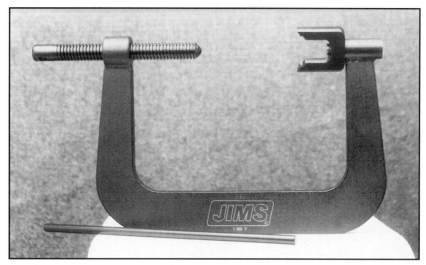

Whether you are working on a Sporty or Big Twin head, this valve-spring tool is necessary to remove or install valves. *Jim's Tools*

Engine Removal

Steam-clean the entire bike, paying particular attention to the engine and transmission.

Secure the bike to a center-stand, or use some means of holding it level and steady. Shake the bike a few times to ensure it won't fall over. The best way to handle this is with a stand that holds the bike frame tightly and allows it to be raised off the floor for easier disassembly. Again, be really sure the bike is stable, because you are going to be yarfing it around quite a bit when the engine is removed and re-installed.

Throw some rags over the front and rear fenders, so if you drop a tool, it won't do any paint damage. Next, remove the seat. Remove one side of the grab strap, then remove the screw and nylon washer from the rear seat bracket. Be sure and save the nylon washer between the seat bracket and fender. This keeps the bracket from scratching the fender. Don't substitute a metal washer.

Slide the seat to the rear and lift off at the same time. The U-shaped bracket at the front of the seat needs to be slid from under the frame bracket. Re-install the rear screw and nylon washer in the fender. Put the seat in a plastic garbage bag and set it somewhere safe. Now is the time to send the seat out to a upholstery shop for any special work. If you are buying a aftermarket custom seat, save the stock one. Put it in the rafters, or a like place. Never throw Harley parts out. If you really want to get rid of them, send them to me, care of the publisher—I'll make the money when they become rare.

Remove the battery cables, starting with the negative cable first. Now that the engine can't accidentally turn over, raise the bike on the stand. The first time you do this, it might help to have a friend steady the bike. It's not going to fall, but with a little help, you will feel better about the whole thing. Once everything is removed prior to the engine coming out, the bike can be set back down on the floor for more stability.

Drain the fuel from the tank(s). Check to see the petcock is shut off and remove the fuel line from it. Attach a rubber hose of the same diameter as the fuel line to the petcock (auto supply store), and drain the fuel into a gas can. Before pulling the bike into the garage for the teardown, ride it until it goes on reserve; this saves having to drain a lot of fuel. Don't forget to remove the crossover line under the tanks; much easier to lift off the tank without it. I only forgot it once—honest!

Remove the two fuel-tank mounting bolts. They are the same on the FXDL, FXD, FXDS, and others. To remove the speedometer on the FXDWG, lift the tank far enough to remove the speedometer sensor wire and ignition harness from the mounting clips. Cut any cable ties holding the wires to the frame. Remove the console from the tank and store it in a safe place. Lift the tank off the frame.

An older tank that has built up deposits from sitting around for many years can be cleaned with a commercial cleaning solvent, or a good detergent soap and water. Double ought (00) lead shot from a gun shop can be added to help break loose the deposits. Count the pellets before throwing them in the tank. Removing all but one will guarantee fuel starvation—usually at the worst possible time.

You may have to pull the rocker boxes to get the necessary clearances for engine removal. If you do, remove the screws holding on the upper cover, remove it and the middle rocker arm cover and gaskets.

Discard the gaskets; mark and tape the hold-down screws. These, and all other Evo fasteners and washers, are specially hardened. If you lose any fasteners from the engine, they must be replaced with correctly rated parts.

Remove the upper cylinder head engine bracket. There are washers between the bracket and frame lug; use the same washers

If all you plan on doing is changing the cam, and don't want to split the case, this cam bearing tool can be used to remove the inner case bearing. *Jim's Tools*

If the cam cover bushing has to be replaced, and you don't want scratches on your chrome cover, this cam cover holding plate will save the finish on the cam cover. *Jim's Tools*

when the bracket is reassembled. Best idea is to wire them to the bracket.

If the engine is going back into the bike with the same spark plugs, now's the time to remove them before they get broken. Presumably, the engine is coming out for some serious work, including new heads, so leave the spark plugs in place to protect the threads, and after the engine comes down, store the heads in a safe place.

Now remove the air-cleaner cover screw, cover, and filter. Remove the breather from the screw on the top right of the backplate, then remove the screws.

Things get a little tricky when it comes to pulling the backplate. The backplate-to-carb screws have to be backed out in sequence, two turns at a time. Pull out the backplate along with the screws. The reason for this is to keep the captive screw threads from catching in the threads in the backplate and damaging the backplate.

Once the screws are free, remove the backplate, baffle (if any), and gasket.

The California-only backplate comes apart slightly differently, what with smog equipment, et al. Disconnect the solenoid wiring connector, and remove the overflow hose from the fitting on the bottom. Remove two screws from the back of the backing plate that hold the baffle and solenoid bracket in place. Remove the small screw on the bottom of the solenoid plunger; remove the solenoid.

All this is only necessary if you are dismantling the backplate to repair the solenoid or clean the butterfly valve. It's not necessary to break down the backplate if you're pulling the engine, especially if the carb and air cleaner are being changed.

Remove the fuel line and, on models that have it, the vacuum-operated electrical switch (V.O.E.S.) hose, and the vacuum hose (CA bikes only) from the carburetor. Disconnect the throttle cables (2) and the enrichener cable.

Take the carb and manifold off as a single item by removing the cap screws holding the manifold in place.

Remove the exhaust-pipe heat shields by loosening the seven screw clamps.

Cheap Horsepower

For those of you with a limited amount of money to spend and who want a little more performance for not much outgo, here are a couple of ideas.

1. The stock jet sizes for 49-state bikes and International, Swiss, and California bikes for 1995 and 1996 are:

49 State Models	1996	1995
Main Jet	170	165
Slow Jet	42	42
California Models		
Main Jet	175	165
Slow Jet	42	42
HDI Models		
Main Jet	180	180
Slow Jet	42	42
Swiss Models		
Main Jet	180	165
Slow Jet	42	42

As you see, the 1995 carb main jets are smaller than the International or Swiss bikes. (Don't ask me—the Swiss have their own ideas—maybe the cold does it.)

Replacing the 165 main jets with the 180 main will fatten up the top half of the throttle.

2. Changing the air filter to a low-restriction, like K&N (800-858-3333), will let the engine breathe better.

3. Opening up the baffles in the pipes by running a 7/8th drill, welded to a steel dowel, through them will relieve some back pressure and make the bike sound more like an 80-incher instead of a 0.080-incher.

All of this will cost less than $25, won't change the looks of the bike, and will give a power boost. Don't expect wheelies, but there will be a difference. Also, everything except the holes in the baffles can be changed back to stock if needed.

1 Drain the gas out of the tank, You can make your life a bit easier if you run the bike until it's on reserve so you don't have as much gas to store.

2 Next, remove the seat.

3 The carb and its related plumbing comes off next. Be sure to plug the intake manifold with a clean rag, keeping unwanted debris out of your engine.

4 Set the carb out of the way and protect it with rags. If you drain the carburetor before you take it off, you'll have less of a mess to deal with at this point.

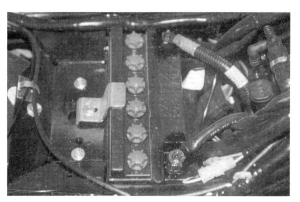

5 Disconnect the battery, positive terminal first, and remove. Be sure and store it on a board; leaving it on bare concrete will eventually drain the charge. If your battery is out for more than a month or so, hit it with a trickle charger for a few hours.

6 One of the problem areas on a Big Twin motor is the alternator case plug. It has a tendency to come loose, so a strap, as shown, should be fabricated to keep it in place. Disconnect this plug and all related electricals on the engine.

7 Remove the tank. Unbolt the spark-plug coil, and remove it and the spark plugs if the engine is coming all the way apart; otherwise, leave the spark plugs in the heads. This bike is coming down to a bare frame, and the primary has already been removed.

8 When you pull the primary cover, make sure an oil pan is there to catch any oil draining out.

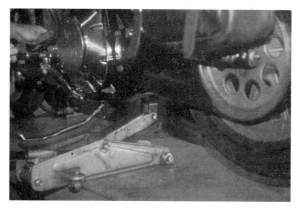

9 Jack up the rear of the bike so the final drive belt can be removed.

10 The carb backing plate is being removed with an air drive wrench. Then remove the V.O.E.S. and all wiring on the top of the engine.

11 This is as far as you have to go on the primary side if only the engine is being removed. The primary chain adjuster must be loosened and then the compensating sprocket nut can be removed; the sprocket and primary chain will come off as a unit.

12 Remove the brake pedal mechanism, footpeg, and exhaust pipes from the right side of the Big Twin or Sportster.

13 On some bikes, the rocker cover will have to be removed for the engine to clear the frame.

14 Remove the motor mount bolts. Support the engine in a sling while the bolts are withdrawn. Use the sling to pull the engine out the right side of the frame.

Unbolt the two header pipe flanges at the head. Remove the clamp holding the header pipe to the gear cover bracket. Also, take off the rear header pipe clamp where it bolts to the transmission side support bracket.

The whole header and muffler system will now come off as a unit. The individual pipes can be separated by twisting at the crossover pipe. If new pipes are to be installed, and they require the original support brackets, the muffler support brackets have to come off the mufflers. Some exhaust systems come with their own support brackets, and the factory units won't be needed.

Remove the right footrest, brake pedal, and master cylinder assembly. The master cylinder assembly comes off by removing the banjo bolt and washers at the brake line. Discard the washers and replace with new. Pry the tine back on the lock washer securing the master cylinder nut. Remove the nut. Back the jam nut off the brake rod and raise the rear brake pedal to allow the master cylinder to move forward and out of the frame bracket. The rear brake line must be bled when the master cylinder is re-installed.

Drain the oil from the tank. On bikes with the oil tank behind the engine, remove all oil lines from it and the oil pump, and mark them as to position. Remove breather lines.

Drain the primary case from the plug on the bottom. Remove the primary cover. Remove the compensating sprocket shaft nut so the compensating sprocket can be removed during engine removal. Remove the four bolts holding the inner primary case to the engine. The inner case and transmission/ clutch will stay in the bike when the engine is removed.

Disconnect the sensor from the ignition module. Remove the

alternator plug from the left engine case. Unplug spark-plug wires.

Remove the clutch cable bracket from the engine. Disconnect the wire on the oil pressure switch.

Remove oil lines from the oil pump.

Remove the nuts and washers on the front and rear engine mounting bolts. Position a jack under the engine, or a hoist cable around the engine, so the engine weight can be taken off the bolts and the bolts removed. The bike must be upright to do this, which is one of the reasons for a bike stand.

Take some tension on the hoist cable to free up the bolts, then remove them. Here's where another set of hands comes in handy. Lift the engine slightly and remove it from the frame. Set it on the bench in an engine stand.

Transmission Removal

Special Tools
HD-38515A clutch spring
   compressing tool
HD-94660-37B mainshaft
   locknut wrench
HD-41184 transmission sprocket
   tool

Removing the transmission is going to require one specialized tool to compress the diaphragm spring and release the retaining ring. Trying to do the job without the compressor can result in getting center-punched by flying

parts. There's enough power in the diaphragm spring to stick it in the far wall, providing something soft doesn't interfere with its flight, like your head. Loosen the jam nut on the mainshaft and remove the jam nut and adjuster screw.

Thread the forcing screw of the H-D compressing tool into the threaded hole on the clutch release plate until the hex head on the forcing screw snugs up against the release plate.

Turn the handle clockwise to compress the diaphragm spring and push the clutch spring seat inwards enough to remove the retaining ring. The ring can be removed with a pair of snap-ring pliers, or use a screwdriver to lift the ring from its grove.

Remove the compressor, taking the diaphragm spring and pressure plate off at the same time. Do not loosen the spring compressing tool until the clutch goes back together. The diaphragm spring can become off-center if the compressor is removed, causing difficulty in finding neutral.

Place the transmission in fifth gear and lock the rear brake. Remove the left-hand thread mainshaft nut from the end of the transmission mainshaft.

Remove the primary chain adjusting shoe by unbolting the two bottom bolts and removing the center nut. Replacing the shoe will require a new center nut.

Remove the engine compensating sprocket, clutch assembly,

and primary chain with adjuster, all as a unit. The compensating sprocket, primary chain, chain adjuster, and clutch must be re-installed as a unit.

Remove the starter. Hold the pinion gear in place and remove the long center jackshaft bolt and lock washer. Remove the end cover.

Remove the starter Allen head bolts and washers. Disconnect the battery lead and solenoid wire. Remove the starter from the right side of the bike.

Remove the three inner primary bolts attaching it to the transmission, and remove the inner primary.

Remove the four Allen screws and lockplate from the transmission sprocket. Use the transmission sprocket tool to hold the sprocket in place while removing the transmission sprocket nut with the mainshaft locknut wrench. The nut is a left-hand thread.

Run the rear-axle adjusting nuts all the way back so the rear axle can be moved far enough forward to remove the sprocket and rear drive belt.

Remove footshifter rod from the shifter lever. Run clutch cable adjuster nuts all the way in and remove the cable from the clutch arm. Unbolt and remove the transmission mounting bolts, supporting the transmission as the bolts are withdrawn.

Remove the transmission from the frame.

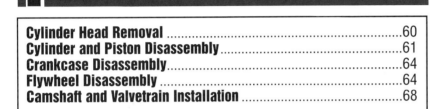

Once the engine is out, the fun begins. To turn your powerplant into a fire-breathing beast, it must be disassembled. Don't forget to clearly mark parts, and place them in places you can find them all as they come off. Incidentally, clearly marked storage bins, old coffee cans, and plastic bags constitute "places where you can find the parts." Tossing parts randomly around the shop guarantees a long, expensive, and frustrating rebuild process.

Cylinder Head Removal

Remove the Allen screws holding the rocker covers and lift off the upper and middle rocker arm covers. Rotate the engine so both valves are closed on the head being removed.

Remove the rocker arm retaining bolts and washers nearest the pushrods. Use a metal punch to mark the four rocker arms so they go back in the same place when the engine is assembled. One way to mark them is:

Punch one dot "." on the flat part of the top of the rocker arm near the valve for #1.

Two dots ".." for #2—and so on ...

Using a brass dowel, drive the rocker arm shafts out of the rocker arms. Mark the shafts on their end in the same manner as the rocker arms.

Remove the rocker arms.

Remove the pushrods, and if they are going back in the engine, mark them by wrapping numbered masking tape on the upper end of the shaft. They have to be replaced in the same holes with the same end on top. Discard them when the cam and pushrods are to be changed.

Use a flat-blade screwdriver to remove the spring cap on the

A Big Twin top end can be pulled with the engine in the frame. Be sure and cover any opening to the cases to keep dust and other undesirable items from finding their way into your engine.

The top and middle rocker covers: the rockers and their shafts have to be removed before the head can be unbolted.

pushrod covers, and remove the covers, springs, spacers, lower pushrod covers, and O-rings.

Remove the remaining fasteners from the lower rocker arm cover to the cylinder head, and remove the cover as an assembly.

Loosen the head bolts in an X pattern, backing them out gradually, 1/8th turn at a time. This prevents distortion of the cylinder head, cylinder, and crankcase studs.

Cylinder Head Bolt Loosening and Torquing Sequence

Continue loosening cylinder head bolts 1/8th turn until all bolts are free, then remove the bolts.

Rock the head gently until it comes loose, and remove it and the gasket.

Repeat this operation for the other head. It's not really necessary, but I mark the head bolts as to position, and make sure they go back in the same holes. After an engine has been run in, all bolts and fasteners should be re-installed in the same place after the engine's opened up.

Note: The cylinder head bolts are grade 8; don't use any other type.

Cylinder and Piston Disassembly

Raise the front cylinder just enough to work a clean shop rag under the piston. This keeps crud from falling in the cases. When

1 The head bolts are loosened in order, and with only a 1/8th turn at a time.

2 With the engine out of the frame and in its stand, it can be stripped the rest of the way.

the cases are to be split, this doesn't have to be done.

Mark the cylinder, on the top fin, "FRONT." Lift the cylinder off the cases, being really careful not to scratch the studs or piston. As the cylinder comes off the piston, make sure the piston doesn't fall and strike

the studs. Light scratches can be buffed out. Heavy scratches and you have an ashtray.

Be careful not to apply any force to the studs. Any bend whatsoever can cause stress and lead to stud failure. This is one reason for an engine stand. If the engine falls over and the studs strike anything

4 The cylinders lift off. Be careful not to let the pistons hit the cylinder studs.

3 To get to the pushrods, remove the keepers and lift out the pushrods, tubes, and O-rings. All this has to be done after the heads are removed. To remove the pushrods without removing either the heads or the engine from the bike, the pushrods will have to be cut and replaced with an adjustable set.

5 The cam sits behind the cam cover on the right side of the engine. To remove the cover, the rivets holding the timing plate cover have to be drilled and the sensor and inner plate removed. Then remove the cover bolts and the cover. Here we have the lifter galleys out of the engine, which is not necessary to swap cams.

hard, they have to be replaced. Hard to believe that something as strong as a stud can be damaged by a 12-inch fall, but remember these studs have to take the force of compression every power stroke. Put your hand on the engine next time it's turning 3,000rpm and feel how much vibration is created. This will make short work of any stud that has been stressed.

Cut eight 6-inch-long pieces of 1/2-inch I.D. hose, and slide them over the studs.

The next step requires safety glasses.

Use an awl or small flat-blade screwdriver to pry the snap rings out of the pistons. As the ring comes out, place your thumb over it so it won't end up 6 feet behind you.

Remove the piston pin by sliding it out of the piston. It should not require any force to move. The pin has a tapered end to help seat the snap rings, and Shovelhead, or earlier, pins will not work.

Mark the front piston on the wrist pin boss with a felt pen, "F."

Handle the pistons very carefully. Their hard surface can be scratched easily. A gouge mark will groove the cylinder, causing lost compression and increased oil consumption. Wrap them in a shop rag and put them in plastic freezer bags. The pistons are a complex shape: elliptical when seen from the top, non-symmetrical barrel-shaped from the side. Also, the piston pin is offset. Any damage to the piston will change it's shape.

Note: Now that Evo motors have been around for over 12 years, its possible to buy a bike that hasn't been run in quite a few years—not too probable, but possible. Before trying to start the engine, you should pull the spark plugs and check the bore and rings. Years of storage in anything but a dry climate can cause the rings to rust onto the cylinders.

Turning over the engine without pre-oiling will cause major scores on the bore and might break the rings in the process. You might be better off to pull the cylinders and do a hone-and-ring job before starting the engine. At the very least, squirt a light penetrating oil into the cylinders; wait for a few hours and SLOWLY turn the engine through by putting the transmission in third gear and rocking the bike back and forth until the pistons free up.

Once the engine has turned through for the first time, recheck the cylinders for any scratches. If no scratches are apparent, turn the engine over for five seconds with the electric starter and recheck. No problems evident, install the plugs and fire the engine. It will smoke for a while, but the smoke should clear within 15 seconds. Run the engine until warm, and change the oil and filter. Drive the bike for 100 miles and change again. Oil's cheap, cylinders aren't. The first start after a long storage can put more wear on an engine than 20,000 miles of riding.

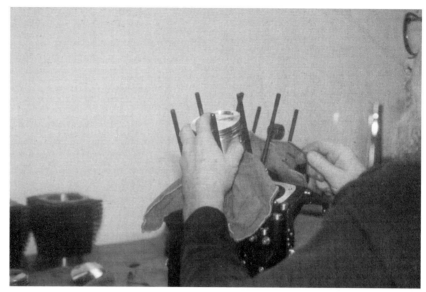

6 Pull the piston pin keepers, and remove the pins and pistons.

7 This is all that's left. The engine is going to get a stroker kit, so the cases have to be split.

Gearcase Cover Removal
Special Tools ⚬━━━━━⊂
Snap-On lock-ring pliers
HD-33418 universal puller

The gearcase, on the right side of the engine, contains gears that drive the cam, ignition timer, engine breather, and oil pump.

Remove the lifter oil screen cap, spring, O-ring, and screen.

Drill out the rivets holding the outer timing cover on, and remove the cover.

Remove the inner cover screws, cover, and gasket.

Remove the cam-position sensor plate and disconnect the wires.

Remove the rotor screw and rotor. Remove the three case cover screws.

Use the puller and an old-style timing cover with screws to remove the case cover. Most shops will have an old cover they will either loan you, or it can be rented for a six-pack of their favorite beverage.

Remove the breather valve washer and breather gear. Remove the cam gear, cam, and thrust washer.

Install a piston pin in the front piston and slide two pieces of wood under the pin to hold the engine from turning over while you remove the pinion gear nut and gear.

Remove the oil pump gear and key.

Use the Snap-On pliers, or any lock-ring pliers, to remove the oil pump gear shaft lock ring; then remove the gear and key.

If the engine's coming all the way down, remove the oil pump mounting bolts and oil pump. The upper inside bolts must be removed with the pump body.

Crankcase Disassembly
Special Tools ⚬━━━━━⊂
Crankshaft bearing removal tool
#HD-94547-80

Remove the seven crankcase bolts and one stud. Only one nut has to be removed from the stud, and it will push out the other side. The stud and left and right bottom bolts are used for case alignment. Mark them as to correct position.

Position crankcase with right side up on two pieces of wood. Tap case with soft hammer until loose, and remove. Remove circlip from pinion shaft and lift off bearing and retainer.

This step will require a machine press for further disassembly of the flywheels and left engine case: a job better left to a shop unless you have the tools at hand and are familiar with Harley cases.

Mount the flywheels and the left case assembly on the press table, supporting the case with two aluminum or steel bars. Set the press up to drive the flywheels out of the case by pressing on the sprocket shaft. Remove the seal with a brass dowel if necessary, then the bearing and two spacers. Leave the lock ring behind the bearing in place.

When replacing the main bearings, the left bearing races must be pressed out using the bearing tool. Leave the inner lock ring in place.

Clean all parts thoroughly in solvent, then allow to air dry. Inspect the oil screen to ensure the mesh is clean and not damaged.

Inspect the cam gear and pinion bushings for any grooves or pits. For purposes of simplification, we will assume either all the bushings and needle bearings related to the cam, gearcase cover, and pinion shaft are serviceable, or have been replaced by a machine shop familiar with Harley Evo engines, as a full knowledge of pressing bearings and bush-

ings, drilling the case and pinning the cover bushing with a dowel, and measuring the shafts for runout takes more knowledge and practice than an average owner will have. Also, your first engine teardown is not the place to learn how to be a machine shop, unless you have lots of prior experience on Harley-Davidson engines.

Flywheel Disassembly
Special Tools ⚬━━━━━⊂
HD-34813 flywheel jig
HD-95635 gear puller (or substitute)
HD-95637-46 wedge
HD-96650-80 flywheel truing stand

Place the jig in a sturdy vice, insert the pinion shaft into the jig.

The wedge clamps around the sprocket shaft bearing, and the puller hooks onto the wedge. Some puller kits come with a bearing wedge as a standard part, simplifying the job. In either case, turn the bearing off slowly, making sure the wedge has a good grip behind the bearing before exerting much force.

Keep the bearing together with its race with a plastic tie. The inner bearing on a one-piece sprocket shaft and flywheel will be ruined by removal and must be replaced.

Remove left flywheel by tapping rim with a soft hammer at a 90-degree angle with the crankpin.

Slip a short piece of pipe, outside diameter less than the connecting rods, over the shaft to hold the rod bearings in place while the rods are removed. Keep these bearings together until replaced in the rods.

Turn the flywheel over and remove the crankpin nut. Press the crankpin out of the flywheel and remove the key.

After cleaning the parts, inspect everything for wear or damage. Check the gear teeth for pitting or wear.

After the flywheels come out of the case and are split, this is what the rods look like on the pin.

This tool presses flywheels from the cases. The cases stay in the stand, and the tool pushes the left case off the wheels first. *Jim's Tools*

To hold the flywheels in proper alignment during reassembly, this jig is used. Very little hammer or wedge work is needed to finish the alignment when this jig is used. *Jim's Tools*

Nothing but the flywheels will be reused, so the rods were removed, and we're going to send the flywheels out to be balanced to the new rods and pistons.

This screw through the front cylinder's spark-plug hole locates TDC for timing. *Jim's Tools*

These torque plates are bolted to the cylinders when they are bored. Torque plates simulate the load of a torqued head. *Jim's Tools*

A regular socket won't do as good a job on flywheel nuts as this one from Jim's Tools. It's machined flat at the nut receiving end to eliminate rounding off the nut.

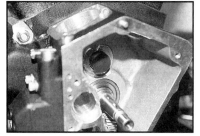

To keep crud out of the engine while the oil pump and cam are worked on, a #6 rubber plug was fit into the cam bushing.

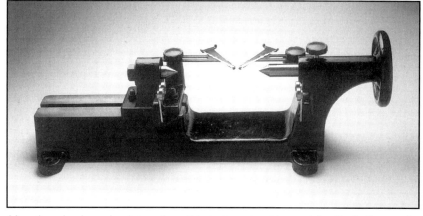

After the wheels go back together, this truing stand is used for final alignment to within 0.002 inch. *CCI*

The Big Twin oil pump is very mediocre for any competition work. Here, the stock pump gears are going to be replaced by a Baisley set. These drive the pump at a 2:1 ratio and move a lot more oil.

Because of the small cost relative to the engine modifications, all bearings, races, flywheel washers, and crankpin should be replaced. Installing a stroker kit will require the replacement of all the rotating parts, anyway.

The Oiling System

The Big Twin oil pump is a very mediocre part for any type of racing work. Based on a design that goes back before 1936, the pump sends oil first to the lifters and valvetrain. Once they have oil and the oil pressure builds to around 15 pounds, the oil pressure plunger is raised against its spring and oil feeds to the bottom end, and then to the pistons. Running below 3,000rpm, the oil

The new gears are installed, and sealant is being applied to the oil pump gasket. Make sure to use only enough sealant for the gasket; don't let any in oil passages.

It's very critical to torque the oil pump cap screws to the values in the chart. This is a torque wrench calibrated in "inch-pounds."

With any new cam installation, don't tighten the valve cover until the cam has been rotated a few times. A high-lift cam may make the rocker hit the inside of the cover. Grind the cover to clear, plus another 0.020 inch.

The oil pump assembled on the engine. A custom three-stage pump would be used if the engine had a turbo fitted. The third stage would feed the turbo center bearing.

pump isn't turning above 1/4 speed, and not enough oil gets sent to the bearings and pistons. Usually the front piston receives the least amount of oil and is the one to loose its oil film and scuff against the cylinder wall first.

Any modified engine needs 20 pounds of oil pressure to ensure correct lubrication. Some mechanics just increase the spring pressure in the pump, but this only creates more of a problem, as then it takes more pressure to divert oil to the bearings.

A much better solution is to replace the stock gears with Baisley (503-289-1251) Big Twin Oil Pump Gears. These drive the pump close to a 2:1 ratio and move a lot more oil.

The best solution is to install a Diversified Products (through Axtell) two-stage, or three-stage, oil pump. This pump has a "gerotor" pump that uses a changeable jet to control oilflow to the bottom end for custom operations when more oil is needed.

The three-stage pump is useful in scavenging the engine during high rpm operation. Or, the third-stage can be used to feed a turbocharger center bearing or supercharger oiling system. The pumps are available for Sportsters and Big Twins. Prices start at $325 for the Sportster two-stage, and rise to $440 for the three-stage pump.

Camshaft and Valvetrain Installation

When installing an aftermarket camshaft:

1. Be sure to check the camshaft bushing in the case. Low-mileage engines won't need a new one, but any motor with over 10,000 miles should have it replaced.
2. Use the correct side clearances with the new cam. Stock clearances are fine.
3. Any cam change will require that the engine be retuned. Carburetion will change.
4. Be SURE to check valve-to-piston clearances. Bent valves make for a poor-running engine. The clay method is covered in the section on engine assembly.
5. Check valve-to-valve clearance by looking through the ports while turning the engine over by hand.
6. Don't buy more cam than the engine can use. Not too many street or touring bikes need a cam that comes on at 4,500rpm and fades at 7,500rpm—unless they tour a lot faster than most.
7. Take your time during assembly. This applies to all phases of engine construction, not just cams. There never seems to be enough time to do the job right, but there's always enough time to do it again. Doing it a second time usually means something broke.
8. Use break-in lube on the cam and lifters. The first few hundred revolutions before the oil has time to reach the parts are the most critical. I use Ford Motorsports Camshaft and Lifter Prelube, part number M-19579-A991, to coat the lifters and cam on any surface that comes in contact with metal. Most cam manufacturers recommend a specific lube; go with their ideas. Some even include it in their kits. Wherever it comes from, make sure it's on the cam.

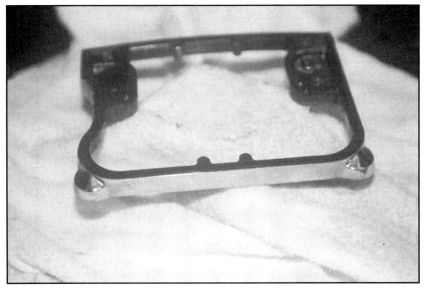

Use break-in lube on the cam and lifters. Dry lifters can gall and shave metal on startup.

Check the inner rocker cover for flatness. It's only a spacer, and a lot of people take it for granted; however, I've seen one warped enough to leak. And I've seen an early aftermarket cheapie that was so porous oil leaked through it!

All cams pretty much look the same. Only by measuring the lobes or checking a part number can most mechanics tell the difference. Big Twin replacement cams can run the same side clearances as a stock cam.

Flywheel Assembly

Replace the flywheel washers when rebuilding the engine or installing aftermarket rods. To remove the washer, it's necessary to drill a 1/4-inch hole through the washer and use a self-tapping screw to back it out.

The original washer was held in place by peening a small amount of flywheel metal over it. The outer edge of the recess needs to be cleaned up so the new washer will sit flat in the recess. Failure to seat the washer fully will leave too little end play for the rods.

Install the washer with the chamfered outside edge facing into the flywheel. Pin the new washers in place with four evenly spaced center-punch holes 0.050-inch deep and 0.050-inch away from the washer.

On a standard rebuild, when an oversized crankpin is fitted, the rods have to be lapped for correct

When all the parts have returned from the machine shop, clean them very thoroughly and air-dry all the pieces. The flywheels will be assembled first. The flywheel washers are punched into the wheels and will have to be removed and replaced. Drill out the punch marks; drill a hole in the washer; then use a self-tapping screw to remove. The new washer must fit absolutely flat for proper rod end play.

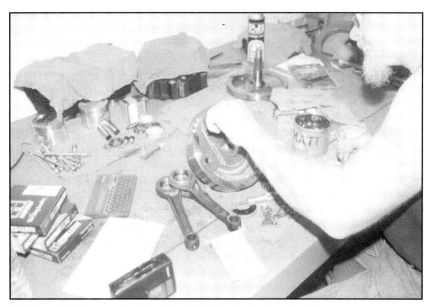

1 Assemble the crankpin to the right flywheel using Loctite.

2 Torque the crankpin nut to 180–200 foot-pounds

3 Mount the rods and bearings on the pin. Use a light grease to hold the bearings in place. The forked rod is for the rear cylinder, and the front rod must be mounted so the curve is to the front of the engine.

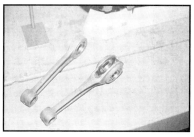

Rod bearing clearances are set by the con rod inside diameter. Rod big end diameter must be within 0.0001 inch and cannot exceed the 1.6270-inch-diameter service wear limit.

clearance. This requires a machine similar to a Sunnen cutter with a lapping arbor, something far beyond your average garage tools. Better to let a competent machine shop handle this operation. They will need both flywheels, new crankpin, rods, and rod bearing. Crankpins are available in two oversize diameters: 0.0010 inch over, marked with a blue dot on the end, and 0.0020 inch over, marked with a red dot.

Rod bearing clearances are set by the connecting-rod inside diameter and the crankpin diameter. These measurements are very critical and need to be taken as accurately as possible. Too-tight bearings can cause seizure and cook the rods and pin. Too much clearance will make the engine rattle like an old Flathead.

You have to be able to determine rod big-end inner diameter to within 0.0001 inch, and it cannot exceed the 1.6270-inch-diameter service wear limit. Let the machine shop deal with setting up the clearances on the crankpin, rod bearings, and replacing the pinion shaft bearing and inner race if necessary. They can replace the rod bushings on the wrist pin side, if necessary.

Once the parts have returned from the shop, you can begin assembly and truing the flywheels. Double-check the parts for cleanliness; inspect all oil passages for

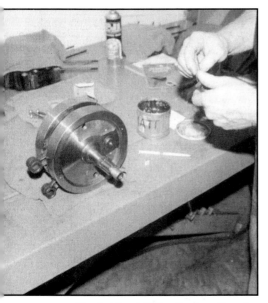

4 Set the left flywheel on the pin. Using Loctite, run the nut on the pin.

5 Torque the nut to an initial 180 foot-pounds with the flywheel jig between the wheels, and insure the rods still turn freely.

crud. Do the final cleaning with a non-petroleum-based solvent like Safety Solvent or any good electrical contact cleaner.

Assemble the crankpin to the right flywheel using Loctite. Torque the crankpin nut to 180–200 foot-pounds.

Set the flywheel in the flywheel fixture with the crankpin up. Mount the rods and bearings on the pin. Use a light all-purpose grease to hold the bearings while the rods are set on the pin. The forked rod is for the rear cylinder, and the front rod must be mounted so the curve is to the front of the engine.

Slide the left flywheel on the pin; run the nut on the pin using Loctite. Set the flywheel assembly jig between the wheels, then tighten the pin nut to an initial torque of 180 foot-pounds. Install the completed assembly in the flywheel truing stand, just tight enough for the rods to swing the flywheels by their own weight.

All the slack must be taken out of the mount with the wheels

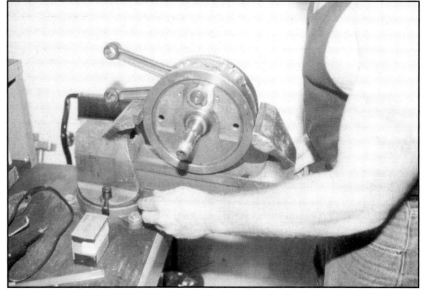

6 Set the assembly in a soft-mouth vice and tighten the clamp to true the wheels. As you tighten the vice, make sure the rods turn free.

Crankpin balancing

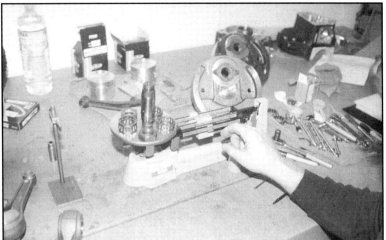

The rods will have to be balanced end for end—big end first, then small end. The entire crankpin assembly, rods, and bearings will have to be weighed and recorded for balance.

still turning smoothly. Set the indicators to lightly touch the flywheels as near the rim as possible. Roll the wheels slowly, watching the indicators for runout. Mark the high point with a yellow lumber crayon or chalk.

Here's where the talent comes in. All the truing must be done within 20 minutes, before the Loctite kicks off. The wheels must be true in all three dimensions. Too wide, and they must be clamped with a C-clamp and pulled together. Too tight, use a wedge made out of a softer metal than the wheels to drive them apart by inserting it in the tight side and rapping the rims near the pin. Too out of round, tap the faces with a soft hammer to bring them true. How hard, how much, and how many of all the above corrections will be based on how good you are with the tools.

Don't hurry; 20 minutes is a long time. But if it looks like you won't get them aligned within the time limit, pull the nut off and clean the threads with Loctite solvent, and start over. The best way to do this is to try to get the wheels as close as possible before they go in the stand. Lots of practice helps. So does having help that has done it before, because this is a relatively tricky job that has to be done right, or the rest of the rebuild is worthless.

Truing must bring the wheels within 0.001 inch. Make sure the flywheel holes are very clean and not worn, nor the pinion shaft worn, or the wheels won't line-up.

Check the rod end play for 0.005-inch to 0.025-inch play by inserting a feeler gauge between the rod and wheel. Too much play can be removed by torquing the nut down to its maximum 210 foot-pounds. Too little play is caused by the crankpin holes being too loose on an old set of wheels that have been apart too

7 Here, a cheater bar is used to torque the crankpin nut. A long bar uses leverage to tighten the nut and is easier on the arms.

many times or the flywheel washers not being fully seated, which means the entire assembly has to come apart and be checked.

If the washers are seated correctly, but there's still not enough clearance, and you don't want to replace the flywheels, the forked rod can be ground down. Only do this as a last resort on an engine not intended for racing.

Once the rod play is correct and the pin nut torqued correctly; check the flywheels again for true. Get out the hammer and C-clamp again if the dimensions still aren't right. Retrue until within the 0.001-inch specification.

8 Set the wheels in the flywheel truing stand. Take all the play out of the mount with the wheels still turning smoothly.

9 Set the indicators lightly against the wheels. Maximum runout is 0.001 inch. Mark the high spots with yellow crayon.

10 Tap the wheels into alignment using a piece of soft metal between the hammer and the rim of the wheels to prevent nicks.

11 A large C-clamp will bring the low side of the wheels into true. Too much squeeze and a metal wedge will have to be used to open them slightly. Truing the wheels requires a lot of practice to get them right. The Loctite only has a 20-minute working life, and if the wheels aren't trued by then, everything will have to come apart and be done again.

12 Use the Harley Bearing Installation Tool #HD-97225-55 and a piece of pipe to drive the sprocket bearing onto the shaft. Make sure the bearing bottoms against the seat.

1 Oil all bearings before assembly with engine oil.

2 Before the cases are assembled, apply a bead of sealant, such as Loctite 819, around the sealing edges.

Crankcase Assembly
Special Tools
Bearing installation tool
#HD-97225-55

Again, I recommend the bearing races and sprocket shaft bearing and seal be installed by a shop. Four different special tools are required for these procedures, and it doesn't make sense to buy them and learn all the tricks if you are only going to do this once or twice over the life of the bike. (At least we all hope you don't have to do this more than every 30,000 miles, or so—too expensive.)

Position the flywheel assembly in the flywheel fixture with the sprocket shaft up and the inner

3 Here, the inner spacer is being measured before installing the outer sprocket shaft bearing.

4 Drive the outer sprocket shaft bearing into the case using the bearing tool.

bearing installed. Set the engine case on the wheels, and position the outer bearing in the case.

You will need a bearing press to drive the bearing against the inner spacer. Spin the case to ensure everything rotates freely.

Remove the engine and install the pinion bearing and retaining ring. Apply a non-hardening sealant to the right case mating edge and slide it against the left case. Install the upper stud and two lower bolts in the cases. Tighten them before installing the other five bolts. Torque in sequence, traveling in an X pattern.

Torque each bolt to 10 foot-pounds. After the cylinders and heads are installed, finish torquing to 15–17 foot-pounds. Wrap rags around the rods, then set the engine in the engine stand.

Check the flywheel end play by installing a dial indicator on the cam side of the engine and the bearing installation tool on the sprocket shaft with enough pre-load to take up the bearing slack.

Rotate the sprocket shaft while pushing it in. Read the end play on the dial indicator. It must be within 0.001 to 0.005 inch, or the bearing inner spacer must be replaced. Spacers are available in 15 sizes, from 0.0925 inch to 0.1205 inch. Thicker spacers give

5 The bearing installation tool pushes on the inner race of the bearing, not the outer race. The bearing must drive tight against the case. Use an air drive impact wrench.

6 Check for freedom of movement with the bearing installation tool tightened all the way down. The rollers must turn freely.

7 Set the cases together. Install the pinion shaft bearing and retaining ring. Turn the cases over so the sprocket shaft, with the tool still mounted, is vertical.

8 Mount a dial indicator on the bearing tool and set the pointer on the case. Use a large screwdriver to press the wheels against the engine case. Record the measurement, and push the shaft the other way and record that play. The total end play must be within 0.001 inch to 0.005 inch, or the bearing inner spacer will have to be replaced. Thicker spacers give more end play. Consult the specifications for this and other measurements.

more end play. Use the thickest spacer for initial installation, or use the original, but record the dimensions.

If you have an Evo unusable sprocket shaft (worn or scored), you can set the clearances another way. Clamp the flywheel end in a vice, and install a bearing half and the old shim. Set the case on the shaft, then the other bearing and seal spacer. Slide a piece of pipe, long enough to tighten the shaft nut, over the shaft. Set a dial indicator on the case with the pointer on the shaft. Rotate and lift the case. Do the same and push it down. The measurement will read end play, and the difference between it and the spacer thickness will give the additional spacer size, less the clearance.

Install new cylinder studs, or if the old ones are used (not recommended), put two drops of Loctite on the threads with the shoulder. Drop a small ball bearing in one of the stud bolts and use it as a driver for the studs. Tighten them with an impact wrench set to 10 foot-pounds. Slide rubber hose pieces over the studs.

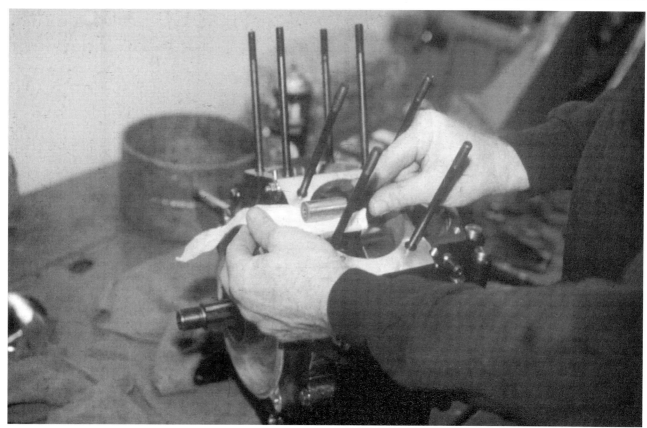

1 Check the base for flatness on the engine cases. Install a new wrist pin in the rod, and rotate the crank until the pin is at its lowest point. A piece of paper should just slide under the wrist pin, evenly on both sides. If one side is higher than the other, the rod is bent and will have to be straightened.

Piston Assembly
Special Tools ⌀━c

HD-34623A piston retaining ring
    installer
HD-96333-51B piston ring
    compressor

Install the pistons. The arrow on top points to the front. Slide the wrist pin into the piston, and install the retaining rings with the gap away from the opening at the bottom of the piston. If Teflon buttons are included with the new piston, install them now. Check the correct position of ring end gaps.

2 The easiest way to straighten a rod is to make a bending bar. Not many rods need bending these days, but the ones in this Evo did, and they had very little mileage on them.

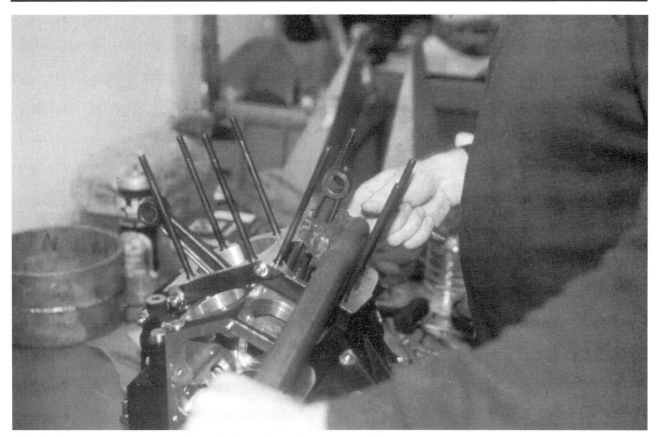

3 Here's where a stand comes in handy. If you try to bend a rod while holding the engine, you'll likely end up with the whole mess on the floor. The rod will have to be bent past true to take care of spring-back. This is also an art: like truing flywheels with a big hammer, it takes time and practice to learn.

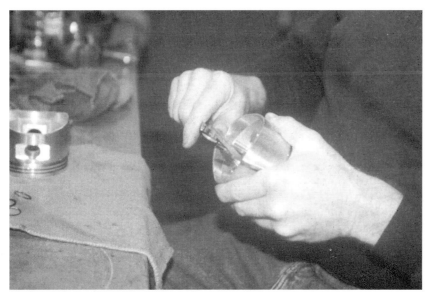

4 Before installing the pistons, check them for bore size. Pistons are barrel-shaped, not round, making measurement all but impossible, but they need to be checked to insure they are the right bore size and not the first size over.

Apply motor oil to the cylinder walls, piston, and inside of the ring compressor. Turn crankpin to top center. Compress the rings. Remove the rubber sleeves from the cylinder studs. Install a new base gasket with a small amount of grease to hold it in place.

Slide one hand under the piston and set the cylinder over the piston. Push the cylinder down until the rings are within the spigot and the ring compressor is at the bottom of the piston. Remove the compressor, and slide the cylinder onto the base gasket. Install the second cylinder in the same manner.

Cylinder Assembly

Check the gasket surfaces for flatness. The head gasket surface has to be within 0.006 inch, and the base gasket surface, 0.008 inch. Bolt the cylinder to a set of torque plates and check with a feeler gauge. Replace any cylinder out of specification.

With the torque plates still in position, measure cylinder bore with an outside mike, or dial indicator. Measure the cylinder from top to bottom of piston travel, and measure front to rear and side to side. Because of the tools and skills needed to perform these steps, a shop should do the work, especially if they have honed the cylinders for final dimension. Provide them with the new pistons, rings, and wrist pins.

1 New or rebored cylinders should have a crosshatch finish for oil retention.

2 Measure the cylinder bores with an inside micrometer. Insert a new ring and check for end gap. Don't file the gaps for clearance, buy new rings.

3 The old cylinder dowels were removed when the cylinders were bored. New ones were driven in, but this one was too small in diameter, and a puller had to be used to remove it. Otherwise, it would have worked around in the cylinder, letting the head shift, and destroying the head or cylinder in the process.

4 Rings are spaced on the pistons, the ring compressor installed, and the cylinder mounted. Use lots of oil, and the cylinder should go on by hand. If it's a little recalcitrant, urge it on a bit with the rubber or wood handle of a hammer.

5 Don't forget the base gasket. Once the rings are in the cylinder, remove the ring compressor and gently slide the cylinder all the way home.

Ask the shop to set up the piston rings for clearance and check the gaps. Don't file the gaps for clearance—replace the rings. Rings must be installed with the gaps staggered. Oil the piston top and ring grooves before sliding rings over piston. Take care not to overly spread the rings, or they will snap. Don't let them scratch the piston either. You might try installing the old rings back on the old pistons, if you've never done this before. Get a feel for what it takes without harming new parts. Make sure the dot on the second compression ring faces up.

If new cylinders are being installed and their bore is 3 5/8 inches or larger, the stock cases should be replaced by a good aftermarket

6 Use two head studs to hold the cylinder in place while the second one is mounted.

7 It's a good idea to leave the head studs on the one cylinder until the other one has the head set in place and torqued.

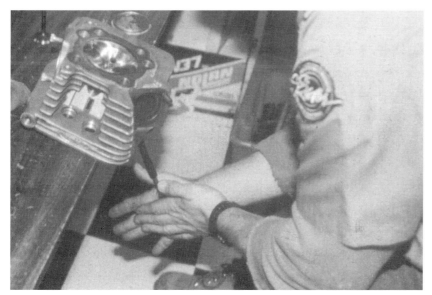

8 The valves are given their final lap into the head by hand. Even the pros at RevTech do it this way.

brand—S.T.D., Sputhe, or Delkron will work. This saves from having to bore out the stock cases, clearance the inner cases for rod travel, and reposition an oil hole at the top of the cases, next to the cylinder bores. Also, the aftermarket cases are much stronger and will handle the bigger engine's power reliably.

Cylinder Head Repair

Up to 16 different tools are needed for work on the heads. Here's another job for the shop. Have them check the rocker arm bushings; replace valve guides—especially if a cam change is in the rebuild; do a triple-angle grind to the valves and seats; and lap the valves and seats.

Have them install the valve seals, springs, and keepers. Measure installed height, spring travel, and coil bind using measurements from the cam sheet.

Head Installation

Install new O-rings over the head dowels before installing the head gasket. Oil the head bolt threads and face of head. Install head, tightening head bolts finger tight.

Tighten the head bolts in sequence to 7 foot-pounds. Then run them to 12 foot-pounds. Again starting at #1, tighten the bolts 1/4 turn.

9 All parts are carefully measured and hand-fitted before going into the head.

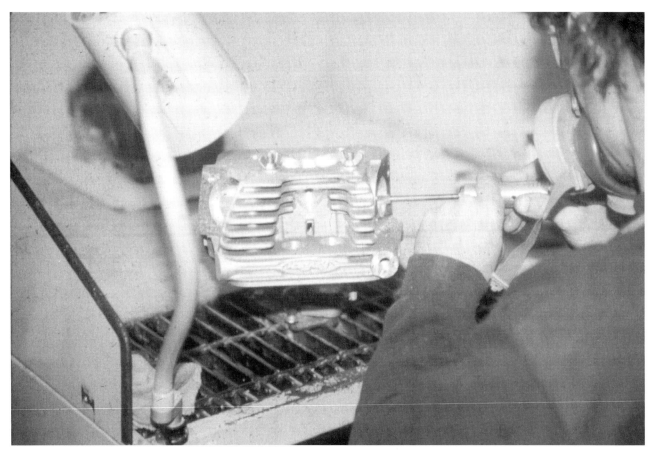

10 RevTech has a large area devoted entirely to porting and polishing heads. They get their heads in rough castings and finish them by hand.

11 Here an air drive grinder is used to open a port. Definitely not a sport for the timid or unskilled. One good slip of the 30,000-rpm grinder and you have a very expensive paperweight.

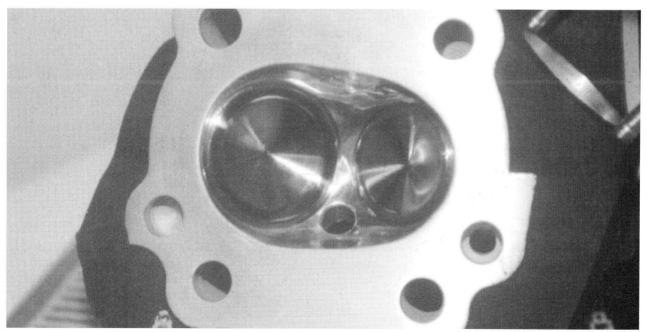

12 Here's what a head should look like after it's been run through a performance shop.

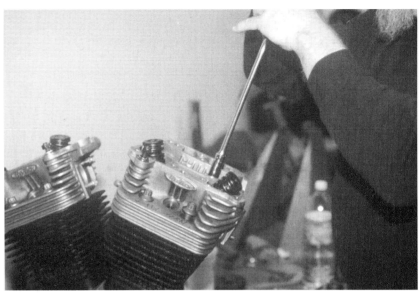

13 Now the top end can be assembled and the heads properly torqued.

14 Another high-performance engine ready to drop in your frame.

1 Lay out all the parts for the cam, timing gears, lifters, oil pump, and cover assembly.

Cam, Timing Gears, and Gear Cover Assembly
Breather Gear End Play

Install breather gear, gasket, and spacer washer to gearcase. Lay a straight edge across the gearcase over the spacer. Distance from straight edge to spacer, less 0.006 inch (gasket compression), is clearance. End play of 0.001 to 0.016 inch is OK. Change spacer to obtain correct clearance.

Place two drops of Loctite red on the pinion shaft threads. Install pinion gear and nut. Tighten right-hand thread nut to 35-45 foot-pounds.

Breather, cam, and pinion gears all have timing marks. Set pinion gear with line between teeth pointing up. Install cam with mark on tooth pointing at pinion mark. Breather gear mark aligns with dot at 60 degrees from cam/pinion gear timing mark. Large dot (if there) on cam gear will point at front lifter assembly.

Install new cover and gasket. Torque screws to 90-120 inch-pounds. Add 1/4 pint of engine oil to gearcase.

Assemble the rest of the gearcase and timer in reverse order of disassembly. Install the lifters and guides as one assembly, using a bent paper clip to hold the lifters in place.

Install rocker arms, shafts, gaskets, seals, and lower rocker covers in reverse order of disassembly. Rotate cam until both lifters on the front cylinder are at lowest point.

Install front pushrod covers, adjustable pushrods and related springs, O-rings, spacers, and caps. Set pushrods according to pushrod specification sheet included with pushrods. Repeat for rear cylinder.

Install lower cover bolts and torque them in an X pattern. 5/16-inch bolts go to 15–18 foot-pounds; 1/4-inch bolts to 10-13 foot-pounds.

Install the middle and upper rocker covers. Make sure the middle cover is in line with the top and bottom covers before torquing the screws to 10-13 foot-pounds in an X pattern.

Install the V.O.E.S. Install the new carb, manifold, and gaskets—follow the carb spec sheet. Install the new ignition components using their spec sheet. You might want to wait on this until the engine is in the bike.

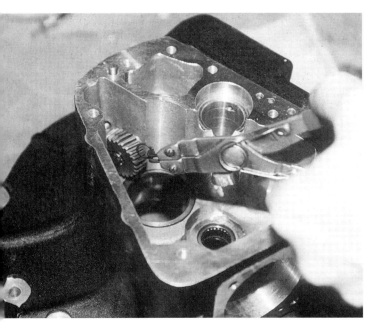

2 Install the oil drive gear and lock washer in the timing case.

3 To install the pinion gear and nut, the sprocket side of the crank must be held stationary. A bar welded onto an old sprocket gear will work well to hold the crank from turning.

4 Now hold the sprocket bar and tighten the pinion nut. Yes, even the pros have the workshop book open to torque values.

5 Install the cam spacer behind the camshaft.

6 The cam, breather gear, and pinion gear all have alignment marks. Paint the marks with white paint to help make them stand out. The marks on the teeth of the cam gear go between the teeth of the breather gear and pinion gear.

7 Use a straight edge to check the breather gear spacer washer-to-crankcase clearance. Distance from the straight edge to the spacer, less 0.006-inch gasket clearance, has to lie between 0.001 inch and 0.016 inch. Change spacer for proper clearances.

8 Install new cover gasket and cover. Recheck breather end play with a feeler gauge.

Getting the Power to the Street

Anyone who's drag-raced a 75–95 horsepower Harley knows the stock clutch works really well as long as it's in a street bike, and thousands of police bikes have proven that H-D made sure their clutch will easily deal with the stock engine's output for many a mile. But that's where the problem begins—stock horsepower. As soon as you begin to ask the clutch to transfer lots of ponies, it goes to sleep. A good percentage of the additional go gets turned into heat when the clutch starts spinning.

A clutch transfers power through friction between fiber and steel plates. Ask it to work above the coefficient of friction of the fiber plates by applying too much power, and it will spin them against the steel ones. You can have all the motor money can buy, but if the clutch won't get the power to the rear wheel, all you'll get is slippage and stink.

Rivera/ Primo, a company that's been building high-performance parts for Harley-Davidson for 23

years, has come out with a clutch/primary belt drive guaranteed to put the torque to the asphalt. They call it the Brute III, a nice choice of words to convey the image of strength, truth, justice, and the American way. Or, at least the idea they're trying to get across is it's not going to give up the first time the throttle is hammered.

Rivera's shop, in Whittier, California, stocks all the parts needed to build a very fast bike. Their 330-page catalog has everything from Accel Ignition to Yankee Engineuity gauge mounts. My reason for getting involved with them had to do with a set of four-valve heads, and I, more or less, became involved with the rest of their products.

Rivera teamed up with Primo, tied in Primo's belt drives with their Pro Clutch, and ended up with a bulletproof package. The clutch uses stainless-steel pressure plates, driven by Alto "Red" fiber plates that have 70 percent more gripping area than stock plates. The clutch uses an OEM-style di-

The Brute III primary belt drive from Primo eliminates wet clutches and all their inherent problems. It uses a dry diaphragm spring and fits without any case grinding.

Below the clutch basket is an optional sealed bearing to replace the open roller bearing on the stock clutch. This eliminates the need for any oil in the case. The adjuster is OEM-style, and the effort at the hand lever is much reduced by the diaphragm spring.

Their Pro Clutch is aimed at older bikes, like my prehistoric Shovelhead, with the idea of better, smoother shifting. It uses a two-row sealed clutch hub bearing, much stronger than the stock caged rollers. And like the Brute III, there's less effort at the hand lever.

aphragm spring, giving much smoother control than a coil-spring setup.

Their primary belt drive and clutch should last long enough to hand down to your kids and brings nothing but advantages over the stock primary chain. It's a lot quieter than the chain, absorbs motor impulses, should only need one adjustment, and you don't have to be built like a gorilla to pull the lever when operating the clutch. It has twice the spring pressure of a stock clutch, with half the pull at the lever. The clutch hub bearing is a sealed, two-row bearing, eliminating the caged rollers and their need for lubrication.

The sealed clutch bearing doesn't have to be pressed on the mainshaft like the OEM part. The new bearing is pressed into the primary case and slides over the mainshaft when the inner primary is installed.

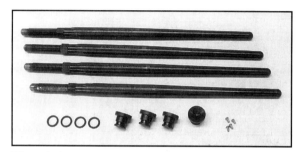

Rivera's just come out with "Taper-Lite" pushrods for Shovelheads on up. Their best feature is that they can be wound down and removed without pulling the rocker boxes or lifter blocks.

Some clutches, built for racing, have a light switch operation—either off or on. This makes for difficult street operation at best. I've ridden bikes where the clutch lever doesn't do anything until the last 1/2 inch of travel—then it locks in tight. One day I really made a fool of myself on a 90-horsepower street bike trying to slip the clutch enough to make a smooth start. I killed the bike at least three times. The owner said the only way he found that worked was to wind the engine up high enough so it could not stall, and just drop the clutch. Worked OK, except the rear tire usually went around faster than the pavement went by, and I couldn't see a long life for the drivetrain, nor a happy time when I tried to explain to the guy in the black-and-white why I was doing burn-outs at every light.

The Rivera clutch has a progressive feel to it and take-up is smooth, plus there's a lot of feedback through the lever, so making easy starts is no problem. Once it's hooked up, it won't slip, and it's been run behind some fairly stout drag-racing motors running in Top Gas and Top Fuel.

Engine Installation

This assumes the transmission and inner primary cover are already installed, the drive sprocket and belt in place, and the bolts to the transmission are still loose. Lay a bead of silicon seal around the two bottom holes on the transmission.

Install a new engine-to-primary O-ring. Set the engine on the mounting pads. Slide compensating sprocket on while installing engine.

Attach the inner primary to the engine. Torque the bolts to 17-21 foot-pounds if the bike is 1995 or older. The 1996 models use grade 8 hardware and are torqued to 25-29 foot-pounds.

Torque the transmission bolts to 33-38 foot-pounds. Bend all locking tabs into place.

Install all engine mount bolts and torque to 25 foot-pounds. A hydraulic car jack will help move the engine around in the frame to get the bolts started. The upper mount torques to 30 foot-pounds on the frame and engine side.

Do not use a hammer to drive the bolts through the mounts. I know I've said in the past that a hammer is used to put screws in, a wrench is to take them out, but don't believe everything I say when it comes to my abilities. I just recently learned which end of the screwdriver to pound on.

Install the starter. Be sure the coupling is installed on the starter motor output shaft before replacing the jackshaft. The end with the countersink goes toward the shaft. Replace all springs, pinion gears, lockplate, and thrust washer; bolt lockplate on shaft. Install retaining ring. Place jackshaft assembly into location. Align lockplate tab and washer slot with shaft key way. Tighten the jackshaft bolt to 7-9 foot-pounds.

Bend the locking tab over bolt.

Install the clutch. With an aftermarket clutch, like a Bandit SuperClutch (from Zipper's), follow their instructions. If only the clutch plates are replaced, the compensating sprocket, primary chain, adjuster, and clutch have to go on as one assembly. The clutch drive may have to be rotated to line up the hub.

Apply red Loctite to the transmission mainshaft threads and run the nut on (left-hand thread) to 70-80 foot-pounds. Same for the compensating sprocket nut. Torque to 150-165 foot-pounds. Either use the primary locking tool, part number HD-41214, or wedge the gears so they won't turn. Do not use the primary chain when wedging.

Bolt on the primary chain adjuster. Adjust the primary chain to 5/8–7/8-inch free play in the middle of the upper chain.

Replace the primary outer cover. Install the three new gaskets, and use a light coat of oil on the outer gasket. Run the screws to 108–120 inch-pounds, using a crosshatch pattern, starting with the bottom bolt between the inspection covers, and finishing with the two bolts on the primary inspection cover. Pour in enough to touch clutch spring, 30–36 ounces. The bike must be upright when checking fluid level. Install the clutch inspection cover with a new O-ring and sealing washers.

Install spark plugs and related wiring. Leave the plugs loose. Use a good brand of aftermarket plug wires (Accel, MSD, or Jacobs).

Install the oil pump with top inside cover bolt and tighten to 60–85 inch-pounds. Install drive gear and key, drive shaft seal with lip toward the feed gears, drive gear lock ring, and idler gear. Replace the gasket on the cover and torque bolts, including top bolts to 90–100 inch-pounds.

Install the oil filter mount, using new seals and O-rings. Leave the oil filter mount fittings and spacer clamp loose until all the lines are installed.

Install all the oil lines to the pump and tank. Use screw clamps or braided metal lines with A&N fittings.

Hook up oil switch wire.

Install clutch cable to the transmission lever, and bolt the cable bracket to the engine.

Install the rear master brake cylinder, right footrest, and brake pedal. Make sure the square body of the master cylinder fits in the bracket hole before tightening down nut over lockplate. Mount pushrod on brake rod with the adjuster nut left loose. Install banjo fitting with new washers and torque to 17–22 foot-pounds.

Adjust brake pedal to 1—1 1/4 inch above the brake pedal, then tighten pushrod nut.

Bleed the brake cylinder with the bike upright. Attach a small clear hose over the rear brake caliper bleeder valve after setting the correct-size box wrench over the flats of the bleeder. Put the other end in a clean container with enough brake fluid to cover the end of the hose. This prevents drawing air back into the caliper. Fill the master cylinder with DOT 5 fluid and replace the cover.

Pump up pressure with the pedal, and holding it down, open the bleeder just enough to release fluid and air. Close the bleeder and repeat the process. Don't reuse fluid. The brake lines are so small that even one air bubble will give spongy brakes. Bleed until all the air is gone, then let the bike sit for a few minutes. Depress the pedal and check for brake action. Repeat bleeding if the pedal isn't firm. Sometimes this can take a while, so be patient. If air continues to come out, or the brake pedal will not firm up, you may need to rebuild the master cylinder. This involves replacing seals and insuring the bore is honed smooth and isn't a big job.

Big Twin Torque Values

Crankpin nut ....180–210 foot-pounds
Pinion gear nut ....35–45 foot-pounds
Oil pump cover bolts..90–120 inch-pounds
Hydraulic lifter guide bolts ....12–15 foot-pounds

Rocker cover

5/16 bolts ....15–18 foot-pounds
1/4 bolts ....10–13 foot-pounds
Cylinder head bolts ....12 foot-pounds plus 1/4 turn
Upper engine mounting bracket...30 foot-pounds
Crankcase stud nut ....see torque sequence
Crankcase bolts..see torque sequence
Gearcase cover screws..90–120 inch-pounds
Timer screws..15–30 inch-pounds
Hydraulic lifter screen plug ....90–120 inch-pounds
Spark plug ....18–22 foot-pounds
Oil pan to transmission case bolts (newer bikes) ....7–9 foot-pounds
Oil fill spout bolts (newer bikes) ....7–9 foot-pounds

If you haven't installed the carb and manifold yet, put it on now. Attach the throttle cables and enrichener wire. Install the exhaust system using directions included with the new pipes.

Replace the fuel tank. The hoses need to be secured with new clamps. Add 1 gallon of gas to the tank and turn on the petcock. Check for leaks.

Add oil to the engine. Install the oil filter.

Spin out the spark plugs and put the bike in third gear. Walk the bike forward to ensure the engine is free and turns easily.

Hook up the battery, and spin the engine over until you have oil pressure on the gauge (optional), or you hear the engine drag down as the oil flows through the pump. Let the starter rest for one minute and turn over again for 10 seconds. Repeat this two times.

Install the spark plugs and start the engine. Hold it at 1,500–2,000 rpm until you feel warmth at the top of the rocker box. Check for leaks or any strange noises. Shut off the engine immediately if you hear anything out of the ordinary. The pipes might make it hard to hear, so use a long screwdriver pressed to the ear or a stethoscope to listen.

Replace the seat and air cleaner.

Check the rear wheel alignment, and tighten the belt.

Take the bike for a short ride, then recheck all the nuts, bolts, clamps, caps, and everything in general.

Break-in

The engine needs to run for 2,000 miles before using extended full throttle. The break-in period should follow Harley-Davidson's instructions in the rider's handbook with the exception of changing the oil and filter after the first 100 miles.

This may sound like a lot more service than needed, but with a fresh, modified engine, 80 horsepower and up, the first 100 miles are critical. Check the oil for any metal particles, or other deposits. In the *Yellow Pages*, under "Oil," you can find companies that will analyze the oil and provide a written report. Airport maintenance shops will also have the phone number of oil analysts.

This test will give the amounts of iron, cobalt, aluminum, copper, brass, and other metals in the oil. Break-in will show a high amount of iron as the rings seat, but this reading should stabilize after two oil changes. Having the oil tested every oil change might be a bit much; however, every 5,000 miles is appropriate. You're not looking so much for iron, etc.; instead look for a change in content. This will tell you just what parts are starting to wear.

After the break-in period, pull the oil screen from the top of the right case and check for deposits. Replace if necessary.

Now go enjoy your bike!

6 | Stage I through Stage III Sportster Engines

The 1200 Sportster—a good starting point to build a high-performance Harley-Davidson. This one's just about to get stuffed full of go-fast parts.

Stage I Engines

A Stage I engine is for the rider who wants more power, but doesn't want to get on a first-name basis with a machine shop. All the modifications to the engine, with the exception of cam changes, can be done without much teardown. Changing the cams isn't really a big deal and is the one change that will really wake up the engine.

There are many ways to go about increasing the output of the Sportster Evo engine; the cam, carb, and exhaust combinations are almost uncountable. The main idea, as I've stressed throughout the book, is to build a balanced package. It does no good to hang a S&S Super D carburetor with a 2 1/4 throat on a stock displace-

ment, stock cam engine. Performance and rideability will go down the tubes. Same for different headers and exhaust. Most of the time, just changing the exhaust will result in the same thing as on the Big Twins—more noise and little, if any, power gain.

The first step should be figuring out the amount of money you have to spend, then add at least 20 percent to that figure for unexpected contingencies. Next, figure out what you wish to achieve by modifying the engine. Is the bike going to spend 98 percent of its time on the street, or will it live a short, happy life hauling you along a quarter-mile at a time? Depending on the end use, the modifications will be quite different.

Here, with the Stage I, we will be looking for more performance on the street, with an occasional race in mind. The main areas of change will be in the carburetion, cam, and exhaust. All changes made to the intake side of the engine must be balanced by similar improvements at the exhaust to produce a reliable, fast finished bike.

You will have to decide what Stage engine you wish to build from the very start. Spending the money to put together a Stage I, then having to change parts, like the cams, to get up to the 100 horsepower of a Stage II is a waste of money. Spend some time with a pencil and your checkbook before buying the newest go-fast part, only to find out it won't do the job.

Rather than starting out with an 883 and having to punch it out to 1200, buy the bigger bike at the start. The difference in price between the XLH 883 Deluxe and the XLH 1200 is $1,000, unless you opt for an 883 Standard, then the differential is more like $2,200.

The 1200 comes with a tach—necessary on a modified bike, and optional on the 883. Additionally a 3.25-gallon tank is standard, instead of the 883's 2.25. One more gallon on a bike with bigger carb, high-lift cam, and tuned pipes will make the difference between making a fuel stop every 60 miles, or going another 25 before stopping. The Sportster pushes fairly easy, but after a couple of miles, your arms begin to tire. An extra gallon of gas weighs 6 pounds, so it's not really a concern where weight is involved.

The stock 1200 puts out 71 foot-pounds of torque at 4,000rpm compared to the 883's 50 at 4,600rpm, so you're already ahead by quite a bit. Plus, the difference in price amounts to maybe $35 over a three-year finance plan, whereas the 883-1200 conversion will eat up $500–$600 right up front. I'd take the hit on the financing to have the extra money for cams and carb rather than duplicate Harley's work just to end up with the bigger engine.

As far as performance, the 1200 Sportster will leave a Big Twin for dead in a roll-on.

For a Stage I engine, budget for a new ignition system, Mikuni or S&S carb, different cams, and a good exhaust system like a Super-Trapp 2 into 1.

The costs look like this:
Dyna, Accel, or Screamin'
  Eagle ignition and coils
  w/wires $200
Mikuni or S&S carb
  w/air cleaner $400
Andrews or Red Shift cams $245
SuperTrapp 2 into 1 $400
Gaskets and miscellaneous
  costs $50
Total $1,295

This will produce an engine with 75 horsepower and will make good power all the way up to 6,500rpm while not giving away anything on the low end. Also, the stock gearbox is more than capable of handling the Stage I motor's output.

Carburetion

The stock carb used on the Sporty from 1988 on is a 40-millimeter constant-velocity Keihin. The table below shows the jet sizes for the 883, 1200, and HDI 1200.

One part that doesn't make the Sportster go any faster, but does wonders for it's rideability, is a 3.25-gallon aftermarket tank. This raises the cruising range by 50 percent. *CCI*

Carburetor Jet Chart

Sizes	Calif 883	49-State 883	HDI 883	Calif 200	49-State 1200	HDI 1200
Main jet	170	160	190	185	170	190
Slow jet	40	40	42	40	40	42

The timing cover has been removed from this 1200 to show the relationship of the four cams. One cam would have to span too wide of an area and the pushrods would be a devil's nightmare, so H-D went to four cams to solve the problem. This means all four have to be changed whenever a cam change is made. The clearances between the gears is quite critical on the Sportster cams. This is one place where careful measurement is very necessary.

You can see that the 49-state bikes run a smaller main jet than their California counterparts; smaller than the International bike too. If a carb and cam change isn't part of your Stage I motor, then the HDI main and slow jets would make a good swap on a stock carb, along with a different air filter and optional pipes.

The air filters made by S&S, Scream'n' Eagle, and K&N will flow at least 2.5cfm more than their stock counterparts. Changing the jets to the 190 main and 42 slow jet, along with insuring the needle is from an XLX-1200, will add 4-6 horsepower to your 883-1200 or 1200.

Another way to go with carburetion is to swap the stocker for a 1 7/8 S&S Super B, Super E, or Mikuni carb. The Super E is 1 7/16 inch shorter than the Super B, making the installed length the same as stock. It comes with a 1 7/8-inch throat, good for stock displacement engines and strokers. The accelerator pump is adjustable for volume, allowing fine-tuning for instant response.

The S&S carbs can be set up with a Thunderjet third fuel circuit that works at all power ranges. Essentially it's a fuel tap off the carb float bowl that allows the intake vacuum pulses to draw extra fuel from a jet in the throttle bore of the carb, before the butterfly. The harder the engine pulls, the more fuel feeds the carb. It's fully adjustable for any size bike and carb. The carb kit retails for $322; add $100 for the Thunderjet.

Mikuni's H-D 40 is designed specifically for use on stock displacement Sportster 1200s and Big Twins. In the past, they had clearance problems with some gas tanks, but Mikuni now says that's been handled.

The Evo Mikuni kit, manifold, choke, Barnett cables, K&N air cleaner, and all hardware

This is what you do on a boring weekend—go race the 883 class. Modifications are limited, and the bikes run pretty much the same. Rider's ability is what counts here.

One of the key differences—for some—between racing and street riding is a back-up bike in case you lose a cylinder, as the bike in the foreground did. The key lesson here is that race motors are great for going fast for a short period of time, but are often too short-lived for street use.

Engine Specifications—883 and 1200cc

General	883cc	1200cc
Horsepower / Torque	55/50	65/71
Bore	30.000 inch	3.498 inch
Stroke	3.812 inch	3.812 inch
Displacement	53.9ci/883cc	73.3ci/1201cc
Compression ratio	90.0:1	90.0:1
Oil capacity	2.8 liters	2.8 liters
Valves Guide fit		
Exhaust	0.0015–0.0033 inch	0.0015–0.0033 inch
Intake	0.008–0.0026 inch	0.008–0.0026 inch
Seat width	0.040–0.062 inch	0.040–0.062 inch
Stem above head	1.975–20.011 inch	1.975–20.011 inch
Outer spring free length	2.105–2.177 inch	2.105–2.177 inch
Inner spring free length	1.926–1.996 inch	1.926–1.996 inch
Rocker Arms		
Shaft to bushing	0.0005–0.0020 inch	0.0005–0.0020 inch
End clearance	0.003–0.013 inch	0.003–0.013 inch
Bushing to rocker arm	0.004–0.002 inch	0.004–0.002 inch
Rocker Shafts		
Fit in cover	0.0007–0.0022 inch	0.0007–0.0022 inch
Pistons		
Compression ring gap	0.010–0.023 inch	0.007–0.020 inch
Oil ring gap	0.010–0.053 inch	0.009–0.052 inch
Piston pin fit	0.00005–0.00045 inch	0.00005–0.00045 inch
Heads		
Valve guide in head	0.0022–0.0033 inch	0.0022–0.0033 inch
Valve seat in head	0.0010–0.0035 inch	0.0010–0.0035 inch
Head surface warpage	0.006 inch	0.006 inch
Cylinders		
Standard bore diameter	30.0005 inch	3.4978 inch
Rods		
Pin fit	0.00125–0.00175 inch	0.00125–0.00175 inch
Flywheel side play	0.005–0.025 inch	0.005–0.025 inch
Crankpin fit	0.0004–0.0017 inch	0.0004–0.0017 inch
Lifters		
Guide fit	0.0008–0.0023 inch	0.0008–0.0023 inch
Roller fit	0.0006–0.0013 inch	0.0006–0.0013 inch
End clearance—roller	0.008–0.022 inch	0.008–0.022 inch
Oil Pump		
Oil pressure @ 2,500rpm	10–17psi	10–17psi
Gerotor clearance	0.003 inch	0.003 inch
Shaft to pump	0.0025 inch	0.0025 inch
Case		
Cam gear shaft in bushing	0.0007–0.0022 inch	0.0007–0.0022 inch
Cam end play	0.005–0.024 inch	0.005–0.024 inch
Rear intake cam end play	0.006–0.024 inch	0.006–0.024 inch
Flywheel		
Runout @ rim	0.0000–0.010 inch	0.0000–0.010 inch
Runout @ shaft	0.0000–0.0020 inch	0.0000–0.0020 inch
End play	0.001–0.005 inch	0.001–0.005 inch
Ignition		
Timing @ 1,650–1,950rpm	40 degrees BTDC	40 degrees BTDC
Spark-plug gap	0.038–0.043 inch	0.038–0.043 inch

comes with a package price of $350.

On either kit, be sure and run the two throttle cables that come with the carb. One cable pulls the throttle open, and the second one pulls the throttle shut. This way, there's no chance of the throttle sticking closed.

Along with allowing the engine to inhale better and provide more air-fuel mixture for combustion; a need exists to ensure a sufficient fuel delivery to the carb. The stock petcock is a finely wrought device and works admirably until called on to exceed its fuelflow capability. If the petcock can't feed the carb fast enough to keep the float bowl full under full-throttle conditions, then the engine will starve—sometimes to the point that it just quits.

Pingel makes petcocks capable of flowing enough for any size Sportster engine. They also manufacture inline fuel filters, both 1 1/2 inch and 3 inches length, to fit any application. Given for what passes through a service station's tanks these days, I'd make the installation of a fuel filter a number one priority. Run for 5,000 miles, then change the fuel filter and cut the old one open for inspection. I sure wouldn't want any of the stuff I've found in the filter inside my engine.

Air Filtration

No matter what type of induction system you run on the engine, carburetion to fuel injection, the air entering the motor must be clean and free of any abrasive particles. This means you can't run one of those slick-looking velocity stacks on the carb with any expectations of long ring and bearing life. The racers at the drags run those stacks because their engines will be torn down long before any noticeable wear can take

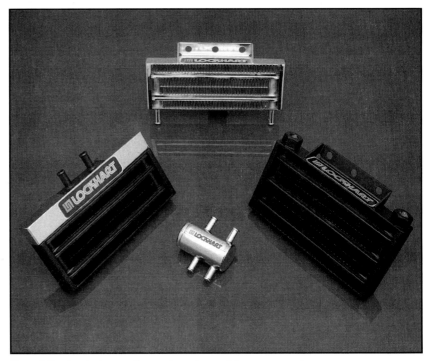

One of the best pieces of speed equipment for your road racer or canyon crusher—an oil cooler. One of these and a tank full of synthetic oil will go a long way towards preventing premature engine wear. *CCI*

RevTech's digital ignition system lets you program advance and redline while providing better control of the sparks. *CCI*

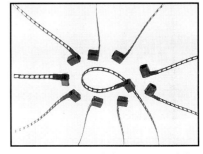

Zip ties are one of the most useful fasteners out there. It's amazing what can be done with a few tie wraps and a little imagination. *CCI*

Dynojet kits allow you to tune the stock carb to new pipes and cams without having to spend a lot of money on a replacement. This kit is for the Keihin CV carb, which was used on Sportsters from 1988 and later. *CCI*

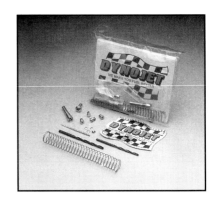

place. Crud in the air is not high on their worry list.

Racers are looking for the last 0.009 horsepower from their engines and so the velocity stack, but I doubt any street rider would be able to tell the difference between a velocity stack and an air filter. At least not until the stack sucks your Levis into the carb and the engine goes quiet.

Newer-design air-cleaner housings actually help direct air into the carb, gaining horsepower over a straight stack.

When a throttle is wide open, there is little or no obstruction to airflow. Here's where the air cleaner must be able to allow the maximum amount of air to move into the carb in order for the en-

Dyno Power drag pipes, shown on an iron-head Sporty, have little or nothing in the way of muffling, but work well on a racing bike. *CCI*

For road riding, Dyno Power's 1 3/4-inch staggered duals work well on the street, without losing much power to excessive back pressure. *CCI*

gine to develop all its potential. RevTech, S&S, K&N, and others make filters and housings that can easily handle all sizes of Big Twin and Sporty street engines.

Cam Changes

As said earlier, cam changes go slightly beyond the scope of a Stage I engine, as far as bolt-on parts are considered. However, the additional performance gained by a cam swap makes the extra expense and installation worthwhile.

Cam overlap is critical on V-twin engines. With too much overlap and low rpm, performance goes away, with the exhaust pressure actually backing up the intake tract, causing the air-fuel mixture to reverse its flow. The exhaust reversion can actually be seen spitting out the charge from the mouth of the carb. With the air cleaner off, you can put your hand in front of the carb and actually feel the pulses and get a gas-covered hand in the process. This is another good reason to run an air filter—little chance of fire should the engine sneeze, or spray on your right leg and ignite off of a hot motor. Remember, gasoline doesn't burn, the fumes do! It's not necessary for your gas-covered leg to actually touch the hot exhaust, just the fumes.

Duration is the amount of time in degrees of rotation that the intake, or exhaust, valve is open. Street Evo Sportys work well with 240 degrees of intake duration and 244 degrees of exhaust, producing a good low-end motor with the power distributed evenly up to the redline. A street-strip engine wants 256 degrees on both valves and will require a valve-spring change. For all-out competition, 257 degrees of duration, plus 0.663-inch lift will really wake up an 88+ci engine; power range is 2,000rpm to 6,000rpm, and a cam and full kit, with

Older pipes that have turned a colorful blue can be cleaned up using Blue Buster, but it will dull the chrome. Besides, some of us like the blue. But remember, too much blue on the rear pipe can indicate a too lean mixture. Run a plug check, and tune as needed. *CCI*

springs, keepers, and pushrods, is required.

For the street, a fairly radical cam with 274 degrees duration and 0.543-inch lift provides a wide mid-range power band and a lot of top end at the cost of power down low. The Red Shift (Zipper's) 543 V2 uses the stock cam gears and grinds new lobes to their specifications. A cam change is a bit pricey though: $435 needed for a set from Red Shift. If you can afford it, and are willing to open up the timing case and replace all the related parts, including the pushrods and valve springs, the horsepower changes will be well worth the effort.

Andrews makes their own cams with lifts from 0.465 to 0.590 inch. Their V2, 240 degrees duration, 0.465-inch lift, is a bolt-in replacement for the stock cams. Most cams with over 0.490-inch lift will require notches to be cut into the tops of the pistons for

clearance. For the Stage I engine, we'll limit cam changes to ones that can be installed without the head coming off. This may require adjustable pushrods and removing the top valve cover to check the rocker clearance, but it's still not a lot of work for someone familiar with wrenches.

Ignition

Most of the manufacturers of Big Twin high-performance single-fire, dual-coil ignition also make a system for the Evolution Sportster. One system not described in the Big Twin section is the H-D Screamin' Eagle Ignition. The entire kit consists of:

1. Braided spark-plug wire sets with integrated ground.
2. Performance coils.
3. Performance ignition modules with 8,000-rpm rev limiter built in, or a variable-position rev limiter with selected redlines.

Whether it's chrome or painted, keep a fresh oil filter on the engine. Clean oil and filters are cheap insurance. *CCI*

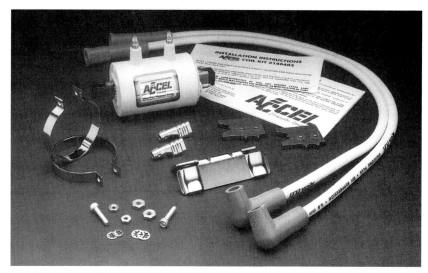

Accel's super coil works on all Stage I- through Stage II-engined Sportsters built from 1965 to present. I guess that pretty much covers the market. *CCI*

The only part of the kit that doesn't do much for me is Screamin' Eagle's SplitFire spark plugs. The manufacturer of the plugs promises increased power, better miles per gallon, and maybe even cleaner teeth. The dyno says different. *Big Twin* magazine took two Harleys—a semi-stock Dyna and a just-off-the-showroom 1995 Heritage Softail with a little over 7,000 miles on the clock at the beginning of the test.

Well, both bikes got to spin the dyno's wheel with stock plugs and the Splitfires. To no one's surprise, the triple throw-down trick plugs not only didn't make more power with the breathed-on Dyna, but also the peak power was down by 1 horsepower.

Next up was the stock bike. Maybe the plugs would work better on the stock engine. Guess what? No difference whatsoever.

The dyno's printer can overlay each run for comparison with the others, and what the total of the 10 runs showed was a slightly fuzzy single line. Not enough difference to make a difference.

Big Twin's conclusion? Save your money. The Splitfires cost over twice what a conventional plug retails for; however, they do

SAE 20-50 oil is recommended for all Evos. My old Shovelhead seems to prefer something a bit gooier, like straight 60 weight, but it uses oil, and Evos don't. *CCI*

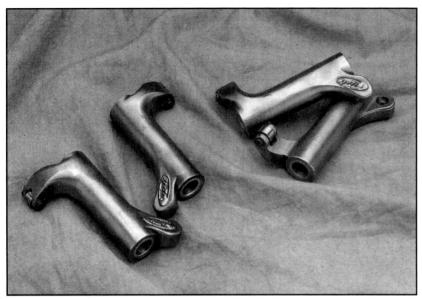

These rocker arms have hardened pushrod cups and replaceable rollers. They work well with aftermarket high-lift cams that use a rocker with a 1.6:1 ratio. *CCI*

This oil cooler is designed specifically for Sportsters and can be ordered with a thermostatic control to bypass the oil until it reaches operating temperature. *Storz*

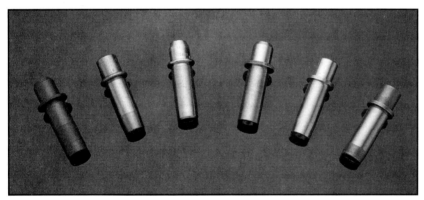

Whether you use CCI, Manley, Rowe, Precision, or other valve guides, be sure and get the right material for the job. Cast-iron guides are self-lubricating and wear well over the miles. The nickel bronze type don't distort during installation and have good self-lubrication qualities. *CCI*

nothing for performance. Advice is to save your money for things that actually work.

Exhaust

Now we come to the end (figuratively speaking) of the Stage I motor. We've got an engine full of hot nasty gases that want to go somewhere. So it's time for a custom exhaust system. If I had a nickel for every horsepower increase claimed by exhaust systems manufacturers, I'd be writing this from under a palm tree. Rather than tell you what doesn't work, we'll just cover the exhaust systems that do really improve performance.

Start off with straight pipes. For maximum top-end performance, they should be 29 inches in overall length. They work well on top end, but aside from neighbors with low tolerance for noise, the main problem with straights is lack of power at normal riding speeds of 2,500–3,500rpm.

Next on the list are the shorty duals. These are seen on a lot of bikes today. Some work OK; some have a problem at high revs. The Screamin' Eagle straight-cut, baloney-slicers, or turn-outs, look most excellent on a set of freshly chromed header pipes, but their internal volume is too small to let the engine breathe like it wants at high rpm.

Racing bikes make use of the 2-into-1 header system with a reverse-cone megaphone at the end. SuperTrapp's stainless-steel 2-into-1 exhaust header/ muffler system is about the best overall performer, street or strip. It's similar to the open megaphone, getting its muffling ability from layers of steel plates. The more plates stacked on the end, the less restriction. This makes for very easy tuning, whether at the strip or on the street. One advantage not touted is a fix-it ticket for loud pipes,

For the best going, Crane Cams makes roller bearing rockers that run on high-quality needle bearings for precise valve control. *Crane*

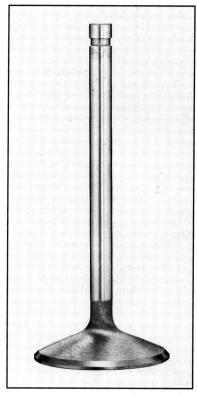

Manley performance valves for Sportsters weigh 30-percent less than stock and follow the cam lobe better in high rpm engines. *Manley*

which can be cured by removing some of the plates, creating fewer square inches for the exhaust to flow through and thereby producing more back pressure and less sound.

Stage I Kits—all 1200cc
Kit #1
1. Dyna Ignition
2. Mikuni carb and air cleaner kit.
3. SuperTrapp 2 into 1 exhaust system
4. Red Shift cam #543 V2

Kit #2
1. Screamin' Eagle ignition
2. S&S Super E carb—Thunderjet optional
3. Drag Specialties Python Pipes
4. Andrews V2 cams

Kit #3
1. Accel ignition
2. Run Roader 2 into 1 Pipes (1986–1993)
3. Quick Silver II carb kit (from Zipper's)
4. Sifton RE-208 cams

Stage II Engines

The 1200 Sportster can be built to produce as much horsepower as a Big Twin motor. This shouldn't come as much of a surprise, as both motors are air-cooled V-twins using the same basic design. Evolution Sportster engines can be built as big as 150 ci, but for street work, 74 ci (1200cc) is about as big as you can go without getting into the esoteric end of the market.

A 1200 Sportster weighs 490 dry weight pounds compared to a Dyna Glide's 598 pounds. This, coupled with a smaller frontal area, gives the performance advantage to the Sporty running the same engine modifications as a Big Twin.

The Stage II engine will involve head work and opening the cases for different flywheels and rods. This engine will be built with the idea in mind that it's going to have to earn its keep on a race track. Expect to see about 100 horsepower at the crank, down to 90 at the rear wheel, due to drivetrain friction and power loss.

Earlier Evo Sportsters suffered from cylinder head leaks due to the lack of a spigot on the top of the cylinders where they fitted into the head. This spigot kept the head gasket from being eaten up by the combustion process. Also, the stock cylinders distorted while they warmed up, causing power-robbing friction, among other problems. Aluminum expands at a different rate than steel, so cylinders grew more than the studs holding them down.

This distortion led to power loss through poor ring seal, and in a 100 horsepower motor, the loss can be noticeable at the drag strip. Axtell and S&S build a set of cast-iron cylinders, bore sizes up to 3 13/16 inches by 5-inch stroke that cut down the distortion completely. They are heavier than the aluminum cylinders, but the added weight is more than offset by the ability to make more power. A set runs in the $850 area, and when the 3 13/16-inch bore cylinders are used, the stock head bolts have to be downsized, along with the heads counterbored and a 30-degree compression relief cut into their combustion chamber.

Axtell's iron cylinders come either finless for drag racing, or with cooling fins for the street. They will sell you a complete Sportster drag-race kit, including finless barrels, forged pistons—compression ratio to request, thicker wrist pins, gaskets, nuts, Teflon wrist pin buttons, and base studs for $913.

One big problem with boring the 883 to a 1200 is in the loss of cylinder wall thickness. The stock walls are thick enough to keep distortion down to a minimum, but when thinned out by a 3 1/2-inch bore, most of the liner goes by way of the boring bar, leaving little for strength. The S&S 1200 kit includes cylinders with thicker liners with much lower distortion rates. They can easily take a clean-up pass with a boring bar when rebuild time comes around.

Bored-out 883 cylinders can't take a cleanup 0.010 overbore without cutting the liner to the point where you can see through it, so if you plan on keeping the bike past the first rebuild, go for aftermarket cylinders rather than boring the stock ones. The initial cost will be higher, but it will be offset in the first rebuild.

If you stay with the stock barrels when you make the 883-1200 conversion, be sure to let everything warmup fully before running the engine hard. The warm engine will let the cylinders grow tight against the head bolts, giving a better seal. Plus, a warm engine makes for longer parts life.

Screamin' Eagle offers a conversion kit with a set of pistons for $135, cylinders already finished for $240, and a template to cut the combustion chambers on the 883's heads. However, unless you plan on staying at the 883 limit,

Manley offers full valve-spring kits compatible with cams in excess of .600-inch lift. *Manley*

Always check any new part for correct size. No one will take back a part if it turns out to be the wrong size after it's been run. *Florida Calipe*

Fuel filters are another form of cheap insurance. Despite their simple installation and low cost, more than a fair share of carbs have plugged due to the lack of a fuel filter. *CCI*

racing strictly in the 883 Twin Sports Racing Series, both road racing and dirt track, start with a 1200 for drag racing or Pro Street.

One big difference to expect when firing up a Stage II, or Stage III, engine is in the noise level of the moving parts. Forged pistons will rattle more than the stock cast-aluminum because of their increased running clearance. The aftermarket cams can rattle if their drive gears are set up too loose. For a rider used to the quiet Evo engine, the increased noise might be a

bother, but that's the trade-off for stronger pistons and different cams.

If you are trying to make the decision between cast versus forged pistons, a short story is in order. It involves a car engine; however, the results are the same for a bike engine.

There's a race in Nevada run over a 90-mile road course on Highway 318 out of Ely, where the idea is to average the highest possible speed within a given class. The course is run on one of Nevada's two-lane highways,

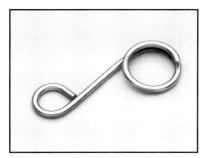

A small piece of wire, granted, but when it keeps your fuel line from laying on anything hot, it becomes fairly worthwhile. This chrome support wire routes the fuel line between the cylinders. *CCI*

For really large Sportys, a Mikuni HSR42 will flow enough air on the top end to produce maximum horsepower. The earlier Mikuni slides sometimes had a bad habit of sticking open when a lot of air was running through them, but the HSR42's slide runs on bearings and doesn't have the problem. *Mikuni*

This tool is designed to hold a Sportster engine at TDC when you're installing cams. It screws into the case at the timing plug hole and holds the flywheel by friction. Sportster engines have a tendency to rotate while the cams are being changed. *CCI*

CCI's "Premium" valve exactly replaces the OEM part, but at a lower cost for those on a budget. *CCI*

blocked off and overseen by Highway Patrol, gate guards, and airplanes, so it features a lot of real fast curves and straights running from 5 to 11 miles, without any danger of meeting a cow or a hay truck as you crest a hill. It's a race where horsepower rules, and tuning for maximum go at that altitude can be fairly tricky.

Any type of four-wheeled vehicle can run, and I've seen everything from a Ford-powered Camaro to a Ferrari F-40 at the starting line. Usually 250 cars are flagged off at 1-minute intervals.

For one race, I entered my Chevrolet SS454 short-bed pickup, because that's all I had at the time. A 2 1/2-inch stainless steel exhaust, different cam, hotter computer chip made the truck run strong, but not enough for my taste. At such high altitude, the engine ran out of breath at about 115 miles per hour, so I did what a lot of people do and bolted on a street supercharger, giving me a theoretical top end in the 140–142-miles-per-hour area— enough to average 125 miles per hour easily, I thought.

Come race day, everything was running fine right up to the 48-mile marker, when the engine

went "clang" and all the horses escaped in a blue cloud out the exhaust pipes. When I finally got the truck back to home base in California, I pulled the heads to see what wasn't there any more. Imagine my surprise when I saw two empty cylinders—no pistons.

I had not changed the stock cast pistons, figuring they could handle the extra 100 or so horsepower of the supercharger without problems. Wrong! Two pistons had turned to chunks of badly distorted aluminum and now rested in the oil pan. I talked to an engine builder who made big-block Chevs go, and he asked what did I expect: The stock pistons had all the tensile strength of a tomato juice can. He told me I should run forged pistons, Carillo rods, and a one-piece nitrided crank.

Another Mikuni carb is available for Sportster engines in the 1200-cc range. If you have any doubt about which size carb to use on your engine, go with the 40-millimeter carb for better all-around performance. *Mikuni*

None of the breakage would have occurred if I had built the engine with forged pistons from the start. I kind of knew that, but I had hoped to make the engine finish one race in one piece.

Point being, the cast pistons are real nice in a stock engine but have no place in a race motor.

There's no reason a Stage II motor shouldn't last as long as a Stage I. Sure there's more power being produced, but with correct care and regular maintenance, both engines will last for thousands of quick miles. The main difference between the motors is the components going inside a Stage II.

Heads

Like the Big Twins, the key to Sportster power is in the heads. More airflow makes more horse-power. A Stage II head, like ones from Zipper's or Branch Flowmetrics (714-827-1463) with flowed ports and bigger valves, will let a 1200-cc engine breathe at 7,500rpm. The stock heads will clean up well; however, they were designed not to produce maximum horsepower but to pass EPA standards, so you're better off with a set of aftermarket heads.

An aftermarket head doesn't have the same restrictions as a factory product. Plus, it is built for performance, not to a cost figure. It is manufactured strictly for performance with little, or no, thought given to what comes out the pipes as far as emissions. Some of these heads aren't legal for highway use and should only be used on racing bikes.

S.T.D. heads come with raised ports for better flow, large valve seats, bathtub-shaped combustion chambers, and dual plugs. The casting is 356 aircraft aluminum, and a bare set retails for $970.

Higher-compression engines sometimes suffer from leaking head gaskets. One solution is to set up the heads for O-rings. The cylinder has to be machined to take O-rings, but a lot of companies sell their cylinders already cut for this purpose. Silicon O-rings will provide an excellent seal on all Stage II and Stage III engines, Big Twin or Sportster.

The only real difference between the two Stages, as far as heads go, is the amount of time and money you are willing to invest to capture that last few horsepower. With high-performance anything, the initial horsepower gains are relatively

The S&S Super B is the equivalent of the Mikuni 40-millimeter carb. S&S can set you up with a fuel mixer for any engine combination up to blown fuel. *S&S*

inexpensive; it's going for the ultimate that costs lots of money.

Ported stock heads require a flow bench to ensure that just making bigger holes does increase airflow. A lot of other factors come into being when reworking heads. Valves are only all the way open for a small number of degrees of crankshaft rotation. Most of the time they're moving up or down, constantly changing flow. A valve does nothing but sit for most of the time, then it has to open and admit the optimum amount of mixture in a short time.

The distance of the valve off the seat constantly changes the cfm through the ports. Every modified engine responds differently to head changes. A lot of money, sweat, and hours has gone into producing the best heads for

racing at the cost of many ruined castings.

To really make a Sportster produce, enough air has to be moved through the heads to make power all the way up to 7,500rpm. A stock head flows in the 85-cfm at 25 pounds of test pressure range. It can be opened enough to flow 145cfm by bigger valves and ports, but soon you reach the point of diminishing returns. To get from 85cfm to 110cfm isn't too hard. The last 30cfm is where the magic and experience comes into play.

Big ports will flow a lot of air at high rpm, but below 3,000rpm the intake velocity can slow to the point where power produced is actually less than stock. It's all a trade-off. If you're willing to live with ragged performance down

low, you can build an engine with a lot of horsepower up in the 5,500–7,500rpm range. For most of us, street riding requires compromise, and we're willing to trade ultimate top end for a broader power band throughout the rpm range.

It's a safe bet that the home tuner can't begin to build a high-flow head without a lot of work and expensive tools. People like Jerry Branch, of Branch Flow-metrics, have invested years of their lives to building better performing heads. Airflow volume, velocity, cam lift, and timing all come into play when designing or modifying heads. A high-lift cam—.550 inch or better of total valve lift—will let the heads flow at their maximum, but valvetrain wear is so high that anything near a 0.600 total valve lift will eat up parts in short order. A good cam to use with a 140-cfm head on the street should have a cam lift of 0.336 inch, 259 degrees of duration, and make power from 3,000 to 7,500rpm.

Some of the newer cams on the market have much better valve-train geometry so that the steep angles encountered with 0.650-inch or more valve lift cams can actually live for longer periods of time. They require some upper case cutting to clear the lobes—a job better left up to a good machine shop—but other than that, they install like any other set. All clearances must be triple-checked before starting the engine. The cams must turn completely through a revolution without touching the lifter support area inside the crankcase. Cams and heads must be matched to get the maximum horsepower out of the engine.

Stage II Kits—1200cc

Almost all the kits listed for Stage I engines will work on a Stage II motor with the addition of better heads and higher-lift cams. Some of the heads, modified and aftermarket, along with cams are listed below.

Heads

1. Branch Flowmetrics modified OEM heads w/valves.
2. Zipper's Performance Stage II heads.
3. S.T.D. heads.

Cams

1. Red Shift 625 V2 for 1986–1990 four-speed Sportsters
2. Red Shift 543 for five-speed 1200-cc Sportsters
3. Andrews V8/N8
4. Screamin' Eagle #25633-86A for 1986–1990 engines, 25647-91 for 1991 and up engines; includes collars, keepers, and springs

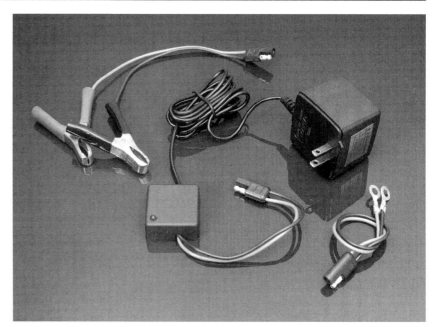

Here's a trick borrowed from touring riders. This trickle charger has the connector at lower right permanently bolted to the battery terminals, so it can be plugged in anytime. For a racer, this will insure the battery stays topped off all the time. *CCI*

SuperTrapp's twin-pipe exhaust system has the pipes up high for better ground clearance, and at the same time, it can be tuned for different circumstances quite easily. The tuning discs on the back of the pipe can be changed in minutes, giving you an unlimited choice of setups for street or track. *CCI*

Stage III Engines—Pro Street

Here's where anything that makes more horsepower will be used. Drag-racing engines are up to 150ci. Street-legal 88-ci Pro Street motors are setting times that a few years ago were the exclusive property of Top Gas engines. Turbos and superchargers combine with nitrous oxide to double horsepower. The idea is to get there fast and worry about costs later.

Our version of a Stage III engine will be an 88-ci Pro Street bike with modifications for better handling and stopping power. Most of the components come from the same manufacturers as Stage I and II engines, but are ranged toward the more radical end of the scale.

Strokers for the Street

Most Sportster riders spend a great percentage of their time below 4,000rpm. Run the engine for any length of time above this figure and vibration can become quite a nuisance. Peak torque on a 1200 occurs right at that rpm, and usually Harley riders like to run on the torque rather than buzzing the engine. Torque is what gives Harleys the ability to grunt and go when the throttle is opened. A stock 1200 puts out 71 foot-pounds of torque at 4,000rpm; a stock Dyna 80ci is good for 77 foot-pounds at 3,600.

What most Sporty street riders are looking for is the ability to wind on the throttle at lower rpms and have the bike jump hard. The best way to achieve this is through an increase in displacement, both by installing larger cylinders and increasing the stroke. New cylinders and a long arm can take a Sportster engine out to 150ci, a little impractical for the street, but just right for drag racing. One is loose on the East Coast, setting records in Top Fuel. This engine

This oil cooler is simple in design and easy to install. It comes with a block-off plate for cold weather, but a thermostatic bypass valve would work better and eliminate covering and uncovering the fins.

The end of this reverse-cone megaphone keeps exhaust reversion to a minimum. The vacuum created during exhaust pulses wants to draw air back into the header. The diffuser and vent channel this air back into the atmosphere so the next exhaust pulse doesn't have to reverse the incoming air before it can pass out the pipe.

runs a bore of 4.25 inches by 4.50-inch stroke. To make the engine stay together while producing consistently high power, the crank was made from a single piece of billet steel. The rods are custom pieces, and the heads are four-valve. A Harley parts man wouldn't recognize anything in the engine.

On a much more practical level, 88–89ci works well on the street and is a fairly reliable engine, depending on how hard and how long the throttle is turned. A stroker engine will not be able to wind as high as a stocker due to higher piston speeds and loads created by heavier rods and pistons. For reliability, the redline might have to be dropped 1,000rpm from the stock bore and stroke engine.

A Sportster Evo engine is reaching piston speeds of 4,700 feet per minute when the engine is turning 7,500rpm. Most engine builders consider 4,000 feet per minute as the upper limit of piston speed when reliability is a factor. If your current redline is in the 7,500rpm area, building an 89-ci stroker will require dropping it to 6,500.

A well set-up Stage III engine will have roughly the same top speed as a big-inch Stage II engine—all other factors being equal. Where the Stage III engine comes into its own is in low rpm pull. The old adage, "Nothing beats cubic inches," is definitely true in this case. An 88-inch Sportster will flat walk away from a Big Twin or Stage II Sportster from a 3,000-rpm roll-on.

Peak power in an 88-ci Sportster is limited by the head's breathing ability. Here is a good place to install a set of high-cfm heads, like Rivera's Four-Valve Billet heads. They aren't inexpensive, but they will get the air into the big stroker engines. With the

For those really concerned about weight on the racer, here's a digital tachometer and hourmeter that weighs less than half a pound. It not only gives rpm but also reads total running time on the engine, just as in aircraft engines.

The drag strip is one place where a megaphone instead of an air cleaner makes sense. This engine only travels a quarter mile at a time and doesn't acquire enough mileage in a year's running to make wear from airborne grit a factor.

capability of filling the cylinders to a 130-percent level, or better, the combination of these heads and 88ci will easily show 125 horsepower. However, unless you have an undying need to spread little pieces of aluminum and steel all over a drag strip, you will have to watch the redline even more closely, because this combination, with a 0.665-inch-valve-lift cam, or better, will continue to make power right up to the explosion. Expect to add $3,500 to the cost of an engine to install four-valve heads, but the end result is well worth the outgo.

Except for the forays to the race track, plan on lowering the stroker's redline by 12 percent. Most of the work is going to be done between 3,000rpm and 5,500rpm anyway, so there's no good reason to wind the engine higher. Shift just past the torque peak and let the stroker do its work down low.

I used to have a sticker on the de-activated speedometer of my 1971 iron Sporty that said: "This engine will turn 8,000rpm—once." I had enough Sifton cam and big carb to let the power run through the ported heads and out the straight pipes all the way up high, but I didn't have enough sense to know when to shift. I'd wind that old beast 'till the valves sounded like playing a xylophone, then grab another gear. It finally told me it had enough mistreatment one night when I was trying to show a Pontiac GTO the error of its ways. I gathered most of the larger pieces and called my friend with a pickup to take the bike home.

Making a stroker will involve a lot more work than swapping cylinders on a Stage II engine. The cases must be split, and everything from the flywheels to the pistons will be changed. Most of the stock engine will end up in a storage bag in back of the garage.

This is the sensor plate that picks up the ignition signal from the rotor. Nothing touches, nothing wears out. No points to adjust—ever.

Drag Specialties offers this 8,000-rpm tach for racers. It mounts in the middle of the bars, high enough to be easily visible. The numbers are clear, and the needle's sweep can be seen without taking your eyes off the track. *Drag Specialties*

The 883 class requires a steering damper on all the bikes. This one's easily adjustable for travel. The damper has to be positioned so it doesn't act as a stop for the steering. There must still be travel left on the shaft when the bars are in full lock in both directions.

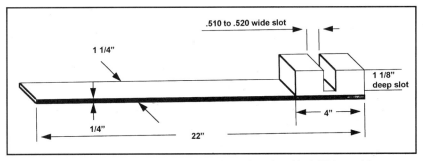

Rod bending tool shown here can be fabricated and welded. This tool is designed to grasp rod immediately below the wristpin end on I-beam section.

Check the size of the silencers on Harley's VR1000. They need to be this big to get the noise level down to the various tracks' limits without sacrificing any power.

The VR1000's disc brakes are full-floating to keep perfect alignment with the calipers. On a street bike you can sometimes hear them rattle, but a little extra racket isn't a factor on a race bike, even if you could hear it over the exhaust and wind noise.

This is how the factory tunes the VR1000 for different tracks with a computer. The mechanic (programmer) is dialing in different parameters for the day. The electronic fuel injection can be adjusted for track elevation, temperature, air density, and many other factors. Each track is different, and Harley Racing Department keeps a computer full of information to help program the bikes. The fuel injection computer is the square box above the mechanic's knee.

Laguna Seca 1995 was a wet outing for the VR1000. With a spare bike, different combinations can be tried without having to wait as changes are made.

Braided stainless steel brake lines are used on the 883 racers. Note how the bolts holding on the caliper are safety-wired so they can't come loose. Class rules spell out what has to be safety-wired on the bike. Things like oil drain plugs are high on the list.

S&S offers their Sidewinder kit that takes a Sportster out to 89ci. Stroke is 4 5/16 inches and bore 3 5/8 inches. It comes with a set of S&S stroker flywheels, rods, rings, wrist pins, pushrods, pushrod covers, intake manifold, and head bolts. The longer cylinders will require a bit of frame modification at the rear where the frame tubes come together above the rear cylinder. This is a job best left to a frame shop, unless you want to take the chance of ending up with a bike that turns one way a lot better than the other.

New motor mount plates are included to bolt the longer cylinders into the frame, since the stroker will be about 1 5/16 inches taller. It might behoove you to go the route of a new frame rather than cut the stock one. Seeing as how everything between the cases is going to end up changed, along with the clutch and transmission door and gears (You didn't think the stock clutch would handle 89 inches, did you? The burning smell is the clutch plates, just before the trans door warps and you bust a few gears.), you might want to think about building a stroker from the ground up.

About the only Harley parts you might use are:

Front end, brakes, bars,
   instruments, cables, and
   fender
Gas tank and seat

Footpeg assemblies and rear
   brake master cylinder
Engine cases
Drive sprockets (unless you
   change ratios)
Wheels—I doubt it.
Wiring and lights

Now if you look at that list and think about your personal preferences, you might even eliminate more than I did. If so, think about buying the oldest belt-drive Sportster you can find, selling all the parts you won't use (stock, straight frames are worth good bucks), and starting with only the parts you actually need to build the bike. Ride your street Sportster while you

Just another basic Sportster engine—with Mert Lawwill magneto cases, hydraulic clutch, and things like the lightened aluminum brake lever. The main point I wanted to make was the size of the air cleaners on this XR-750. Lots of surface area makes for little resistance through the filters. This way a lot of dirt can be picked up without making a pressure drop across the filter.

Axtell's ductile iron cylinders can handle all strokes and go up to 4-inch bore size. *Axtell*

Cheap insurance. Every time the engine comes down, replace these rod races and wrist pin bushings. *S&S*

work on your secret weapon. This way, there's no pressure to get the bike up at any certain time, and you can make sure all's right before it goes hunting.

Another way to end up with an 88-ci motor is to contact Zipper's and talk to them about their Mountain Motor. This engine uses the stock stroke, so the frame doesn't have to be cut to fit cylinders under the frame.

Zipper's uses Axtell 3 13/16-inch cylinders and pistons to get the 88-ci displacement. A Red Shift 625 V2 set of cams, with 0.625 lift, goes in the cases, along with Carillo rods and an improved oiling system. Ported heads have Baisley Pro Street valves and roller rockers. Gas feeds through an S&S Thunderjet Super G carb. Sparks courtesy a dual-plug ignition. All the combustion products exit by way of free-flowing pipes (your choice). Clutch and transmission have been beefed up to handle all the power.

This engine makes near 130 horsepower, with good engine life because the stroke isn't increased. You can send them your engine, or buy one outright. This way would be cheaper than a stroker in a new frame, but still figure on $7,000 to $8,000 by the time you hear noise.

Whichever way you go, be sure to reserve a soft spot in your heart for all the Ninja riders who have never encountered a big-inch Sportster. It does bother me so to watch grown men cry.

Stage III Kits

Kit #1

1. Zipper's 88-ci Mountain Motor
2. SuperTrapp 2 into 1 exhaust system

Kit #2

1. S&S Sidewinder 89-ci kit
2. S&S Super G carb
3. Storz stainless-steel exhaust
4. Dyna ignition

Kit #3

1. Axtell 3 13/16-inch Pro Street cylinders and pistons
2. Andrews BV cams and kit
3. MC Power Arc ignition
4. Mikuni HSR 42 carb
5. Drag Specialties Python pipes, or Python 2-inch drag pipes

Again, these are but a few ways to build a killer Sportster engine. Many other suppliers produce excellent parts that can do the same job. People like Sputhe, S.T.D., Crane, and others have different parts that achieve the same final product. And that is a strong, powerful, 125-horsepower Sportster capable of easily showing everybody its tail light.

What I find interesting on this Sportster-derived drag racer is the use of spoked wheels. Aluminum or magnesium would be a lot lighter and much simpler to deal with as far as maintenance.

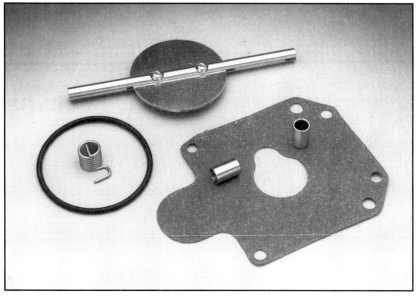

These are all the parts needed to rebuild the body of an S&S Super A or B carb. Not much to wear out, and simple to work on. *CCI*

Go with a set of S&S rods when you want the bottom end to stay together under serious operation. Remember to rebalance the engine when the rods are changed. These are for a Big Twin, but the Sportsters are almost identical. *S&S*

Starting Problems

Once you've pumped an engine up with lots of compression, a full-race camshaft, and big carburetor(s), other problems begin to creep in, such as just getting the fire lit. An electric starter is a wonderful thing, but the stock unit just doesn't have enough grunt to reliably turn over a really high-compression engine. In this case, a lesson from the road racers might be a good idea.

A lot of the knee-on-the-ground racers use a set of rollers to light off the engine, for a couple of reasons: First, it makes for a lighter bike if you don't have to run an electric starter, huge battery, relays, and wiring. Second, rollers mean you don't have to resort to pushing, and being able to start and run the bike while sitting still is a real benefit.

The rollers let you, or your mechanic, watch everything while the engine is turned over. Two rollers are mounted in a frame wide enough to let a pickup or car put a wheel on them while still leaving plenty of room for your bike's rear wheel. The vehicle's engine provides the necessary power to spin the rollers to start the bike, while its differential means the car or pickup stays put.

Put the rear wheel on the rollers, put the bike in second gear or higher, clamp on the front brake, and spin up the rollers. Ignition on, fuel on, and drop the clutch. Once the engine catches, pull in the clutch lever. Stop the rollers and then pull off. Staying upright while going through this procedure takes a bit of getting used to, but once you have it nailed, you will never go back to bump-starting. A couple of trips up and down the pits trying to push-start the bike while wearing leathers in 100-degree weather will soon convince you of the wisdom of rollers.

You can also use the rollers to lube an engine before it's lit off. Pull the plugs, make sure the fuel is off, and crank the engine by hand to insure nothing binds or drags. Go through the same drill as starting, only this time just use the rollers to turn the engine over, driving the oil pump and pushing oil throughout the engine. Considering most engine wear occurs when the cylinders and bearings are dry, this is a good way to extend engine life.

My semi-lucid, certifiably crazy, road-racing brother warms up his bike in third gear while sitting on the rollers. This way he can catch any leaks or other problems before running out on the track, and the bike doesn't have to be pushed back to the pits should something decide to quit working.

A really clean way to go on an exhaust system is with a one-piece header and muffler. These staggered duals work well on an engine with a healthy cam, 10.5:1 compression, and an S&S carb. They also fit the original mounting brackets. *CCI*

117

Most repairs don't require the removal of more than the heads and cylinders. However, if a stroker kit is planned, or the rods are going to be changed, the engine/transmission will have to come out of the bike and be torn down.

All the aftermarket go-fast parts, carbs, cams, lifters, heads, etc., can be installed without total engine teardown. Installing a stroker kit is the only reason to open the cases. Making an 883 Sportster into a 1200 only requires a cylinder change, but opening up the engine to 1,340cc means the transmission and clutch will need to be modified. The stock bottom end can handle 82 horsepower without modifications, but the thing's sure gonna' vibrate.

We will cover the complete teardown in case a rod change or a stroker kit is in the works. A lot of the teardown is similar to the Big Twin, and will be so marked with a "*."

Steam-clean the bike, paying particular attention to the engine.

Remove the seat.*

Disconnect the battery, ground cable first, then positive cable and green wire running to the starter. Remove the battery and tray.

Remove the two screws holding the air cleaner cover in place. Remove the backing plate and disconnect the two hoses. Put everything in a bag as it will be replaced by a new less-restrictive air cleaner.*

Disconnect and remove the spark-plug wires, ignition coil, horn, throttle cables, and clip.*

Drain gasoline, remove tank.*

Loosen enrichener control at carb.* Disconnect V.O.E.S. hose at carb and V.O.E.S. wire from ignition module.*

Remove the carb and intake manifold.*

Remove exhaust system by removing heat shields and nuts and washers from head studs. Remove master-cylinder mounting bolts and lift brake pedal to get at the front muffler locknut. Remove rear muffler locknut, freeing the rear muffler from the support bracket. Remove the exhaust system as an assembly.

Disconnect and remove the clutch cable by removing clutch inspection cover (TORX T-27 screwdriver), remove the spring and lockplate from the adjusting screw. Turn adjusting screw clockwise to drive the ramp assembly toward the cable. Unscrew adjusting screw nut. Remove coupling from ramp, then remove cable from slot in coupling. Remove cable from primary cover. Remove and store O-ring on end of cable.

Drain primary case.*

Remove top engine bracket. Keep shims together with nuts and V.O.E.S. switch.

Remove the front engine mount from the head.

No more needs to be removed to work on the heads and cylinders.

To continue teardown, remove rear master cylinder and disconnect banjo fitting and linkage.

* Remove the three sprocket cover screws, and remove the footpeg, pedal, cylinder support, and cover as a unit.

Disconnect oil pressure switch and neutral-switch wire.

Unplug ignition timer wiring from the harness. Disconnect the alternator from the regulator at the plug below the regulator.

Disconnect the ground cable from the rear crankcase bolt.

Drain engine oil. Remove all oil lines from pump to engine and tank. Mark lines with masking tape.

1 Between the clamp and the straps, this Sportster is pretty well tied down, making engine work easier. The hoist brings the bike up to the mechanic rather than having the mechanic go down to the bike.

2 The top rocker covers, rockers, and pushrods come off first. Mark the rockers to be sure they'll end up back in the same place.

Remove front engine mounting plate.

Remove bolts holding rear of engine to frame.

Lift engine slightly. Tip to clear while removing it from the right side of the motorcycle. Set in engine stand, or upright on bench.

Remove upper, middle, and lower rocker boxes with rockers attached.*

Remove the rocker shafts and rockers.*

3 Remove the heads, backing out the head bolts 1/8th turn at a time.

4 After the heads come off, remove the pushrod tubes and retainers.

Loosen head bolts following pattern for Big Twin engines, but only turn the head bolts 1/8th turn at a time.*

Remove the heads.

Remove pushrod tube retainers from four pushrod tubes. Remove pushrod covers and retainers, then pushrods.

Unbolt plates from the side of the lifter galleys. Remove the two pins holding in the lifters. A small vice-grip pliers will help. Pull lifters out of galley.

Check to ensure no dirt can get into the engine when the cylinders are pulled.

Lift the cylinder off the studs.* Install hose on studs.* Remove the snap rings and wrist pins from the pistons.* If the pistons and pins are to be reused, mark the end of the front pin "F," and the piston likewise.

We will assume you're going to build a stroker, or a 1200cc out of an 883cc, so the stock pistons, pins, rods, and flywheels will not be used in a stroker, and the pistons and pins won't be in the 883-1200 conversion.

The assembly of the top end is similar to the Big Twin.*

While tearing the engine down, look at the pistons for wear spots on either side. If one side near the wrist pin is shiny while the other side has carbon on it, the piston isn't running true in the cylinder, and during rebuild the rods must be straightened.

Gearcase Cover and Cam Removal

Drill off the heads of the timing case cover rivets.* Remove outer and inner covers. Disconnect the sensor wiring connector. Most connectors on the bike are mounted in T-brackets to keep them in place, prevent wear, and cut down electrical problems. To remove a connector from the T-stud support, push it toward the rear and lift off. Depress the external clips on the connector and separate it with a rocking motion. The sensor two-pin connector only has one clip; larger connectors have two.

Mark the position of the sensor-plate screws on the sensor plate. This will help with setting timing during the rebuild. Remove the sensor plate and rotor.*

Remove gearcase-cover screws. Position a drain pan under the case to catch the oil, and lightly tap the case to remove. Use a soft hammer to tap, not a screwdriver to pry. I know it's tempting to slip a screwdriver between the cases with a hammer, go ahead—the parts people at the dealership will love you.

Remove cam gears; clean fully and give to friends for souvenirs. This is the last time you will see the stock cams. Remove

5 Be sure to plug open holes to the crankcase with a clean rag or other sanitary item.

6 Remove the cylinders, carefully keeping the rods and pistons from hitting the crankcase studs.

7 The rear piston is laying against the studs. We're not going to use it again, so it doesn't matter if it gets scratched. However, if you plan on reusing the pistons, slide a piece of hose over the studs.

8 The new pistons will up the compression while increasing the bore. The pistons have thicker walls and crown to handle higher loads.

the pinion nut (it's Loctited, so be careful), pinion gear, and oil pump drive gear.

Cam gears are built with CAD/CAM equipment and are matched closely. Different-diameter gears have different color codes. If individual gears are changed, the same color code must be used. With an aftermarket cam (Andrews, Sifton, etc.), the gears are matched. The likelihood of mixing up gear sets is small, but you must ensure it doesn't happen.

Harley has seven different color codes, indicating gear diameters, for their stock cams. The changes are small, but enough to where the engine can rattle like two skeletons roller skating on a tin roof if the gears are mismatched. New cam sets aren't a problem.

Red Shift cams (Zipper's) require the stock cams be sent in and new lobes ground on them. Two reasons for this. One, Harley tightened gear lash on 1980 and later Sportster engines using a multitude of gears cut to blueprint manufacturing tolerances to ensure the engine runs quietly but not too tight. Two, these are not mass-produced cams, and doing it as an exchange keeps the correct clearances and holds costs down.

Sifton sells new cams outright but requires that cam gear diameters be checked before ordering the new cams. With cams of 0.480 lift, or higher, the clearance between the cam lobe and gearcase on the #2 and #3 cams must be checked, and the cases ground for correct clearance.

With any high-performance cam, the entire valvetrain, lifters, pushrods, valve springs, keepers, and seals need to be changed to take advantage of the increased horsepower. On a street engine, I'd stay with hydraulic lifter cams because of their low maintenance. Racing is a different story. Lifters have to be solid for reliable oper-

9 The engine is coming out eventually, so the mounting bolts are removed. Keep them in order and bagged.

10 All engines should be so clean. This one only has 14 miles on it, and already it's in pieces. It's going to go on a stand for developmental work and will show back up in the bike as an 88-horsepower tire-shredder.

11 Drill the rivets off the timing case cover and remove the outer and inner plates. The position of the sensor plate is then marked, and the sensor removed. Next, remove the gearcase cover screws.

ation at high (6,500+) rpm.

Have the machine shop check and replace, if necessary, the cam bushings in the cover and right engine case. They have to be pinned and reamed after installation, so this is definitely a shop job.

Check flywheel end play before splitting the cases.* End play must be between 0.001–0.005 inch, or the inner bearing spacer must be changed. The shims run in size from 0.0975 to 0.1145 inch.

Remove the two screws holding the oil pump to the engine case. The pump will drop when the screws are out, so have a pan underneath and hold the pump as the last screw comes out.

At this point the oil pump can be disassembled and checked, or the rotor assembly changed if more oilflow is required. Remove the two screws holding the cover on the oil pump body and slide the cover off. Slide the two rotor assemblies out; clean and inspect for wear. The maximum clearance between rotors is 0.004; replace both as a set if larger gaps are found. A new pump-to-engine gasket, retaining ring, and pump body O-ring will be required. Rebuild is just the opposite of teardown. Cover screws torque to 125–150 inch-pounds; pump-to-crankcase screws take the same.

Primary and Clutch Removal
Special Tools
HD-38362 sprocket locking link
HD-38515A clutch compressing tool
HD-38515-91 clutch forcing screw

Remove the shift lever and left footpeg. Unscrew the primary chain adjuster on the bottom of the primary. Remove the primary outer cover.* Remove the two starter bolts and take the starter off.

Install the sprocket locking link and remove the engine sprocket nut. Loosen the sprocket.

12 Remove the gearcase cover carefully, or you might end up with lots of parts on the floor. Keep a pan underneath the engine to collect what little oil remains in the case.

13 The cam bushings should be measured with a micrometer and replaced if necessary. In this case, the cam bushings are new, so they won't be changed.

Remove the adjusting screw assembly and snap ring from the pressure plate. Remove the clutch hub left-hand thread nut, then pull the clutch, primary chain, and engine sprocket off as a group.

Don't attempt to teardown the clutch without a spring compressing tool, because the diaphragm is under a lot of spring pressure and will remove skin and extremities if it comes apart. For a graphic illustration, picture all those plates coming at you at around 60 miles per hour.

With the compressor, put only enough pressure on the diaphragm to remove the snap ring and spring seat. Remove the diaphragm assembly, then release the spring tension from the compressor and remove the snap ring and diaphragm from the pressure plates.

Remove the retaining ring and adjusting screw. Pull out the clutch pack and replace with aftermarket plates.
Clutch plates are stacked
Clutch hub -F-S-F-S-F-S-F-SP-
F-S-F-S-F-S-F- diaphragm assembly
F=friction
S=steel
SP=spring

Assembly is the reverse of disassembly.

Transmission Removal

Place trans in first gear. Remove the two screws holding the lockplate on the output hub and remove the lockplate. Remove output shaft left-hand thread nut.

Remove cotter pin and loosen rear axle nut. Back off adjusters to loosen rear belt. Remove right lower shock bolt and belt guard. Remove the belt from the rear hub. Lift the belt off the front hub and remove the output hub.

Remove the TORX screw and retainer from the countershaft. Remove the shifter assembly.

14 The lifters are held in place by pins through the galley. Unbolt the cover plate to get at the pins.

15 The pins are hardened and can be pulled with a pair of pliers. Be very careful to protect the rod, as a tiny nick can develop into a crack. In this case, the rod is going to be changed, so no rags protect it from the case.

Pull the five bolts holding the transmission door, and slide the transmission out of the case.

Engine Case Teardown

Remove the oil filter. Remove the case screws and rear engine mount bolt.

Set the case's gearcase side up, and tap them with a soft hammer to break them apart (tap, not TAP).

Mount the flywheels and left case in a press, and press the sprocket shaft to remove the flywheels. If the pinion shaft, or sprocket shaft bearing, needs to be replaced, a crankshaft bearing tool and access to a press will be needed. Don't try to remove the retaining ring from the right-hand case as the case is easily damaged when removing the ring.

Separate the flywheels, rods, and crankpin.* Do not try to remove the retaining ring in the left case; damage to the case can result. Clean all the parts and go take a well-deserved break. Next we'll put it back together.

16 This shows the relationship between the lifter and its locating pin.

17 Inspect the roller on the lifter for any wear or pitting. Replace if needed.

18 After the lifters came out, the locating pins were put back in place, and now the cams are going to be changed.

19 The cams slide out easily. Check the cam bushings in the case for wear. Now the pinion nut, gear, and oil pump drive gear can be removed. The factory uses Loctite on the pinion nut, so use a smooth pull rather than a sudden force to remove it. The two screws holding the oil pump can be removed along with the pump.

Before we get too deep into rebuilding the Sporty engine, there's one idea I want to pass along. Providing you plan on working on more than one engine during your life as a racer, buying an engine cradle will provide you with an extra set of hands when it comes to replacing cams, torquing bolts, and manhandling cases around on a workbench. Something like Rivera's Sportster cradle does wonders for working on an engine.

I got tired of trying to hold a torque wrench, hold the case, and keep the socket from slipping off the bolt head. Turns out the job required one more hand than I had. That, and not having a buddy around when I needed grunt labor, convinced me that the next engine goes in a stand, or cradle.

The one advantage to a cradle is always having the engine right where you want it, instead of the other way around. It runs more money than you want to spend if you are only working on one engine, but comes in really handy about the third engine you pull down.

Clean all the parts and look over everything for wear, grooving, or pitting. Have a shop check any questionable part. Much easier to replace a worn, or out-of-tolerance, bearing or crankpin now, rather than after the cases are back together.

For this rebuild, we will plan on converting a 883 to a 1200 in the process. The stock flywheels and rods will be used, and the flywheel washers and rod bearings will be replaced.

The flywheel washers are replaced by the same method as in the Big Twins. Just be sure to drill the hole only slightly deeper than the washer. Remove as little material as possible. Clean up the outer lip where the flywheel was punched to hold in the old washer. It's really important to seat the new washers fully in the flywheel. An incorrectly seated washer will result in too little rod side play. The washer's beveled edge faces the crankpin bearing.

Reassemble the flywheels and check for true.*

Sprocket bearings, pinion-shaft bearings, engine main bearings, and all their races are installed and clearanced the same as the Big Twin.*

Rod Installation

Before rebuilding the flywheels, the rod's bearing-race inside diameter needs to be checked in four directions and, if out of round or grooved, lapped to the next size or replaced. The machine shop will need the crankpin as well as the new bearings.

If the rods are to be replaced, S&S makes a 4140 chrome-moly steel rods with wider I-beams, heavier radiuses where needed, and they are heat-treated and shot-peened. S&S can supply rods with the stock 0.946-inch wrist pin length, or with the same width as Big Twins, 10.073 inch for bores 3 7/16 and up. They will fit stroker flywheels up to 5 inches without additional rod-to-rod clearance.

All S&S rods weigh more than the stock item, so the flywheels must be rebalanced. Any clearance work done on the rods can only remove material from certain areas as shown in the directions included with the kits.

Some places to check for correct clearances, both on Sportster and Big Twin rod installations are:
1. Female rod bearing end to mainshaft nut—0.030-inch minimum.
2. Female rod bearing end to inner flywheel—0.060 inch.

A set of Axtell stroker pistons are going in the engine. They come as a kit with rings, wrist pins, and Teflon buttons. *Axtell*

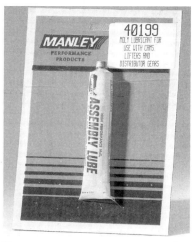

Use a good assembly lube on all the rotating parts in the cam case. The first few seconds of life are the most critical as far as wear. Moly lube will protect lobes and gears until a sufficient oilflow is established. *CCI*

3. Wrist pin end of both rods to the flywheel edge—0.060 inch.

Set up the right flywheel, crankpin, and rods with bearings in the right crankcase half. Install the pistons and cylinders. Check for rod-to-crankcase clearance on the front and back of each cylinder; 0.060 inch is necessary. Don't cut the rods for clearance as that will weaken them. Instead, take material off the point of contact on the flywheel rim, mainshaft nut, crankcase, or cylinder spigot.

All S&S rods are shot-peened to reduce the possibility of stress cracks. Polishing or grinding the rods will remove the shot-peening and isn't recommended.

When assembling the S&S rods on their forged flywheels, torque the engine's crankpin nuts to 400 foot-pounds on the Big Twin, and 350 foot-pounds on the Sportster. The stock crankpin and flywheels only go to 150–185 pounds, so be sure of the numbers before twisting a torque wrench.

If the teardown showed the pistons were running crooked in the bore, the rods must be checked and bent to bring them true. Sometimes tolerances in the cases, cylinders, or pistons can cause the rods to run to one side or the other.

To straighten the rods, a tool like the one in Figure 1 can be built to bend the rod straight. With the lower end rebuilt, install the pistons without rings, and bolt the cylinders, with gaskets, in place. Hold the front piston toward the right side of the engine and rotate the crank in the normal direction of travel three times. Check the side clearances visually. Push the piston in the other direction and repeat the procedure. If the piston is crooked in the bore, the rod must be bent to bring the piston straight in the bore. I recommend professional help in this operation as it takes some experience to know just how hard to twist the rod to have it snap back straight. Every time you bend the rod, the entire checking process must be duplicated until both pistons run true.

Crankcase Assembly
Special tools
HD-37047A sprocket shaft bearing and seal installation tool (8 pieces)

Check the left crankcase half to ensure the retaining-ring gap is aligned with the oil supply hole. The sprocket shaft bearing races should already have been installed by the shop. Install the flywheels in the flywheel support with the sprocket shaft up. Wrap the rods with towels to protect them. Install the inner bearing and spacer (rounded end up) on the shaft using the nut driver in the installation tool. Run the nut driver all the way to the bottom of the threads.

Repeat the procedure using the rest of the included spacers until the nut bottoms against the shaft shoulder.

Slide the left case on the shaft. Place the end-play spacer on the shaft. Install the outer bearing with the small end toward the flywheels. Place the flat side of the outer spacer against the bearing. Run the bearing down with the nut driver. Use the kit spacers to draw the bearing into the race until both bearings rest against the inner spacer.

Install the oil seal with the kit spacer and driver. The open side faces out. Drive the seal in until the

1 Seals and O-rings are cheap. Replace all of them during any tear-down. *CCI*

2 When the flywheel is balanced, a weight equivalent to the rods and pistons is bolted to it for the correct balance factor.

3 To lighten the wheel, a hole in the side of the rim is cut using a drill bit in a press—not by hand.

4 Most of the Sportster's assembly is similar to the Big Twin except when it comes to the cams. Each of the four replacement cams have to be checked for proper clearance. Cams are sold as a set, or in some cases, your cams are reground and reinstalled, which maintains stock clearances.

5 Cams install in sequence. Because of the larger-diameter additional gear on the outboard end of the rear intake, the rear exhaust and front intake must be installed before the rear intake cam gear.

6 The rear intake cam gear goes in last. Be sure all the timing marks align as on the front two cams.

7 The pistons and cylinders assemble in the same way as a Big Twin. We're laying a new head gasket in place prior to installing the head.

8 The pushrod tubes get new oil seals before installation.

spacer contacts the bearing cage.

Set the case and flywheels in the engine stand. Spread a layer of 3-M #800 sealant, or similar, over the crankcase faces. Install the right case and bolts. Tighten the 1/4-inch bolts to 70–110 inch-pounds, the 5/16-inch fasteners to 15–18 foot-pounds.

Oil the pinion shaft and install the outer bearing. Secure it with a new snap ring.

Install the cylinder studs.* Pack the cases with clean shop rags, not paper towels.

Mount the engine back in the frame.

Install the transmission in the case. Hold the gears so the mainshaft enters fifth gear, and the countershaft and shifter shaft slide into their bearings. Install the five transmission door bolts with a couple of drops of Loctite Blue on them. Here's a good chance to gain some strength in the transmission by using a billet tranny door with a double-row bearing instead of the stock single-row. For competition use only, a full-coverage iron door set up with a double-row bearing will handle all the horsepower you can put through it. The iron door fits all four-speed Sportys but won't accept an alternator.

9 Now the heads can go on, and the rest of the engine can be reassembled.

While you are in the transmission, think about installing a set of Andrews close-ratio drive gears, and a Bandit SuperClutch designed for the 1971–1984 Sportster. This combination makes for a bulletproof, racing setup.

The five door bolts torque to 13–17 foot-pounds. Slide the shifter pawl over the pins and set the shifter shaft on the transmission studs. Install the washers and locknuts on the studs, leaving them loose for alignment purposes. At-

tach the detent arm spring over its grove on the lower post.

Set the detent plate over the shifter drum pins. Rotate the plate until the holes in the back of the plate align with the pins on the end of the drum shaft. Install a NEW snap ring on the detent plate shaft.

Shift the transmission into third gear. Slide a #32 drill bit (.116-inch diameter) through the hole in the detent plate, and between the pawl and drivepin at the end of the shifter drum shaft. Put some weight on the shifter shaft, but not so much as to rotate the drum. This aligns the pawl and the drum. Now tighten the bottom shifter shaft nut to 90–110 inch-pounds, and then the top nut to the same torque.

Slide a new quad ring over the fifth-gear shaft, up to the taper. Install the spacer, tapered end toward the transmission, up to the bearing.

Dip the lips of the shaft seal in transmission fluid and drive it, lips to case, until it's flush with the case. It can be driven up against the retaining ring—an additional 0.030 inch.

Install the transmission sprocket and the rear drive belt onto the mainshaft.

Set the trans in first gear. Apply a few drops of Loctite Red to the transmission sprocket nut, and run it on the shaft with the machined side against the sprocket. Torque the nut counterclockwise to 110–120 foot-pounds. Install the lockplate over the nut so that two holes align with the holes on the sprocket, and install two new screws, with the thread locking compound on them, to 90–110 inch-pounds. The sprocket nut can be tightened further if the holes won't line-up, but do not torque past 150 foot-pounds.

Install the rest of the transmission parts in the reverse of removal. Adjust the rear drive belt tension. Fill the transmission with 32 ounces of fluid through the clutch cover. Make sure the oil comes to the bottom of the clutch diaphragm spring with the bike level.

Install the oil pump and new gasket on the engine. Torque the pump screws to 125–150 inch-pounds. Install oil lines with new hose clamps. Use Teflon pipe dope on the threads of any fittings removed.

Cylinders and Heads

Install the pistons and rings.* Here's where the changes to an 883 to make it a 1200 come into play. The 1200 kit consists of a set of 3 1/2-inch-bore pistons with rings, standard wrist pins, and gaskets. Zipper's offers a kit for $130 with a set of optional tool steel wrist pins for another $40. Head work will be necessary to raise the compression, or a set of Wiseco (800-321-1364) pistons with dished domes can be used. They will give a compression ratio of 10:1 on 1986 and 1987 engines, and between 8.7 and 9.5 on the newer bikes.

Later engines can use a flat-top piston to raise the CR to 10.2:1. This way the heads don't have to be milled. Here, a rebalance is definitely needed, unless you think the bike needs a little more vibration above 4,000rpm.

The Wiseco pistons weigh within a few grams of the factory units; however, a flywheel rebalance is still advised.

The stock cylinders need to be taken out another 0.5 inch to accept the pistons. The shop will bore the cylinders close to this measurement and then finish the walls with a hone, leaving cross-hatching in the cylinders for oil control and compression seal.

Zipper's will do all the machine work on the heads and cylinders needed for the 883-1200 conversion. Send them your stock cylinders and heads; they will bore the cylinders from 3 inches to 3.5 inches and finish hone, using torque plates, machine the combustion chambers and pistons for whatever CR you want, then fit the wrist pins and rings on the new pistons. All this will set you back $255. They will also balance your flywheels to the new parts and have the facilities to handle any machine shop services, from head porting to complete engine building.

Remember, though, punching out the stock cylinders is cheaper, but it doesn't leave much meat in the walls. It's still a better idea to go with new cylinders if you already own an 883. As recommended, the better solution is to buy a 1200 and work from there.

Now install the heads.* Use new head gaskets with new O-rings underneath. Use care in positioning the head on the cylinder, as the gasket can shift. A couple of drops of head gasket adhesive will help keep it from moving.

Torque the head bolts.* Use three different stages:
1. Torque to 7–9 foot-pounds
2. Go to 12–14 foot-pounds
3. Turn each bolt 90 degrees

Rotate the engine until the front cylinder's cams are all the way down. Dip the lifters in engine oil and install with the flats facing front to rear so the pins will clear. Do the same for the rear cylinder. Insert the pins, place O-rings over the pins, and install pin plate with screws.

Install pushrod tubes, new seals, and O-rings. Install retaining screw to 15–18 foot-pounds.

Install pushrods, using correct color code for intake and exhaust.

Pushrod Table
Exhaust: Three pink bands—10.800 inches
Intake: One brown band—10.746 inches

Set the lower rocker box on new gaskets with gasket bead upwards. Place the pushrods into rocker sockets. Make sure all pushrods can be turned easily before rotating engine. Install lower cover bolts; tighten with a cross-pattern, one turn at a time. Install the middle cover and gasket with breather valve on intake side. Repeat for back cylinder.

Install oil pump drive gear and pinion gear on pinion shaft.

Align the timing mark on the pinion gear tooth with inside keyway. Install nut on pinion shaft with Loctite Red. Torque to 35–45 foot-pounds.

Apply engine oil to all cam bushings, shafts, and gears. Install all cams with the timing marks aligned. The rear exhaust cam and the front intake cam must be installed before the rear intake cam because of the rear intake cam's larger-diameter gear.

Install the gearcase cover with a new seal and gasket.

Check cam end play by turning the engine until #1 cam lobe is on the top. Use a screwdriver to pry the cam gear toward the gear cover. With a feeler gauge, measure the clearance between the crankcase bushing and cam gear shoulder. Clearance must be between 0.005–0.024 inch on all gears except the rear intake. Rear intake clearance is 0.006–0.024 inch.

Engine Installation

Place the engine in the frame from the right side. Install the four rear mounting bolts and torque to 25–30 foot-pounds. Install lower front engine brackets, and torque.

Install upper front engine brackets. Tighten engine side first, then frame side.

Install top mounting bracket, connect V.O.E.S. and ignition switch.

Connect all oil lines with new hose clamps.

Connect ground wire to crankcase bolt.

Bolt positive battery cable and green wire to starter.

Plug in regulator, and attach neutral switch and sensor wire. Connect oil pressure switch.

Install clutch cable.

Install stock, or aftermarket, carb and intake manifold. Use the air-cleaner backplate as a centering guide. Attach throttle cables and enrichener.

Install rear belt cover, brake pedal, and linkage. Mount right footrest and master cylinder.

Install new exhaust system.

Bolt on fuel tank; hook up fuel lines, horn, throttle cable clip, and ignition coil. Install air cleaner and battery. Charge the battery if necessary.

Replace oil filter; add engine oil, and primary case oil if necessary.

Plug in spark-plug wires. Connect battery cables, negative last. Mount the seat.

Use the same break-in procedure as for the Big Twin.* Recheck the timing.

Torque and Tuning Specifications for Sportster 883 and 1200

Ignition System

Timing during cranking	5 degrees BTDC
Timing at 1,650–1,950rpm	40 BTDC
(set timing at this speed)	
Spark-plug gap (6R12)	0.038–0.040 inch
Engine speed at idle	950–1,050rpm

Torque Values

Crankpin nut	150–185 foot-pounds
Pinion gear nut	35–45 foot-pounds
Oil tank mounting nuts	3–5 foot-pounds
Oil pump mounting screws	125–150 inch-pounds
Pushrod-tubes plate bolts	15–18 foot-pounds
Gearcase cover screws	80–110 inch-pounds
Rocker cover	
5/16 bolts	15–18 foot-pounds
1/4 bolts	10–13 foot-pounds

Rear Engine Mount Bolts

Frame to crankcase	25–35 foot-pounds
Negative cable nut	65–80 inch-pounds

Lower front engine bracket bolts:

Crankcase	25–30 foot-pounds
Frame	25–30 foot-pounds

Upper front engine bracket bolts:

Head	25–30 foot-pounds
Frame	30–35 foot-pounds

Top center bracket bolts:

Head	25–30 foot-pounds
Frame	30–35 foot-pounds
Timer screws	11–18 foot-pounds
Spark plug	43–48 inch-pounds
Rotor bolt	80–110 inch-pounds
Lifter plate screws	15–20 inch-pounds

Engine

The following is a list of several problems that will make the bike not turn over, start, or run correctly.

1. If the starter doesn't turn the engine over, or doesn't run at all, aside from a dead battery, look for a bad starter solenoid, relay, or bad wiring in the circuit. If the starter spins, but doesn't engage, look for a bad pinion gear or overrun clutch.

2. The engine will turn over, there's gas in the tank, fuels on, but it won't fire; make sure the vacuum hose to the stock petcock is clear and hooked up correctly. The new vacuum-operated petcocks on 1996 H-Ds have been somewhat of a warranty item, and quite a few have been replaced because they won't feed reliably. A Pingel petcock and gas filter won't have this problem.

Make sure the fuel filter is new, the spark plugs are new, and the engine didn't get flooded when first starting the engine. Overuse of the enrichener can flood the engine.

Check the battery connections for looseness, both at the battery and the starter.

New spark-plug wires will prevent shorting or arcing. A bad ignition coil will make for hard or no starting and engine missing. It can be easily checked with an Ohm meter. Resistance across the primary circuit (12 volts) must be between 2.5–3.1 Ohms. Secondary (high voltage to the plugs) resistance runs between 10,000–12,500 Ohms. An aftermarket coil can be even higher, but if there's no resistance, or an open circuit, the coil is bad.

The ignition module on newer bikes can be faulty. On 1996 bikes and newer, it's mounted on the inboard side of the electrical side panel. The 1995 bikes have it on the left-side ignition module bracket. This requires more sophisticated testing, and normally it isn't a problem. Electronics usually fail in the first month, if they're going to fail. I'd look for other causes before replacing the module.

Be sure the timing is correct. An engine badly out of time won't run very well.

Installing the pushrods incorrectly will cause a valve to hang open with the chance of valve-to-piston contact.

3. Hard starting can be due to most of the above, and an almost-dead battery can turn the engine without leaving enough juice for the plugs. If the fuel tank has sat around for a long time, or the fuel is old, the engine will be hard to start and run like "expletive deleted." An air leak at the manifold can lean out the engine until it won't run or has no power.

Make sure the vent hose and/or vapor valve isn't plugged, starving the engine. The enrichener cable can be incorrectly adjusted, holding it on after the engine's warm.

4. A missing engine might have incorrectly adjusted valves, wrong valve timing, or broken valve springs. I've seen brand new valve springs break the first time the engine's started. Granted it was a while ago, but it can happen and will drive you to drink trying to figure out the problem.

Weak valve springs can cause the engine to flatten out or miss at any rpm above idle. I once had a motor that wouldn't pull above 4,000 on the dyno before it just flattened out and quit making power. We replaced almost everything before finding a solution. Took a while, but the problem was traced to soft valve springs. Of course I only found it after many hours and much diagnosis. At first I thought it was a bad coil or plugs going to sleep. Maybe the ignition module was breaking down. Finally we pulled the heads, looking for broken parts, and tested the springs. They were down to 40 percent of their rated tension when compressed. They went in the scrap pile, and a set of Crane springs cured the problem.

A bad V.O.E.S. will retard the timing, causing power loss. It can be tested with the engine idling by removing the vacuum hose from the carb and plugging the fitting. The timing will retard and the idle will drop. Reinstall the hose and the idle will pick back up. If this doesn't happen, check the V.O.E.S. wire connection to the ignition module or the ground wire.

The ignition module has a connector at the crankcase that when dirty, or oil soaked, can cause poor sparks or no sparks.

5. Fouling plugs are due to worn or broken piston rings, bad plugs, worn valve guides or seals, or too fat a mixture (incorrectly jetted carb). This can happen especially when setting up a new carb for the first time. Be sure and start with the smaller jets, or the initial set in the carb, then slowly make changes upwards.

6. Detonation and/or pinging can be caused by too much carbon in the combustion chamber, or a build-up on the piston. Detonation on a new engine is due to low-octane fuel, wrong plugs, too much ignition advance, or a bad V.O.E.S.

Occasionally an engine builder picks too high a compression ratio for the gas available. Anything over 10:1 is going to require a higher octane than the available 92 octane on the street. Mixing racing gas for street running is all well and good but becomes a problem when on a ride of any duration. A hot summer's day and a lot of squeeze in the engine is a surefire way to remove the tops of the pistons.

7. New engines are tight and can create a lot of heat in a short

When installing a new ignition system, make sure the wires in the plugs make good contact. All connectors need to be checked to insure the wires didn't come loose when they were pulled apart.

This sounds basic, but one low cell in a battery can leave you stranded. A voltmeter test must show above 14.2 volts, or the battery is weak. Use distilled water and the battery will last more than one year. Keep it on a trickle charger if the bike has to sit through those gentle Wisconsin winters.

period of time. Overheating, a hard problem to spot, usually is due to low oil levels, poor oil circulation, a leaking valve, or too retarded timing. A leaking valve shows up in a compression test. Low oil level is self-evident. Poor oil circulation is harder to spot.

Check the oil return line in the oil tank. Warm oil should be visible flowing into the tank. The newer bikes, with the oil tank under the trans, can be harder to check. A flashlight will help spot oilflow.

Usually the oil pump is extremely reliable; however, a piece

The newer vacuum-operated fuel valves have a bad habit of not working, or of working intermittently. This is a surefire way to take the bike home on the back of a tow truck, as there is no easy way to bypass the vacuum valve.

Due to the equipment required, you are typically better off having a shop do the machine work on the engine. Most of us don't have a garage with one of these surface cutters in the aft corner.

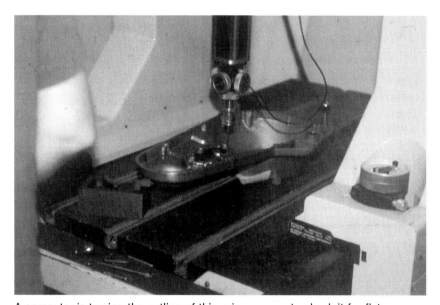

A computer is tracing the outline of this primary case to check it for flatness. The case has an oil leak that's really hard to locate, and as it turned out, the case had a rise in one of the edges around the adjuster cover that wouldn't seal.

of metal or hard carbon can shear the key or chip gears. If no oilflow is evident into the tank, or turning over the engine for the first time doesn't produce oilflow, tear down the oil pump and look for a broken key on the scavenger gear or feed gears. Starting the bike after a long spell in cold, wet weather can introduce condensation slush or ice into the oil passages. Preheating the engine will eliminate this problem.

8. Too much oil usage is caused by bad rings, incorrectly timed breather, or worn valve guides. Very seldom can a plugged oil filter push oil out, but it can happen. Oil can leak though, and Harleys have been known to drip a drop or two in the past. The Evo engine should be oil-tight if assembled correctly. An overfilled oil tank, plugged breather hose, or restricted return line can cause leaks. Loose parts will too, but we are all excellent mechanics and that doesn't happen—does it?

9. A bad alternator can be quickly checked with a simple voltmeter. Read the voltage across the battery terminals with the engine off—13.2 volts, or so. Then start the engine and check the voltage at 2,000rpm. It should be at least 14.3 to 14.7; less means the regulator or alternator is bad;

over 15 will cook the battery. Check for a good ground on the regulator base with an Ohmmeter between the base and the ground side of the battery.

Unplug the regulator connection at the engine, and check each pin to ground. Replace the regulator if any pin shows a circuit to ground.

Check the alternator connections at the case for resistance from both pins to ground. There should be zero continuity (no movement of the Ohmmeter's needle) between them. Any reading indicates a grounded stator. Resistance between the pins should be 0.1–.2 Ohms; lower indicates a bad stator.

A crack like this one on the inside of a transmission might only cause missed shifts until it decides to let go, usually under a lot of strain and high rpms.

A valve spring compressor is used to compress the valve spring so the keepers can be put in place. This is done after the valve spring tension is checked and recorded.

As the transmission is being assembled, everything has to be checked and double-checked. The stock Harley tranny will handle 20–30 more horsepower without problems; it's when you go beyond that point that problems start appearing.

The alternator puts out AC voltage; the rectifier changes it to DC. Running the engine at 2,000rpm must show 32–40 volts AC across the pins on the case, or the rotor or stator is bad.

10. Excessive engine vibration is due to loose mounting brackets, worn primary chain, unbalanced tires, incorrect drivetrain alignment, internal engine problems, or a broken frame. Especially on a race bike, check the engine mounts and frame welds before every race.

11. Upper valvetrain noise is caused by lack of oil, bad lifters, worn cam gears, or a bent pushrod. Use a stethoscope to localize the noise, or hold the end of a long screwdriver to your ear and run the tip over the engine to discover where the noise is loudest.

Transmission

Once the engine is making all that horsepower, it has to be able to transfer it to the ground. The stock Harley transmission is quite capable of dealing with 20–30 more horsepower without loosing any reliability, but much more than that will cause, at the least, premature wear of the gears and shafts. A 96-inch stroker and an aggressive throttle hand will only aggravate the problem. If you like to use all the power all the time, some modifications must be made to the transmission to ensure smooth shifting and a reasonable life. Note I said "reasonable." Any time engine or transmission components are put through the rigors of full-throttle power shifts at 7,500rpm, frequent replacement will become necessary.

Drag racing puts an incredible strain on OEM parts that were designed to last 100,000 miles of fairly easy street riding. Let's face it, no motorcycle manufacturer, including Harley-Davidson, designs its parts for competition. Probably less than 1 percent of owners will ever see a set of starting lights and a quarter-mile of rubber-dusted asphalt. Most Harley street riders haven't had the engine over 5,500rpm, unless they miss a shift.

For those of us who do spend a lot of time trying to twist the throttle off the bars, a trouble-free transmission is a necessity. Miss a power shift at 6,500–7,000rpm and you can easily bend, or break, some very expensive pieces of metal.

Once a transmission has 20,000–30,000 miles on it, or 10,000 hard miles, the stock parts can wear to the point of failure. Recently, I had the chance to baby-sit an 88-inch Dyna, replete with lots of S&S and other aftermarket parts inside the engine, for a few months. Being the nice, polite gentleman that I am, I offered to take the bike out for a little well-needed exercise now and again. The owner agreed, providing I pay for anything I break. I felt as though the bike, being rather new—a 1995, if memory serves—might respond better to outings a quarter-mile in length on a private, well-supervised track, rather than extended travel on the nation's roads.

Prior to taking the Dyna into the bright lights of nighttime racing, a little testing was in order. After all, no one wants to show up at a race track with an untried bike. So, one Sunday morning, the Dyna and I went down to a little-used road behind the campus of Sun Microsystems for a short workout.

Imagine my embarrassment when the Dyna absolutely refused to go into fourth gear when shifted hard. Stirring the shifter from first through third went smoother than a spoon through tapioca; however, when I reached for fourth in a hurry, the transmission decided not to cooperate, going into neutral instead. So much for going racing.

This damage was the result of an air cleaner base-plate screw that worked loose and fell into the engine. The owner said the bike was just idling and quit and couldn't be started. Judging by the damage, it must have its idle set at 6,000 rpm. The top of the piston was wedged in the cylinder, and it took a five-pound hammer and a block of wood to move it. The lesson? Loctite is cheap; so is double-checking every nut and bolt.

When the owner returned, we had a discussion about the problem, and he admitted having run into the same thing a few times. Between the transmission's lack of shifting, and thoughts about what would happen if it really broke under hard acceleration, we decided it was time for the transmission to be brought up to the same level as the engine.

Andrews Products (312-992-4014) has been in the business of building high-performance transmission parts for over 20 years. They manufacture gears and shafts capable of dealing with big engines while providing excellent reliability. The Evolution's five-speed can be beefed up using the following parts. Prices are only approximate, but close. Due to time lag from writing to reading, prices can change. Contact Andrews for current costs.
1. Mainshaft #296850—$134
2. Countershaft #296700—$75
3. 1st gear 2.94 close-ratio(c/r) set #296110—$135
4. 2nd main/3rd counter gear #296220—$56

This aftermarket swingarm is typical of what's being sold these days. To properly set the rear belt tension while insuring the wheel stays straight, careful measurements must be taken from the same fixed point on both sides and the axle set to the points.

5. 2nd main/3rd counter gear #296330—$56
6. 4th main gear #296445—$56
7. 4th counter gear #296440—$30
8. Main drive gear #296585—$144
9. Counter drive gear #296555—$44

Earlier Big Twins with four-speed boxes can take advantage of either a 2.44 first gear, good for lighter bikes, or a 2.60 gear for Electra Glides. You can also install a set of super close ratio gears for drag racing that features a 2.24 first, 1.65 second, and a 1.35 third gear.

Sportster owners have the option of installing a wide-ratio 2.68 first gear, or a close-ratio set of main drive gears that can be held in the case by a 7075-T6 aluminum trap door from Bandit Machine Works (through Zipper's).

Andrews uses high nickel, heat-treated steel in their gears, many of which are shot-peened for stress relief. The key ways in the shafts are tougher, making the possibility of a spun gear slight. The gears are beveled on their lead-in ramps for smoother engagement. This lets the dogs on the shifter engage on a high-rpm shift. The close-ratio first gear lets you add about 5 miles per hour to first and brings it closer to second. Starts with the taller gear aren't noticeably different from stock.

Don't try to use the Andrews gears on your stock mainshaft or countershaft. By the time the trans is opened, either shaft can be bent enough to render it useless for competition. Even low-mileage shafts can have 0.003–0.004-inch runout, which is too much when used for racing. Reliable shifting at high rpm demands stronger, true shafts.

Wet-clutch Evos built between 1984 and 1989 have a weak spot in the clutch hub. The key way between it and the mainshaft is cut too close to the end of the hub. Along with that, a lot of the factory hubs have a sloppy fit on the shaft. This can cause the hub to spin on the shaft, destroying both in the process. Zipper's installs a steel reinforcement collar for more support around the key way, then hand-laps the hub to the mainshaft for a tight fit.

Transmission Troubleshooting (Both Engines)

1. Hard shifting. Check the clutch adjustment for drag. A bent shifter rod will make shifting imprecise. Worn or bent shifter forks in the transmission, worn shifter clutch dogs, a broken return spring, or lack of oil will make shifting hard.
2. Inside the transmission, a bad shifter drum, worn shifter parts, bent shifter forks, or damaged gears will cause the transmission to jump out of gear.
3. Installing an aftermarket clutch should cure any dragging, slipping, or chattering; however, the stock clutch could have worn or warped plates, not enough spring tension, or too much oil in the primary.

This bike wandered all over the road when the front brakes were applied. Upon opening the forks, less than 1/2 ounce of oil was drained from both of them combined. A fill with Torco 15 weight, and all the problems disappeared.

A lot of street bikes get their mufflers swapped for a set of straight pipes. The owner thinks the noise makes him go faster, but the bike develops flat spots and is actually slower than with the stock pipes. This bike had what looked like mufflers, but there was nothing inside them to regulate sound.

Forced Induction and Nitrous Oxide

10

Nitrous Oxide

Nitrous oxide is a true bolt-on piece of equipment that will make all your friends hard to see in the rearview mirror. Other than a stainless-steel or aluminum can, there's nothing to be seen. The engine doesn't have to be stepped on real hard to make use of the increased horsepower; a stocker will benefit greatly from an nitrous bottle.

Nitrous oxide is composed of two atoms of nitrogen and one atom of oxygen. Its sole purpose is to provide a source of oxygen straight into the intake manifold, behind the carburetor. Two different spray nozzles are drilled and tapped into the manifold: one for the nitrous oxide and one for the extra gasoline that can now be burned. Both fuel and nitrous oxide nozzles are controlled electrically by solenoid valves activated through a push-button. It's extremely important to have an adequate fuelflow to feed the electric fuel pump, because any fuel starvation will cause a lean condition and surging.

Nitrous oxide doesn't add any power in itself, it just allows more raw fuel into the combustion chamber along with enough oxygen to burn it. Nitrous oxide is made up of 36 percent oxygen by weight. When heated to above 572 degrees on the compression stroke, nitrous oxide breaks down and releases the O2, which allows the extra fuel to burn. When pressurized nitrous oxide is injected into the intake manifold, it turns from a liquid to a gas at -127 degrees. This drops the intake charge by 65–75 degrees. The cooler mixture packs more densely in the combustion chamber, making even more power. Generally, every 10 degrees reduction in the cylinder incoming charge adds 1 percent more horsepower. Seventy-five degrees can, and will, add 7 percent more power just from the cooling alone.

The nitrogen released during combustion acts as a buffer to the combustion process, smoothing out the flame front.

Originally when nitrous oxide appeared for hot-rodders, it was the identical gas used by dentists, with all the same affects to the nervous system. Well, the Drug Enforcement Agency put short shrift to that. Now the gas in the bottles is tempered with 100 parts per million of sulfur dioxide, which will deter anyone looking to use nitrous as a stimulant. Sulfur dioxide has a remarkable similarity to rotten eggs—only more so. Your own body's gag reflex will keep you from tapping the bottle twice (I know you wouldn't do it, but there are a few who might try—once!).

Nitrous oxide should only be used on a fresh engine because the tremendous increase of power can put a load on an older engine that worn bearings can't take. As the energy released in the cylinder increases, so does the load on the rods, bearings, and related parts. The most popular kit, manufactured by Nitrous Oxide Systems (NOS) (714-821-0580) is designed for use on demand and only at wide-open throttle. They highly recommend it only be installed on a fresh motor.

NOS kits are available as a direct port injection system for Harley-Davidson's 883cc and up; the super-strong Harley bottom end can take more instant horsepower than other designs. With the jets included in the kit, you can regulate horsepower increase up to 30–40 percent on a stock engine.

The ex-World War II fighters, like P-51 Mustangs and P-38 Lightnings, that run in the Reno Air Races use nitrous during qual-

The NOS bottle mounts upright and tilted forward on the frame so the internal spigot can draw all the liquid. The bottle can be mounted anywhere there's clearance, and smaller bottles can be ordered. *NOS Systems*

ifying and on demand in the actual races. Tipping the bottle can result in as much as 400 horsepower, or more, for short periods of time in the big Merlin and Rolls-Royce engines. With the largest jets in the kit, large H-D engines can produce 35–40 horsepower gains on demand.

For this type of power increase to be used regularly, the engine must be modified to handle the additional stress of 15–20 horsepower per cylinder. Forged pistons will take the strain better than cast, but they should already be on the menu for a highly modified engine. The timing will work better when kicked back 1 to 1 1/2 degree. Higher-octane fuel, 100+, will be required. For maximum sustained use, the rods should be replaced with Carillo or S&S type. Due to the increase in cylinder pressure, correct torquing of all fasteners is imperative.

A standard bottle of nitrous oxide will last up to two minutes at wide-open throttle on a big Evolution engine. Two minutes might not sound like a long time, but it's

True "bolt-on" horsepower, nitrous oxide uses the oxygen in the nitrous, along with extra gasoline to increase horsepower. Nitrous by itself doesn't increase power, it only lets extra fuel be burnt on every compression stroke, and that's where the power originates. This size bottle is good for two minutes of wide-open throttle, which, when you sit and count to 120 with an imaginary throttle in your hand, is a long time. *NOS Systems*

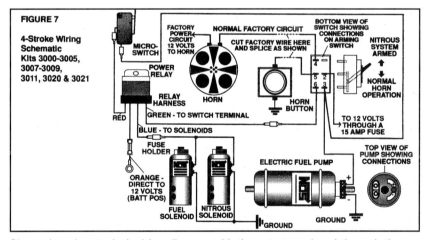

Shown here is a typical wiring diagram with the actuator relayed through the horn button, so it can be used as a horn or trigger for the nitrous. *NOS Systems*

more than enough for 5–6 runs down the strip, or two passes over a measured mile at El Mirage Dry Lakes. Normally nitrous oxide is only used in top gear and for 10–20 seconds of continued use.

High-compression engines can make good usage of nitrous, provided the right proportions of nitrous oxide and fuel are maintained. Generally the higher the compression ratio, the more ignition retard must be dialed in. Racing gas of 110 octane may be necessary to prevent detonation and take advantage of all the potential.

If the engine is being built specifically to run nitrous oxide, then a cam with more exhaust overlap and duration will work the best. However, in 99 percent of motorcycle use the nitrous oxide isn't in, so pick a cam for general operating conditions. There are specific cams available for nitrous use which have more aggressive exhaust lobe profiling, but since cam selection really depends on bike weight, intended use, and final gearing, stick with the cam recommended for your particular installation.

The kit can be installed with no special tools in about four hours. The only semi-trick part is wiring the NOS and fuel solenoids to your horn button. A relay is included to allow you to switch between horn operation and solenoid activation. Additionally a micro switch fits near the throttle so the solenoids can't be activated until the carb is wide open. Be sure the micro switch and related wiring don't interfere with throttle operation throughout full shaft travel.

Installing the bottle only requires enough space to keep it upright and away from your leg. Play around with bottle positions relative to your leg. Throwing your foot over the seat and accidentally clipping the supply valve on top of the bottle with your calf will make a lasting impression.

Startup and final checking is easy.

1. After the kit is mounted and all wiring connections double-checked, start the engine.

2. Turn the arming switch into the "on" position.

3. Run the engine at 2,500rpm and briefly hit the horn button. The engine speed should drop due to the rich mixture. Then release the button.

4. Holding 2,500rpm, turn the bottle on. There must be no change in engine operation, idle speed, or exhaust note. If there is, the wiring is incorrect and must be repaired before riding.

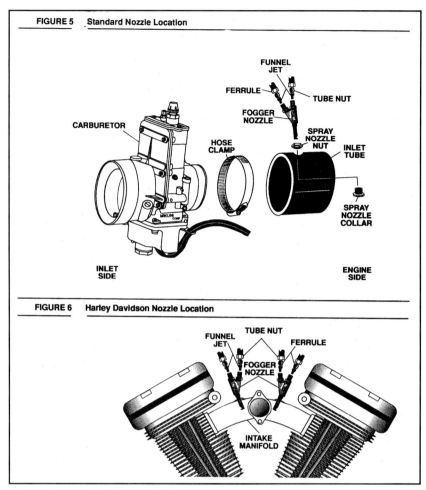

The nozzles go directly into the intake manifold on a Harley; gas and nitrous tie together and enter through a common spray bar. Make sure all your wiring and plumbing are correct, because this setup provides its own oxygen and fuel and can make power even with the throttle fully closed. *NOS Systems*

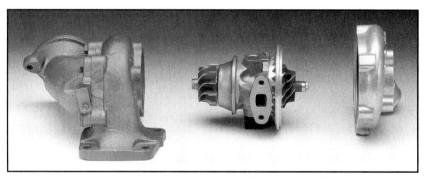

A turbocharger is a very simple device. One side of the cartridge in the center has a turbine wheel that is powered by the hot exhaust gases. The other side has a smaller wheel that compresses the incoming charge into a denser, more powerful mixture. *Garrett*

A preset valve, called a waste gate, bleeds off the excess exhaust when the boost reaches an adjustable set point. This controls total turbo boost and is usually set between 9 and 14 pounds for best performance and reliability. The waste gate can be screwed down to give 15–19 pounds of boost, but the heat produced will turn the pistons into peanut butter.

The impeller on the left is about 6 inches long on motorcycle applications—a rather compact package for all the power it develops. It spins up to 150,000rpm at high boost, making oil feed to the central bearing very critical.

What looks like a huge radiator is actually an intercooler to help cool down the incoming mixture after the turbo has compressed and heated it. This is an air-to-air intercooler. On some water-cooled vehicles, the intercooler is water-to-air, which provides quicker warming up and steadier operating temperatures.

The right side of the bike shows the waste-gate valve behind the turbo exhaust outlet. All the turbo components that work in the exhaust stream are wrapped with insulation to help keep the heat in the turbo, where it makes horsepower, and off the rider, where it makes barbecue. The bike really didn't do all that well at the dry lakes. If memory serves, it only ran 185 or so in the measured mile, but was still spinning the rear tire going into the timing lights.

First Choice Turbo Center offers the Aerocharger for Harleys. Instead of using the bike's mediocre oiling system, it carries its own supply of lubricant: enough for 700 hours of running. It can be installed on any H-D, from Buell to Battleship, in a few hours. Power improvements at maximum boost are on the order of 110 horsepower and 120 foot-pounds of torque at the crank. A run on a Dynojet model 150 dyno showed a little over 102 horsepower on an otherwise stock 1995 Buell.

This show bike mounts a supercharger on the right side of the engine, fed by two carbs on a custom-made manifold. The drive comes from a belt takeoff on the primary side, runs in front of the engine, and turns again to drive the puffer through a right-angle drive. I never saw it run, so power is a question; however, it sure was hell for complicated. I wouldn't want to be aboard if a shaft let go at 6,000rpm, or so.

5. Inspect all lines for leaks, nitrous oxide leaks can be spotted easily by frost build-up at the leak. Also, make sure the bottle is off when the bike is put away.

With an nitrous oxide system, elevated performance can be had for a much smaller dollar outlay than boring cylinders and porting heads or building a stroker—kit prices run in the $430 range for all Harley applications. Installation requires only hand tools and can be accomplished in three hours, or so.

The fuel system must be able to flow at least 0.10 gallons per hour per horsepower. The fuel pump in the NOS kit is capable of handling all requirements regardless of engine size. Street engines will run satisfactorily on 92-octane pump gas; higher-output engines require more. The petcock must be able to handle the increased flow.

Mounting a Nitrous System

1. Disconnect the battery.

2. Make sure the bottle is not mounted near any heat source like the exhaust pipes. The bottle has a siphon tube inside and must be mounted with the bottle facing up and the label on top. The siphon tube is bent so it points at the side opposite the label. If the bottle is to be mounted upside down, the siphon tube must be removed. Be sure the bottle is empty before trying to remove the valve. Non-siphon tube bottles can be ordered from NOS.

3. Next install the nitrous solenoid and the fuel solenoid. Both solenoids must be mounted above the spray nozzles. Then position the fuel pump and attach the lines to the tank and pump. At this time, the tank should be empty and a new high-flow, dual-outlet (Pingel) petcock installed. All piping connections must be made with Teflon paste pipe dope, not Teflon tape.

Excess tape could get into one of the lines, blocking the flow, causing intermittent running problems.

4. Install the nozzles in the intake manifold, and run the lines from the two solenoids to the nozzles. Start off with the smallest jets included in the kit, and work up from there. All lines must be tie-wrapped securely to prevent chafing, and mounted in such a way that they don't rub anywhere.

5. Follow the wiring diagram in the kit to hook up the arming system to the horn button. Most Harleys activate their horn circuit through a grounding circuit, but some use a +12-volt circuit and must be wired slightly differently. Check your horn wiring with a DC meter to establish correct voltage flow, or read your wiring diagram.

Mount the arming switch within easy reach. This switch must be turned on before the horn circuit can fire the solenoids. Mount the rest of the relays and wiring as per the provided wiring diagram. Wire the fuel pump to the positive pole of the arming switch, and ground the negative wire.

Reconnect the battery and replace any equipment removed during the installation. Test the bottle as shown above.

Turbocharging

A turbo takes the waste energy coming out of the exhaust pipe as heat and converts it into mechanical motion to force-feed the incoming charge into the cylinders. A lot of energy goes out the exhaust, and it can be used to provide a great deal of power increase on the intake side.

The turbocharger is a rather simple device, considering all the power it is capable of producing. It consists of a single shaft, mounted in a bearing, with an exhaust impeller on one end and an intake impeller on the other. Both impellers run inside a housing, one side being fed by the exhaust and the other connected to the intake.

The hot exhaust gases spin the exhaust impeller at speeds up to 120,000rpm. This, in turn, drives the intake impeller, forcing more fuel-air mixture into the cylinders. The center bearing is fed with its own oil supply from the positive-pressure side of the oil pump, and oil returns to the oil tank. Some applications on water-cooled engines have a water jacket around the bearing, aiding in heat transfer. One side of the turbo can get so hot from the exhaust that it can be clearly seen at night by its cherry red color. I have measured over 600 degrees at the exhaust outlet one minute after shutting the engine down.

The inlet side of the turbo sees the fresh intake charge, which is compressed by the impeller and forced into the engine. In the process of compression, the intake charge picks up a lot of heat, and

sometimes an intercooler is placed between the turbo outlet and the intake manifold.

Intercoolers act like a big radiator, transferring the heat of the incoming charge to the outside air, in the case of an air-to-air cooler, and into the engine's cooling system on an air-to-water cooler. The inlet temperature can drop as much as 70 degrees through an intercooler. A cooler incoming charge will be denser, packing more oxygen and producing more power. A nitrous kit will cool the incoming charge even more, so it makes good sense to install both kits at the same time. Together, they can produce as much as 105 horsepower at the rear wheel of a 1,340-cc machine.

As the throttle is opened, the exhaust gases grow in volume, temperature, and speed, all of which help spin the exhaust turbine up from idle to an rpm where power is produced by the intake impeller. Depending on the size of the impellers, the time it takes to spin up to speed can vary by 1–3 seconds. This is called turbo lag and is responsible for the hesitation between the time the throttle is cracked open and the boost pressure goes positive.

Newer installations make use of variable-angle vanes, smaller scrolls, and lighter impellers to eliminate most of the lag, but some still remains. I've owned a number of turbo bikes and rather enjoy the feeling of power as the boost goes positive. A good setup will make every gear feel like first.

Get the bike rolling in second gear at 2,500rpm and crack the throttle. Watch the boost gauge go from running a vacuum to producing positive pressure. Then feel the arm-stretching power kick in as the tach rushes toward redline.

My first bike had such a big impeller in the turbo that nothing happened below 3,000rpm. But when the turbo did kick in, the engine spun up so fast in first and second that the rev limiter shut it down for a few seconds, usually at the worst possible time. The front wheel would launch into the air, hanging two feet above the ground until the engine went to sleep. Then the gravity monster grabbed the front wheel and slammed it to the pavement. All this was going on while the ignition was trying to sort itself out and turn the sparks back on as I picked another gear. The fire would relight, and the front wheel would go away again.

I thought I'd have to get off the bike and pull the front wheel back down to the ground, since it hung up there so long. Then the tach hit 6,800rpm, and the engine and I went through the game of shift-and-wait-for-the-fire-again.

I finally got wise and learned not to wind the engine so high in the lower gears before shifting. My eyes watched the tach hit 5,000rpm, and by the time my brain told my body to locate another gear, the engine had run up another 1,500rpm. That turbo was set up with an adjustable waste gate, and I had it set for 15 pounds of boost, which probably added another 40 horsepower to an 85-horsepower engine.

The waste gate is controlled by an actuator connected to manifold pressure. At a given pressure, it opens a bypass in the exhaust side of the turbo, causing some of the hot gases to route around the impeller. This limits the boost and puts a cap on horsepower.

My waste-gate actuator had a valve in the pressure line running from the manifold to the actuator. I could turn this valve off, and the manifold pressure couldn't make it to the diaphragm on the actuator, so the waste gate wouldn't open. With the waste-gate opening normally, the actuator limited the boost to 8–9 pounds. With the valve closed, and no limit on the turbo, I saw better than 15–17 pounds of boost. The engine would keep making more power right up to where the rev limiter kicked in.

A lot of extra stress was generated by the higher boost, and the pistons were in danger of melting down into the crankcase, but that motor sure made power. The limiting factor in top speed was my chicken factor, not horsepower. The bike would pull right up to 6,800rpm in fifth gear, no problem whatsoever. Things got mighty hot if I ran like that for many seconds. The turbo was mounted on the right side of the engine, below my leg. A few times I was kind of worried about cooking parts of me that I highly favored, so I wrapped all the hot parts of the turbo and exhaust with heat-shield tape. This brought the temperature down to something livable.

The engine finally had one too many high-pressure runs, and I liberally coated the rear wheel with very hot engine oil. Luckily I was going slow. Unluckily, I was going slow in a corner. Luckily, I didn't fall down. Unluckily, the large oak tree in the corner's apex is what kept me from falling.

When I rebuilt what was left of the engine, I made sure the boost control valve wasn't in the line any more. Eight to nine pounds of boost was still enough to drive the bike to top end, just not quite so rapid, but a great deal more reliably.

Most new turbo kits have some method of limiting the boost, either through backing down the timing or opening the waste gate when detonation is sensed. The timing can be elec-

This dragster mounts a set of four-valve heads; that's why you see a carb sticking out both sides of the engine. Both feed a common plenum between the cylinders, letting each cylinder draw from both. Check the "gas tank." It's got a screw fastener right through the center to hold it on. It's only a glass shell; the real tank sits much lower between the frame tubes.

tronically retarded at onset of detonation, but this will limit total power output.

The best way to handle detonation is to start off with a low boost setting and keep bumping it up until the onset of detonation, then back down a pound or two. Better fuel will let you handle more boost, but the trade-off is in increased wear. Figure on 50 percent of your nonscheduled maintenance will be caused by the turbo.

On my last turbo installation, I O-ringed the heads to keep the head gasket from blowing, installed an intercooler between the front frame down tubes, and set my boost control on a solenoid, actuated in the same way as a nitrous system—through the horn button. The solenoid stayed open when no power was applied. Hit

the horn button, the solenoid closed, and in less than one second the boost doubled.

I installed a boost gauge, an oil temperature gauge on the turbo bearing housing, an exhaust gas temperature sensor in the turbo outlet, and an inlet temperature gauge between the intercooler and the heads. I ran synthetic oil and changed it and the filter every 1,000 miles; a bit expensive—but cheap insurance.

The engine compression ratio was dropped to 7.5:1, total boost limited to 14 pounds, and inside the engine, I put the best stuff money could buy. The bike would easily cruise at 100 miles per hour. Twisting the throttle at that speed set me back on the seat. The second owner has over 30,000 miles on the bike, and the engine hasn't been torn down yet. We only had one fuel problem, and a dual-outlet petcock solved that. Under full power, mileage wasn't too good, though. No boost and 50 miles per gallon; play with the throttle, and you got 15 miles per gallon. But, lord was it fun. It didn't have a lot off the line, but from 50 miles per hour and up, it could humiliate anybody. I saw 6,600rpm on the tach in fifth gear, which works out to 145+ miles per hour.

When running a turbo, a few things need to be done that you wouldn't do on a normally aspirated engine. The tremendous heat near the turbo's center bearing can cause the oil to turn to coke and form hard deposits in the bearing, shortening its life. Once the engine quits turning, there is no more cool oil going into the bearing, so let the engine idle for at least one minute after running hard. This will help carry away most of the excess heat.

When running a turbo engine, take care to ensure a correct air-fuel mixture. A little richer mixture will provide extra cooling. Timing is also critical, as too much advance will cause the fuel to explode ahead of the flame front, causing massive detonation. Too little advance will cause the combustion temperatures to soar, also causing detonation.

Higher cylinder pressures, imposed by the turbo, will require a good ignition system capable of delivering a fat spark. The rate at which a turbo motor revs will require the use of a good rev limiter, preferably a "soft" type that backs down the timing as redline approaches, then turns off the spark.

A missed shift can send the engine into the stratosphere before you can react, so along with a rev limiter, make sure the transmission is in excellent shape. Going from second to nothing, when shifting at

full power, will definitely make for a few anxious moments.

First Choice Turbo Center (716-226-2929) deals with a turbo system called the "Aerocharger." The turbo bolts on the left side of the engine; is fed exhaust from a header pipe that winds from the rear cylinder around the front, picking up the front cylinder's exhaust port in the process; and blows high-pressure air through an intercooler into a custom-pressurized carb.

Harleys aren't noted for their high oil pressure, nor do they have a lot of extra pumping capacity to handle the center bearing on the turbo, so the Aerocharger comes with its own supply of oil. The center bearing is an air-cooled, low-friction ball bearing, and there's enough oil in the supply tank to run 700 hours at full boost. This eliminates the extra expense of a multi-stage oil pump and related cooler. You'd still be better off, though, installing an engine oil cooler to handle the increased heat thrown off by the raise in performance. The lube for the turbo is different from engine oil, meaning a supply must be carried if you anticipate traveling a long distance on a heavily loaded tourer.

There are a few problems that can occur with a turbo installation. These problems don't necessarily involve the turbo as they do the engine's ability to dissipate heat when the boost is up for a long period of time, such as when you're pulling the above-mentioned touring scoot over a high mountain range on a hot day. Detonation could result from all the extra heat, and the engine oil will get quite hot—the reason for the cooler.

About the only way to keep the heat load down is to drop down a gear and slow a bit until the engine cools. On a lightly loaded Big Twin, this won't be a problem. However, doing this

could create another source of engine stress. Turbochargers are self-limiting in boost by way of a waste gate that releases the excess exhaust gases when the intake boost pressure rises to a preset psi. A stock FXR, with only the addition of the Aerocharger, tested on CCI's Dynojet 100 made 106 horsepower with 11.5psi of boost. This was at 5,500rpm, no less!

Well then, if 11.5psi makes so much power, what would happen if the boost were dialed up to its maximum? After all, the turbo will keep spinning harder as the exhaust flow increases, making more boost up to its design limits, so why not see what 16–19psi can do?

What overboost can do is rapidly melt your pistons, if detonation doesn't cause the power to go away first. This is a situation where a little is good, a little more is better, and a lot more is very harmful to moving parts.

Stick with 8psi of boost for maximum engine life, only bouncing up to 11, or so, for racing. It's easy enough to increase the boost for a short period, so there's no need to ride around with the turbo maxed out, and just wearing out parts. The lower boost rate will limit you to a measly 80–85 horsepower, but that should be enough to give you a whole new attitude about performance.

Installation is rather straightforward. The turbo system will consist of a new exhaust, the turbo, new intake piping, an intercooler, oil lines, and possibly a new carb. The turbo can either draw through the carb or blow through it, depending on the kit. A draw-through system eliminates the problem of a pressurized carb and is slightly cheaper because of this, and maintenance will be less.

Figure on one full day to install the kit, and a few hours mak-

Someone has been around aircraft. This bike's switch panel uses military-type quick kill switches on an aluminum plate mounted in front of a gas cap of an airplane design.

ing everything run correctly. With the right engine components, and a little care when it comes to the throttle, 30,000 miles on the engine isn't impossible. Any mechanic with average to good skills shouldn't have trouble installing a kit. No special tools are required.

The stock intake and exhaust have to be removed, a petcock changed, and the new parts bolted on. Start the engine and check for any exhaust leaks, and you're ready to roll. Be aware that using the turbo's boost will cause the fuel gauge to drop at a greatly accelerated rate. Figure on 60 percent more fuel to make 60 percent more power. Full throttle won't have to be held as long, but you'd

still better plan on more frequent gas stops.

On a long trip I took three years ago, from San Jose to Palm Springs, I stuck to the back roads, which don't suffer from CHP infestation, and was able to run in the high 80s for long periods of time. Boost was running right around 3–5psi at that speed, no matter how little the throttle was open. The turbo just made that much boost at that rpm— 3,300–3,500. Gas mileage went down the toilet. I only got 80 miles between fill-ups, so something had to be done.

I set up the turbo to bypass all the exhaust through the waste gate by using a clamp to hold the actu-

ator all the way open all the time, but this wasn't too cool as I had to remove the clamp when I wanted to make serious horses. Otherwise the engine just ran like a stocker. Finally I ended up changing the waste-gate actuator spring to one that opened at 5psi instead of 8; this made a difference in mileage—not a lot, though. I could have slowed down—I guess. But 20-mile-long empty straights and an 80-horsepower bike don't mix well at 65 miles per hour.

Years ago, if you wanted a turbo engine, pretty much all the pieces and to be hand-fit and a lot of car turbo parts adapted. Today, companies provide a kit with everything from intake to muffler to take care of any size and horsepower bike. There's no reason not to go this route if you want to keep the engine stock and still have a lot of power available within seconds. Actually, this might be a better idea than going the cam, carb, compression, and increased displacement route, and having to live with a rough idle and reduced driveability all the time.

The Big Twin Aerocharger kit retails for $3,995. Options available include:

1. Upgraded turbo for larger (95ci and up) engines..............................$120
2. Engine brace.....................$320
3. Intercooler upgrade..........$120
4. VDO boost gauge (necessary if you want to read boost) $59

The kit for the Sportster or Buell S2 runs slightly less—$3,495.

Picture a Buell with 120 horsepower and 120 foot-pounds of torque! First Choice says the Buell kit is for the advanced rider only, and it's easy to see why. All that power in a light frame will definitely give you stories to tell your grandchildren.

Supercharging

A supercharger is another way to force air into the engine. The supercharger was originally developed as a blower for diesel engines in order to scavenge the combustion chamber on big oil-burning motors, such as GM 4-71, 6-71, and 8-71 engines. The number 71 denotes the size of one cylinder in cubic inches, and the other number denotes the number of cylinders (i.e., 8-71 would be 568ci). Hot rodders adapted the blowers for drag racing as far back as the fifties.

Now blowers are starting to turn up on Harleys. They aren't driven by exhaust, as turbos are, but by a direct drive off of the engine's crank. Usually an external pulley turns a belt that drives the supercharger. The induction system, injectors, or carburetion sits on top of the blower. The engine turns the blower, and the air-fuel mixture is compressed by rotors inside the blower, forcing the mixture into the combustion chamber under pressure.

The ratio between the pulley on the motor and the pulley on the supercharger determines the amount of boost. The blower can be underdriven, turning slower than the motor; driven 1 to 1; or overdriven faster than the motor. Eight to ten pounds of boost is standard for most street installations. Depending on the size of the impellers and the rest of the induction system, a blower can push more charge through at 8 pounds than a turbo will at the same psi.

Installing a blower takes a little more effort than a turbo. A drive off the engine has to be fabricated, usually with an outboard bearing to help take the load, as a blower requires a lot of engine horsepower to drive it. Mounting the blower can be quite a challenge.

One setup I saw recently had the blower mounted directly on an intake manifold and two S.U. carbs feeding through a forward curved runners into the blower. The drive for the blower came off the engine sprocket, went through two right-angle bends, and one belt drive. It was on a show bike, so I really don't know how it worked, but it was incredibly complicated.

Blowers take a lot of horsepower to turn them over. A few years ago in an experiment, a 350-ci Chev engine was hooked up to a GMC 8-71 blower, just to see how much power it would take to turn the fan. The 350 couldn't get above 4,000rpm before it ran out of grunt and stalled. A blower on top a 500+ci engine running nitro methane can easily suck up 400 horsepower to turn it at racing speeds. A bike blower will eat up a minimum of 25 horsepower to run. Of course, it makes a great deal more power than it consumes, so it's worth the installation.

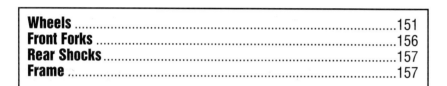

"Go fast, turn left, and don't do anything stupid!"

So went my introduction to dirt-track racing. Back then almost all the racing parts needed to make a Harley turn or stop on a dirt or asphalt track had to be fabricated out of whatever could be adapted from another type of bike, made in the shop, or purchased from Harley's racing department.

Today that isn't the case. Now, if you want to make a Sportster turn corners and handle well on the street, or want to see how well you do battle on a race track, many suppliers are ready to help you build a racing machine.

I only remember one person who actually campaigned a Big Twin on a race track. He had built a sidehack rig using a Shovelhead engine mildly warmed over. When he wasn't out running over other racers, he actually got the thing to go fairly fast. Not fast enough for pro racing—the Europeans dominated that, but fast enough to place well on a few local tracks. Other than his, all the good handling, racing machines

have been derived from Sportsters in the last 20 years.

My philosophy on fast bikes is that it's as important to make them handle as it is to have a 100 horsepower, toad-stompin' motor. Every road has a turn, and how the bike brakes, goes through the apex, and performs when power is applied coming out of the turn are just as important as making it go fast down the straight.

A lot of racers consider a race track a series of straights connected by corners of various entry speeds. A lot of racers get the doors blown off them by other riders who can carry more speed through the corners because their bikes don't slide out from under them, shake like a Waring blender, or weave out of a corner like a drunk on roller skates.

Here again, it's balanced performance you're looking for. It does no good to have a set of brakes that go from 100 to 0 in two bike lengths if the forks can't take the force and the front tire washes out before maximum braking comes into effect.

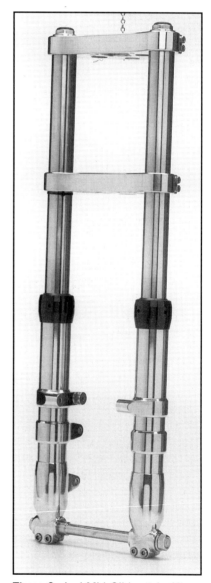

These Ceriani Mid-Glide-style 43-millimeter front forks will fit either a Big Twin or Sportster.

148

To make a Sportster handle, both ends have to be treated as a unit. A lot of handling problems blamed on the front end actually originate at the swingarm. The first place to start is by making the bike go up and down when you want it to, not when the soft suspension wants it to.

Harley-Davidson and the American Motorcyclist Association have teamed up over the last few years to run a class called "883 Sportster." The name pretty much explains the class. Only 883-cc Sportsters are legal for the series, and modifications are tightly controlled.

Engines can only be overbored 0.010 inch; the air cleaner can be replaced with a specified Screamin' Eagle high-flow kit; and the exhaust can be changed as long as its noise level meets the track's regulations. D.O.T. tires are required, and only shocks, springs, and brake pads can be swapped for better equipment.

The 883 racers also run on the dirt, which requires the front brake and fender to be removed, and a seat more suited to riding sideways to be installed. Other than that, everything has to be as from the factory. This leaves a wide latitude for using parts that exactly meet the specifications as listed by the factory, but ensures that all the bikes are pretty close to each other in the power and turning department.

Luckily for you, you're not bound by rules as far as what you can do to make your street bike give Ninjas fits. The Japanese 1,100-cc bikes might have the advantage over you in ultimate horsepower; however, your 90-horsepower, 1,200-cc Sporty can be built to let the rice rockets have a short, fleeting look at your license plate when you reach the turns. Eat them alive in the turns, and soon they will be fond memories in the rearview mirror.

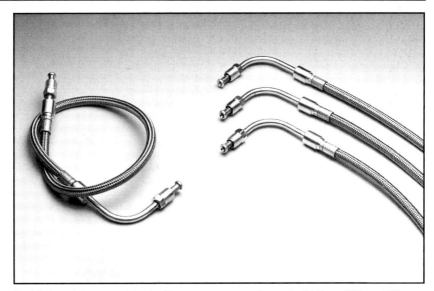

Braided stainless steel brake lines are a necessity on fast bikes. CCI and Storz offer prefabricated lines for any Harley. *CCI*

Performance Machine's spun aluminum wheels are used on road racers and drag racers all over the world. Their wheels are lighter, which reduces unsprung weight; stronger, which eliminates flex; and look good in the process. *PM*

The front forks can benefit from a spring change and a steering damper. You may not think a steering damper is a wise investment, but the first time you encounter a high-speed wobble that slaps the handgrips against the tank, you'll definitely consider a different hobby.

Running any bike over 125 miles per hour at the dry lakes or Bonneville requires a steering damper. I once ran El Mirage Dry Lakes on a bike that didn't have a damper and got to enjoy a wobble that left me sweating and dry-mouthed for a long time afterwards.

This was on a street bike with a lot of power and box stock suspension. The course is 1 mile in length, and the start is similar to a drag strip. The biggest difference is that dirt doesn't have anywhere near the coefficient of friction as pavement, so traction becomes a problem. It's not uncommon to find yourself in third or fourth still trying to get the rear wheel to hook up. Twist the throttle, and the engine makes a lot of noise, the tach climbs 3,000rpm, and the rear tire spins five times faster than the front.

I was working my way through third gear on a four-speed bike, 5,000rpm and near 110 miles per hour, when the front end gave a little shake. I gained another 500rpm, and that's when the front end went on strike. The bars started shaking in wild oscillations. No way was I able to hold them tight enough to stop them from dancing around. The front wheel actually bounced off the ground. All this happened a whole lot faster than it takes to tell. Two choices were available: turn off the power and ride it down with the front brake applied very lightly, or keep the throttle pinned and hope the bike could run through the wobble.

Well, I'd sat in line for three

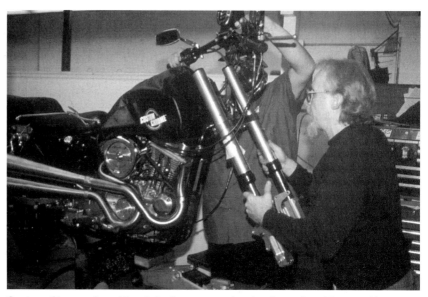

Custom Chrome is getting into the suspension business in a big way. Here a set of upside-down front forks are being mounted on one of their research Sportsters. These forks aren't even in the catalog yet, but you can bet they will show up fairly soon. The bike is one of their high-compression, big-displacement, 95-horsepower Sportsters that are ridden every day for evaluation. Sometimes the rider has to run 200 miles per day or better—anybody for a job?

PM's six-piston calipers and full-floating 13-inch discs are the same equipment found on Buell Motorcycles. If you're going to play in the canyons, you couldn't do better than install a pair of these on the front end. *PM*

hours to make the first run, and it was going to take at least that long to get back through the line if the steering problem could be fixed, so I just held on and hoped. Now understand, all this happened in the space of 500rpm in third, so the decision to keep going was not based on a long period of thought. Today I wouldn't do it again; however, I seem to learn most things by doing them wrong the first time, and this was no exception.

The bike did run through the wobble after another 15–20 miles per hour, and it finished the run. I don't remember how fast it went, but I do remember that the checkering on the grips left a pattern on my palms—through the gloves—that took a half hour to fade.

Steve Storz (805-641-9540) is the person to call for performance parts on your bike. A G.C.B. steering damper for Evo Sportsters with 35-millimeter to 54-millimeter fork tubes runs less than $250. A dual-rate fork tuning kit, springs, and preload spacers runs $70. For the ultimate in front suspension, a set of Forcelle Italia inverted forks, or G.C.B.'s upside-down racing forks retail at $1,650 and $1,900, respectively. The G.C.B. forks will take Brembo calipers and discs, and the Forcelle Italia will mount stock Harley discs or Performance Machine brakes.

The rear end responds well to Works Performance or Progressive Suspension shocks—$550 or so. If you're not quite ready to drop $2,000–3,000 into the suspension, but still want to improve handling, Storz has a performance suspension kit, consisting of new fork springs, dampening rods, fork oil, and rear shocks for $325. This way you gain a big improvement in the bike's handling without spending the kid's college money.

Significant upgrading in the brakes department can be done

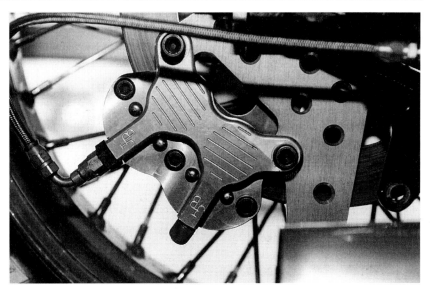

Other brands of disc brakes are available for many different requirements. Here a JB caliper stops the rear wheel of a dragster. The braided line runs into the top piston, and the bleeder is on the bottom. Seeing as how air goes up, this requires the caliper to be reverse-bled by pushing brake fluid through the bottom bleeder port until no more air comes out the master. If the master sits lower than the caliper, it will have to be elevated while being bled. Don't spill any brake fluid on painted surfaces, unless you want to remove the paint.

with Ferodo brake pads and Russell braided steel brake lines—brake pads for under $30, lines $120. Changing brake lines to braided steel may look like a visual-improvement item only; however, they will make a difference in stopping power. The stock rubber lines swell slightly when the brakes heat up and transfer that heat to the brake fluid. Squeezing the lever some more just results in bigger hoses, not better braking. The non-expanding steel lines, in combination with Ferodo pads, will surprise you with the improvement in stopping distances and braking control.

Changing lines and pads are easy; bleeding the brakes, as mentioned previously, is a little harder, but very important.

For those of you who like to play in the dirt, Storz offers almost everything necessary to build a 883 for dirt track racing, from footpegs to 7/8-inch handlebars.

Storz Performance has ex-

hibits at motorcycle shows in Cincinnati, Ohio; Daytona Beach, Florida; and San Francisco and Anaheim, California. Their tech people can show you the actual equipment and make suggestions as to what will work best for your needs. This isn't supposed to sound like an ad, but Steve Storz has been around Harleys as everything from a factory racing tuner to a performance parts business owner, and he knows what it takes to make a Sporty work in the corners.

Wheels

This may sound simple, but the first place to look for better handling is at the tires and wheels. All the trick suspension parts in all the fancy color catalogs won't do you any good if the parts that transfer the power to the ground are worn or installed incorrectly.

Check the tires at least once a week for correct pressure. Different tires require different inflation, depending on their intended

Buell Motorcycles

Although there is a certain satisfaction in building your own Harley-Davidson that handles like a dream, Buell motorcycles offer a simpler alternative. Out of the box, the light, strong chassis will allow the machine to carve through the turns with ease.

In 1983, Eric Buell began marketing five very limited production bikes based as the XLCR was, around the standard Sportster engine assembly. They used different frames and suspension; however, the cafe—sport bike—look was back. These continued to appear until 1993 when Harley-Davidson acquired 49 percent of Buell Motorcycles.

Today, mid-1996, Buell offers three models: S2 Thunderbolt, S2T Thunderbolt Sport Touring, and the S1 Lightning. Each bike fills a niche in the sport-riding market.

The S2 Thunderbolt frame holds an Evolution Sportster 1200 engine in a patented isolation system that tames the 1200's vibration. The perimeter frame, made from chrome-moly steel, is very light and rigid, much more so than the standard Sporty frame. But, Harley never intended the stock Sportster to run and handle like Eric Buell's creations.

The only engine changes are to the intake and exhaust system. A lot more horsepower hides under the tank, just waiting for the right owner and a few parts. But pure speed isn't the reason for the S2. Sport riding with a reliable, fast bike is its forte. The S2 begs to be taken out on a twisty road and allowed to show what it can do.

The new frame, with fully adjustable suspension at both ends, takes care of the handling; a six-piston brake caliper wrapped around a 13.4-inch rotor gives the rider the ability to perform "brakies" at will. For those of you unfamiliar with the term "brakies," picture a bike stopping so hard that the back wheel lifts off the ground. Super sticky tires and humongous front brakes make it easy for some racers to carry the rear tire for 40–50 feet. Interesting, but a tad scary for the uninitiated.

The next bike in the line-up is the S2T Sport Tourer. This isn't the bike for the person stepping off an Ultra Glide and looking for something a little lighter. This is a bike for the rider who takes sport touring seriously; like 400 mile days, all on back roads. The S2T may come with saddlebags, two front-fairing softbags, higher bars, and touring

The S-2 Sport Touring is the top line of Buell Motorcycles. Built for the rider who takes sport touring seriously, it is more for the person, male or female, who wants to go run with the BMW crowd, rather than for someone who stepped off an Ultra Glide looking for a smaller tourer.

mounted footpegs, but it's definitely more at home with the BMW R1100 RT riders, straightening corners and beating the speed limit to death, than with the heavy touring set. If my body bent like it used to, before the last decade took such a toll, the S2T might find a place in my garage.

Buell, and Harley dealers, say the S2T is popular with women because it is smaller and easier to ride; plus, more than a few female riders have said they delight in showing their taillight to the thundering herd.

Single-purpose bikes are a lot like specific finest-quality implements. The Japanese Katana sword blades were built by craftsmen for the specific purpose of enabling a Samurai warrior to remove heads with finesse and ease. Wesley-Richards Nitro Express double rifles have a two-year waiting period and start at $35,000, and go up rapidly, but they are built for the specific purpose of providing a quick second shot when African dangerous game like the Cape Buffalo decides its 1,800 pounds is going to occupy the same spot as your 180 pounds, and your heart is playing the *Anvil Chorus* while your legs are working at being somewhere else. At that time, the dollars spent aren't a concern; a loud bang with the correct results will suffice, thank you.

The fully adjustable rear shock lays sideways under the frame. The exhaust canister is just visible behind it.

The front brake is a 340-millimeter cast-iron floating rotor running through a six-piston Buell PM caliper with braided stainless brake lines. The rear brake is a 230-millimeter rotor with Brembo caliper. Stopping isn't a problem.

A lot of work went into making the bike pass EPA and DOT noise regulations. The air cleaner had a lot of engineering to make it meet regulations while still flowing enough air to make 91 horsepower. Just think what an ignition chip, a SuperTrapp, and a good set of cams would do for this bike.

The Buell S1 Lightning is a lot like the two items mentioned above. It exists purely as a precision instrument for those who want the finest in V-twin handling and power. At 425 pounds and 91 horsepower, it's the epitome of sport racers. The bike has the ability to make you feel like you are 50 pounds lighter, 4 inches smaller, and 10 seconds slower. Trying to reach the limits on this bike will put you right up there with the best super bikes around—Kawasaki ZX-11s and the like. They may have more sheer horsepower than the S1, but a better-than-average S1 rider will give them a hell of a run when the road turns a corner.

The engine's 91 horsepower comes by way of reduced crankshaft weight, Screamin' Eagle cams, more squeeze, and a head casting unique to the Buell engine. A new ignition curve solves the detonation that occasionally visits the 1200 Sporty and earlier T-bolts.

Trying to make the mufflers quiet while still allowing the engine to breathe took the combined talents of Harley engineers, Harley's muffler supplier, and an acoustics design consultant. The result is the large, semi-quiet muffler mounted under the frame. The larger volume of the silencer box on the end of the headers allows the incoming gases to slow down to the point where the mufflers and the air intake together make less than 80 decibels. The airbox is a bit large—needed ram tubes and resonators fill the space to keep the intake tract quiet while still allowing the engine to put out 91 horsepower at the crank. Power losses through the clutch and transmission, among other things, cut the rear wheel horsepower down to 75, almost 50 percent more than a 1200 Sportster engine.

The bike will run a quarter mile in 11.80 seconds at 112 miles per hour. A long straight will see 130 miles per hour on the clock. Base price for the S1 is under $10,000; the S2 is a few thousand above that; and the S2T Thunderbolt Sport Touring is about the same amount as the S2.

use. Individual operating pressures are determined by many factors—track temperature, air temperature, available traction, different rubber compounds. All must be considered when setting tire pressure.

Heat will increase tire pressure. You may start out the morning at the track with 32 psi in the front tire, only to find out that as the day grows warmer and the tire heats up on the course, pressure will have increased by as much as 5 psi. This means tire pressure must be checked before every heat or qualifying run. Buy a good tire-pressure gauge, and keep a record of pressures used at different tracks with various tire compounds.

Stock pressures for Sportster street tires are 30 psi front, 36 psi rear. A heavily loaded bike requires higher pressure in the rear, 40 psi. Big Twins use the same pressures. All spoke wheels manufactured by Harley-Davidson use tube-type tires. Cast and solid disc wheels use tubeless tires. Be sure the right tire is on the correct wheel.

As far as the wheels are concerned, inspect them before each event for nicks, dings, and dents. On a street bike, visually inspect the wheels and tires while the bike warms-up. Today's tubeless tires, on aluminum wheels, are not very susceptible to going flat unless punctured; however, tube tires on spoke rims can have problems with broken spoke ends piercing the tube. Some wheel manufacturers have spoke wheels built for tubeless tires, and mostly this alleviates the problem. The spokes attach to the outside of the rim, and the tire mounts inside on a tubeless bead.

Before going racing, check both the front and rear axle nuts for correct torque. Front nuts go to 50–55 foot-pounds, rears to

A four-piston caliper and the same 13-inch floating disc is available for those who don't need all the brakes of a Superbike but want improved stopping capabilities. *PM*

60–65 foot-pounds. Get the front end off the ground, preferably on a bike stand, and check for excessive side play or up-and-down play in the hubs. Replace the wheel bearings if more than 1/8-inch play exists. The factory sets wheel bearing end play between 0.002 inch to 0.006 inch; more than this can cause front-end oscillations.

Spin the front tire and check for run-out or out-of-round; 1/16 inch is maximum allowable from side to side. Out-of-round tires, or rims, go to the scrap heap. Any time a tire is changed, the wheel needs to be rebalanced. One way to avoid large amounts of wheel weight is to mount the heavy side of the tire 180 degrees opposite the heavy side of the wheel. This will require deflating and reinflating the tire, turning it on the rim, then rechecking the balance. Mark the valve position on the tire so that you know how far to turn the tire.

A bubble balancer will make this job fairly easy. You can come close by setting the rim on the balancer and then the tire on top of the rim. Rotate the tire until the

best balance is achieved, then mark and mount the tire. All further balancing should be done dynamically for street tires, but race tires absolutely must be done with a dynamic balancer. Static balancing will be close, but close only counts with hand grenades and horseshoes.

To remove the front wheel on all Harleys, unbolt the brake caliper(s) and wire it up so it doesn't hang on the brake line. Don't squeeze the front brake lever with the caliper removed; the pistons can pop out, and the caliper has to be torn down to reseat them.

The axle nut comes off next, then the pinch bolts can be loosened and the front axle pulled. Support the tire while removing the shaft. Be sure to remove the spacer and felt washer from the brake disc.

Rear wheel removal is a tad more involved. I've found an easy way to deal with rear tire changes, and that is to let the shop do the work. All of you aren't as lazy as I am, so you will probably want to do your own, especially at a track where changes can be necessary once a day, or more.

Lift the rear wheel far enough off the ground to slide the wheel out from under the fender. Loosen the axle nut and adjusting nuts. Slide the wheel all the way forward to remove the belt from the sprocket. Remove the cotter pin, throw it away, and remove the axle nut and washer. Always use a new cotter pin when changing tires. No, a bent piece of coat hanger won't do.

Rap the end of the axle with a soft hammer until it slides out of the swingarm. Having another set of hands to support the tire helps. The spacer will drop out, and the rear wheel is free to come out. Here again, don't depress the brake pedal while the wheel is off the bike. At this point, the discs can be removed, and the wheel bearings repacked or replaced. A TORX screwdriver will remove the T-40 screws holding the disc on the wheel. Use new screws for reassembly. These five screws transfer all the braking forces from the disc to the hub, and you can't afford a broken screw.

Spoke wheels will require retruing if the spokes have been changed. A four-across pattern is used for strength. This means each outside spoke crosses four inside spokes. Outer spokes have shorter heads, while inner spokes are longer. Lacing and truing wheels is an acquired skill—used along with magic—and shouldn't be attempted by the inexperienced. If you want twisted spokes in your wheels, or are building a spoked wheel for the first time, let a shop with the correct Harley truing stand do the work. It's really easy to lay up a wheel and find out it's 1/2 inch to the right of true.

The same truing stand can be used to check cast wheels for runout. In this case, however, any radial runout past 0.040 inch and

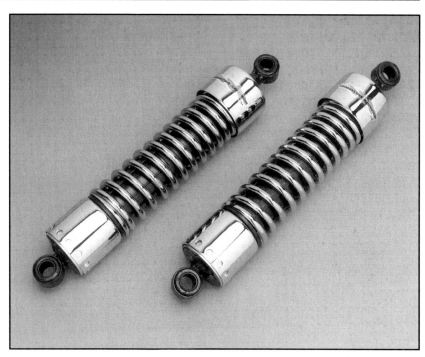

New shocks on the back of your bike will do wonders for handling improvement. Sometimes what seems like front-end problems can actually be caused by a set of worn-out shocks in the back. *CCI*

the wheel becomes an expensive conversation piece. In the same vein, don't ever try to pound out a dent on a cast wheel. It can be done, and it may look good, but the structural integrity of the wheel will have been weakened. Having the wheel fail as you clear 120 miles per hour will definitely give you a chance to test your helmet and leathers.

Whenever replacing a tube tire, change the tube. Rim protectors (Harley part number HD-01289) and tire tools, not screwdrivers, will be necessary to remove a tire from either type of rim. Usually a bead breaker is needed to roll the beads off the wheel flange. Start the upper bead over the rim at the valve, and work from there.

Use a new rim strip on tube-type wheels. This strip will keep the tube from rubbing against the spoke heads. Apply a good rubber lubricant on the beads and

rim flanges, then carefully work the first bead over the rim. On a tube-type rim, the tube goes in next. Use talcum powder, or rubber lube, on the tube to ensure it doesn't pinch while installing the last bead. Put enough air in the tube so it holds its shape, and start with the valve stem first. To help hold the stem in the rim while the tube is being mounted, a stem nut can be threaded a short ways onto the stem.

Work the bead onto the rim, starting opposite the stem. Take your time and don't get the tube caught between the rim and the tire. After the tire is on the rim, inflate it slowly until it seats. Deflate the tire to allow the tube to unwrinkle. Sometimes bouncing the tire on the ground a few times helps align the tube. Inflate the tire to correct specifications and remount to the bike. Any leaks will show up as bubbles around the valve stem, but some air may get trapped between the tube and tire, so let it escape before thinking you have a leak.

Tubeless tires are removed and installed the same way as tube-type, but with the advantage that you don't have to worry about the tube. It's a good idea to replace the valve stem with every tire change. Always use a metal valve stem. Different-diameter wheels take different stems. The 19-inch wheels use a stepped stem, while 16-inch wheels use a straight stem.

Front Forks

Improving the operation of the front forks mostly consists of changing the fork oil, damper rods, and springs. Drain the fork oil by removing the drain screws on the bottom of the fork legs and pumping the forks up and down.

Do only one at a time.

Make sure the forks are fully extended by supporting the front wheel off the ground. Remove the top caps from the top of the forks. The springs can be changed at this time.

Depending on whether the forks are dry (completely disassembled and rebuilt), or wet (just the oil drained), different amounts of oil will be required.

Fork Capacities

FXD	Dry	Wet
models	10.2 oz	9.2 oz
Sportster	10.2 oz	9.0 oz
Hugger	12.1 oz	10.7 oz

Replace the springs, install any preload spacers, and replace the caps. Hold the front brake while bouncing the forks up and down to check operation.

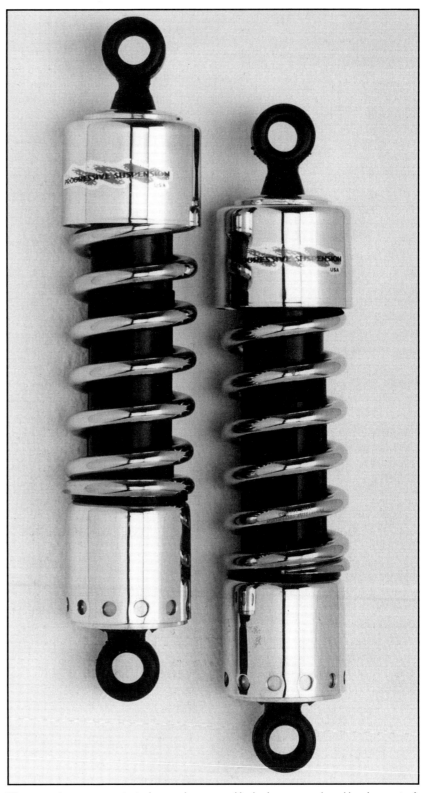

There are improvements to be made on any Harley's suspension. Here's a set of Progressive Suspension rear shocks for a Dyna Glide. These shocks have stiffer springs to resist bottoming, and better damping for performance in the turns.

Rear Shocks

The stock shocks work well to keep the fender off the tire. For any purpose other than mild street riding, better components must be installed. To change shocks, lift the rear of the bike off the ground, remove the top and bottom shock nuts and bottom bolt, and slide one shock off at a time. The other shock will hold the wheel in position. Progressive Suspension (619-948-4012) has a set of shocks that cover all Harleys from 1949 FLHs to 1996, and Sportsters from 1953–up.

Shocks are available as stainless steel, stainless steel adjustable, aluminum, and aluminum adjustable. Depending on your requirements, you can order shocks from 11.5 inches to 14.25 inches long. The aluminum adjustable shocks have five different rebound damping settings. They can be set soft for the street, then cranked down firm for racing. They are rebuildable, and their springs are said to last for a lifetime. Every couple of seasons, they should be opened up and rebuilt.

Even the Softail models, with a frame designed more for looks than performance, can benefit from a new set of shocks. If the rear suspension bottoms when going off a curb or through a pothole, consider shocks with higher spring rates, variable spring rates, and adjustable damping.

Stay away from air shocks on a racer. They are designed to carry heavy loads and shouldn't be used to sort out handling problems. They are engineered for those who like to pack everything from hair dryers to souvenir commemorative lead bars, two people, a small dog with matching helmet, and enough gear to cross the Gobi Desert on their large, heavy touring machines. Air shocks provide quick and easy adjustability for varying loads, but steel spring shocks offer superior racing performance.

Frame

The main consideration for a frame is to ensure it's not bent. On an assembled bike, check that both wheels travel in the same plane. Roll straight down a dirt road and check the tire tracks. The front wheel has to be dead center in the rear tire track.

Have someone else ride behind you and look for out of alignment conditions. Should the bike take a hard fall, look for crazed or cracked paint on all the frame tubes. Any signs of damage and the bike needs to go to a frame shop for straightening. Severe damage can be fixed, but don't use a repaired frame on a race bike unless the shop specializes in building competition equipment and knows how to correctly fishplate a frame for strength.

Some big stroker bikes require a taller frame to accommodate the longer cylinders. This can be accomplished by moving the top mounts or frame tube upwards, or replacing the entire frame with one setup for a stroker.

The main reason I advocate building the bike on paper, before turning any wrenches, is to avoid problems like tall cylinders in short frames. Have all the changes worked out on paper, and everything will go together correctly. You don't want to find out half way through that some part won't fit and major modifications must be made. Go look at a few other bikes with similar changes in order to get an idea as to what you'll encounter with yours. Talk to the people who have been there and done that, so you won't repeat the same mistakes. This is the cheapest education you can get.

Summation

Everything in this book is intended to let you enjoy more performance out of your Harley. There's almost an unlimited number of different modifications that can be done to a Big Twin, touring bike, or Sportster. You can find some type of competition every weekend from April to October. Go to a few events that interest you. Volunteer to work as a flagman, communications worker, or tech inspector. All racing events rely heavily on unpaid workers to help run events. From Vintage Racing at Laguna Seca to setting land speed records at Bonneville, there's something you can do.

Work on a pit crew for a couple of seasons. Go find performance shops open on the weekends and see if they could use you without pay for a few hours. The education you will acquire through any of these outlets will be worth more than money. Watching what other racers do, learning from their mistakes, and seeing how the winners operate is an education money can't buy.

Above all, go enjoy yourself. The people you meet, the bikes you see, and the pleasure you get out of racing is what the sport is all about. Go get involved, and say "Hi" if our paths cross.

Appendix A
Performance Parts and Services

ACCEL Products
PO Box 142
Branford, CT 06405
(203) 481-5771

Airflow Research
10490 Ilex Avenue
Paconia, CA 91331
(818) 834-9010

Andrews Products
5212 Shapland Avenue
Rosemond, IL 60018

Avon Tire
Hoppe & Associates
PO Box 336
Edmonds, WA 98020
(800) 624-7470

Axtell Sales, Inc.
1424 S.E. Maury
Des Moines, IA 50317
(515) 243-2518

Bandit Machine Works
222 Millwood Road
Lancaster, PA 17602
(717) 464-2800

Barnett Engineering
PO Box 2826
Santa Fe Springs, CA 90670
(310) 941-1284

Branch Flowmetrics
556 Corporate Drive
Cypress, CA 90630
(714) 827-1463

Bub Enterprises
22573 Meyer Ravine Road
Grass Valley, CA 95949
(916) 268-0449

Carl's Speed Shop
9339 Santa Fe Springs Road
Santa Fe Springs, CA 90670
(310) 941-9385

Carillo Industries
990 Calle Armanecer
San Clemente, CA 92672
(714) 498-1800

Champion Spark Plug
900 Upton Avenue
Toledo, OH 43607
(800) 537-8964

Corbin Pacific
11445 Commercial Parkway
Castroville, CA 95012
(800) 538-7035

Crane Cams
530 Fentress Boulevard
Daytona Beach, FL 32114
(904) 258-6174

Custom Chrome, Inc.
One Jacqueline Court
Morgan Hill, CA 95037
(800) 729-3332

Delkron Manufacturing
2430 Manning Street
Sacramento, CA 95815
(916) 921-9703

Drag Specialties
PO Box 9336
Minneapolis, MN 55440
(800) 222-3400

Dunlop Tires
PO Box 1109
Buffalo, NY 14240
(800) 548-4714

Earl's Performance Products
189 West Victoria
Long Beach, CA 90805
(800) 533-1320

EBC Brakes
12860 Bradley Avenue
Sylmar, CA 91342
(818) 362-5534

Edelbrock Corp.
2700 California Street
Torrance, CA 90503
(310) 782-2900
Web: http://www.edelbrock.com

Fueling R&D
2521 Palma Drive
Ventura, CA 93003
(805) 650-2598

First Choice Turbo Center
1558 West Henrietta Road
East Avon, NY 14414
(716) 226-2929

Gerolamy Co.
3250 Monier Circle
Rancho Cordova, CA 95742
(916) 638-9008

Harley-Davidson Motor Co.
3700 West Juneau Avenue
Milwaukee, WI 53208
(414) 342-4680

Jacobs Engineering
500 North Baird Street
Midland, TX 79701
(800) 627-8800

Jim's Tools
555 Dawson Drive
Camarillo, CA 93012
(805) 482-6913

K&N Engineering
561 Iowa Avenue
Riverside, CA 92507
(800) 858-3333

Kerker/SuperTrapp
3910 Seaport Boulevard
West Sacramento, CA 95691
(916) 372-8000

Kosman Racing
55 Oak Street
San Francisco, CA 94102
(415) 861-4262

Loctite Corp.
4450 Cranwood Parkway
Cleveland, OH 44128
(800) 321-9188

Manley Performance Products
1960 Swarthmore Avenue
Lakewood, NJ 08701
(800) 526-1362

Mikuni America
8910 Mikuni Avenue
Northridge, CA 91342
(818) 885-1242

MSD Ignition
1490 Henry Brennan Drive
El Paso, TX 79936
(915) 857-5200

Nitrous Oxide Systems
5930 Lakeshore Drive
Cypress, CA 90630
(714) 821-0580

Performance Machine
15535 Garfield Avenue
Paramount, CA 90723
(310) 634-6532

Pingel Enterprise
2076 C 11th Avenue
Adams, WI 53910
(608) 339-7999

Pipe Dreams
PO Box 1918
Andover, MA 01810
(800) 927-4737

Progressive Suspension
11129 G. Avenue
Hesperia, CA 92345
(619) 948-4012

Red Shift Cams
8040 Washington Boulevard
Jessup, MD 20794
(301) 799-9451

Rich Products
12420 San Pablo Avenue
Richmond, CA 94805
(510) 234-7547

Rivera Engineering
12532 Lambert Road
Whittier, CA 90606
(800) 872-1515
(310) 907-2600

Russell Performance Products
2645 Gundry Avenue
Signal Hill, CA 90806
(800) 394-1120

S&S Cycle, Inc.
Rt.2, County G
Box 215
Viola, WI 54664
(608) 627-1497

Sifton Motorcycle Products
943 Branston Road
San Carlos, CA 94070
(415) 592-2203

Snap-On Tools
2801 80th Street
Kenosha, WI 53141
(414) 656-5372

Sputhe Engineering
11185 Lime Kiln Road
Grass Valley, CA 95949
(916) 268-0887

S.T.D. Development Co
PO Box 3583
Chatsworth, CA 91313
(818) 998-8226

Storz Performance
234 Olive Street
Ventura, CA 93001
(805) 641-9540

V-Thunder by Competition Cams
3406 Democrat Road
Memphis, TN 38118
(901) 794-2833

Wiseco Pistons
7201 Industrial Park Boulevard
Mentor, OH 44060
(800) 321-1364

Works Performance
8730 Shirley Avenue
Northridge, CA 91324
(818) 762-5407

Zipper's Cycle
8040 Washington Boulevard
Jessup, MD 20794
(410) 799-8989

Appendix B
Racing Organizations

All Harley Drag Racing
    Association (AHDRA)
PO Box 1429
Elton College, NC 27244
(919) 229-4877

American Motorcycle Racing
    Association (AMRA)
PO Box 50
Itasca, IL 60143
(708) 250-0838

Bonneville Nationals, Inc.
22048 Vivenda
Grand Terrace, CA 92324
(714) 783-8293

FLASH Racing and *Thunder
    Alley* Race School
(203) 425-8777
Usually held in August at Sturgis,
    South Dakota, in conjunction
    with the Rally.

East Coast Racing Association
    (ECRA)
219 East Horse Pike
Galloway Township, NJ 08201
(609) 652-1159

International Drag Bike
    Association (IDBA)
3936 Raceway Park Road
Mount Olive, AL 35117
(205) 841-0553

PROSTAR
PO Box 182
Atco, NJ 08004
(609) 768-4624

Southern California Timing
    Association (SCTA)
12534 Cypress Ave.
Chino, CA 91710
(714) 627-9260

Index